Using
TEST DATA
in CLINICAL
PRACTICE

We would like to dedicate this book to all of our students and clients, who have taught us so much about teaching and assessment skills.

Using
TEST DATA
in CLINICAL
PRACTICE

*A Handbook for Mental
Health Professionals*

Kathryn C. MacCluskie
Elizabeth Reynolds Welfel
Sarah M. Toman

Cleveland State University

SAGE Publications
International Educational and Professional Publisher
Thousand Oaks ▪ London ▪ New Delhi

For information:

Sage Publications, Inc.
2455 Teller Road
Thousand Oaks, California 91320
E-mail: order@sagepub.com

Sage Publications Ltd.
6 Bonhill Street
London EC2A 4PU
United Kingdom

Sage Publications India Pvt. Ltd.
M-32 Market
Greater Kailash I
New Delhi 110 048 India

Printed in the United States of America

Library of Congress Cataloging-in-Publication Data

MacCluskie, Kathryn C.
  Using test data in clinical practice / Kathryn C. MacCluskie,
Elizabeth Reynolds Welfel, Sarah M. Toman.
     p. cm.
Includes bibliographical references and index.
  ISBN 0-7619-2188-5
  1. Psychological tests. 2. Psychometrics. I. Welfel, Elizabeth
Reynolds, 1949- II. Toman, Sarah M. III. Title.
  RC473.P79 M33 2002
  616.89'075--dc21
                              2002006457

This book is printed on acid-free paper.

02 03 04 05 10 9 8 7 6 5 4 3 2 1

Acquisitions Editor:	Jim Brace-Thompson
Editorial Assistant:	Karen Ehrmann
Copy Editor:	Gillian Dickens
Production Editor:	Sanford Robinson
Typesetter:	Siva Math Setters, Chennai, India
Cover Designer:	Sandra Ng

Contents

List of Tables

List of Figures

Preface

Our motivation to write this book arose from our collective concern about promoting client welfare. We each had experiences with motivated students who wanted to help clients yet who encountered difficulty in translating test findings into information that could help inform the treatment process. Each of us developed our own strategies for teaching about how to accomplish that integration through our own respective work with our clients. Yet we wondered how many others there were beyond our narrow purview who also struggled with the same challenges to make meaningful use of test data. Thus, we agreed to pool our knowledge and experience in testing, in the hope that it might help some professionals with this challenging aspect of test use. This book is intended for use by any mental health professional who is going to conduct testing or who might be a consumer of testing done by someone else. Although we do offer some straightforward definitions of commonly used statistical terms, the assumption is made that readers will have at least a small amount of background in basic psychometric concepts such as standardization.

We organized the book into sections that parallel the domains of our specialty areas. Thus, after an introductory chapter, we offer two chapters each in the domains of cognitive ability, personality, and career interest assessment. Each chapter offers standard features—a summary and discussion questions. In addition, some chapters feature a resource list. For those readers who are using this text for a course, the discussion questions can be used in a group format. For those readers who are practicing professionals and using this text as a reference, the discussion questions might raise some questions to generate further consideration and discussion with a supervisor or colleagues. We also created a client for a case study chapter, again pooling our respective clinical experiences to craft a rounded client presentation that offers numerous clinical issues.

This book is intended for a broad audience—students learning how to administer and interpret tests, as well as practitioners who are currently working with clients and wish to develop or enrich their skills in handling test data. Due to the applied nature of the information, in a graduate-level introductory course on the WAIS-III, MMPI, or career development, this book would best be used as a supplement to a book that covers more of the basics of test administration. However, it would be quite appropriate for an advanced testing course, an internship in assessment, or postdoctoral fellowships in psychology or counseling.

We have a number of people to thank for making this book possible. We wish to thank our colleagues at Cleveland State University, who served as sounding boards on a variety of issues related to this book. Thanks also to our graduate assistant, Elizabeth Richmond, who worked hard on the projects we asked her to do. Our students, in their own wisdom and ways of being, always help us learn more and also help us learn how to be better teachers of assessment techniques. Jim Brace-Thompson, our editor at Sage, has been incredibly supportive and encouraging. Working with him has been a joy. Also, our sincere appreciation is extended to Dr. Donald Zytowski for his attention to the career assessment chapters. His guidance and suggestions were invaluable.

1

Introduction to Testing in Clinical Practice

Testing and assessment have traditionally been the domain of both psychologists and counselors. During the second half of the 20th century, however, a trend toward subspecialties and differentiated identities of various mental health practitioners emerged. This trend meant that other areas of mental health service delivery became involved with testing. Despite efforts among the mental health disciplines to differentiate themselves, the amount of shared knowledge between the subareas is significant (MacCluskie & Ingersoll, 2001). The subject areas shared among numerous mental health disciplines include developmental psychology, normal/abnormal psychology, ethics, treatment, and assessment.

In mental health disciplines, in contrast, measurements on individuals are based largely on *hypothetical constructs*. A hypothetical construct is a framework of assumptions, developed by theorists and researchers, intended to enable subsequent observations to be understood. Another term for construct is *domain*. For example, the constructs of intelligence, personality, and career interest are defined as constructs because none of them exists as a physical entity that can be directly measured. Instead, attempts are made to measure behaviors or attributes that are considered to be the result or expression of intelligence, personality, or career interest. There is no irrefutable proof that any of them, per se, exist within people. However, individual differences between people's behavior are measurable. Some of those differences are assumed to be the result of varying levels and types of intelligence. The same principles hold true for other domains of attributes within individuals, such as personality and career interests.

Psychologists continue to have mandatory coursework in psychological assessment and diagnosis as part of their academic preparation. In addition, 17 states now permit licensed counselors to diagnose and treat mental and emotional disorders, and 21 additional states permit licensed counselors to treat mental and emotional disorders. Other mental health professionals (e.g., social workers, substance abuse counselors), who may not have the training or credentials to administer psychological assessments, may nevertheless have occasion to review test scores from assessments that have been administered by another clinician. Becoming adept with applying test data to the therapeutic process offers an opportunity for building and strengthening one's professional identity. Occasions on which test data would be generated by another clinician might include a therapist working with a client who completed tests during a psychiatric hospitalization, a client who was assessed by a school psychologist due to academic problems, or a client who was assessed at a college counseling center as part of an intake screening.

Regardless of whether a practitioner is the individual who administers standardized instruments, there exist inherent components of clinical activity across the mental health professions. These clinical activities transcend professional identity or affiliation and include assessment of client problems, client strengths, and level and quality of interpersonal functioning. The term *assessment* refers to a continuum of procedures that range from unstructured, such as intake or mental status interviews, to highly structured, such as standardized intelligence and personality tests.

The Scope of This Text

A meaningful conceptualization of the assessment process and purpose served by this test can be illustrated by means of a diagram.

Figure 1.1 illustrates the process from referral (determining when tests would be helpful) to diagnosis, treatment planning, and the

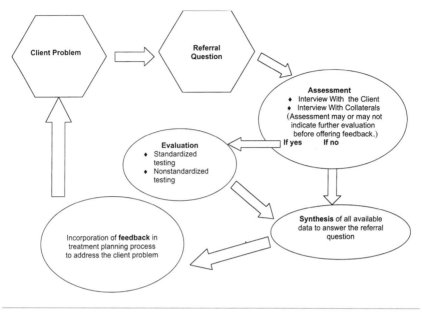

Figure 1.1   The Process of Evaluation

gaining of self-knowledge. We begin with the referral question, of which a paraphrase would be occasions when tests could be beneficial to the helping process.

There are myriad occasions when it may be beneficial for a client to participate in structured clinical assessments using standardized tests (more accurately referred to as *instruments*). Examples of occasions on which test data might be highly informative include the following:

- Generating a differential diagnosis
- Illuminating the scope and extent of psychopathology in the context of a comparison group
- Generating insight about a client's strengths and coping ability
- Gathering information for appropriate treatment planning to assist in the career decision-making process
- Better understanding a client's lack of progress in counseling
- Determining whether a client meets eligibility requirements for inclusion in a particular program (e.g., a client might qualify for special arrangements in the workplace or college classroom based on certain test scores suggesting a learning disability)

- Evaluating a student in a school setting and doing multifaceted assessments to meet requirements for identifying special needs students
- Using test scores as a baseline for comparison for response to treatment by testing before, during, and after therapy

This text focuses specifically on data generated in the evaluation phase—data that originate from structured, standardized instruments. The text gives readers background information about and straightforward examples of how test data can inform the treatment process with individual clients in personality and intellectual functioning and career development.

Our description begins with the block labeled the "Referral Question" in Figure 1.1. In this context, we are concerned with three broad purposes: (a) classification and diagnosis (normative comparison), (b) treatment planning, and (c) self-knowledge. Our developmental focus is on clients ranging from adolescence (age 16) through adulthood. The focus begins with adolescents because there are separate instruments developed specifically for use with children, yet a thorough discussion of interpretive techniques for those instruments is beyond the scope of this book.

Diagnosis

One broad use of tests can be conceptualized as identification of pathology, meaning problems in the domain being tested, of sufficient severity as to qualify for a formal diagnosis. Bearing in mind that diagnosis of psychopathology often involves looking at a person's symptoms in the context of a reference group, testing offers a structured, formalized method for making the comparison. Sometimes symptoms needed for a diagnosis of psychopathology are ones that most people do not experience. Other times, the diagnostic criteria for a disorder lie not in the unusualness of the symptom but rather in the intensity and/or frequency of the symptom. In either case, determining a diagnosis is an exercise in comparing one individual to society at large—base rates in the population. Using standardized instruments can provide one avenue for making a comparison of one individual to a larger group of individuals—in the case of testing, comparison to the standardization group. There are clear implications here regarding variables of diversity and the dangers of making normative comparisons in diagnosis. These implications will be addressed later in this chapter.

Even in the absence of a formal diagnosis, the diagnostic process consists of the clinician using skills to accurately conceptualize the client's presenting problem. Draguns (1996) noted that determining a client's disorder in a category of distinct mental disorders represents a restricted definition of diagnosis. A somewhat broader conceptualization of assessment includes prognosis, severity rating, evaluation of strengths and resources, and social supports (Ridley, Li, & Hill, 1998). The present discussion expands the term *diagnosis* to be synonymous with the multimodal conceptualization of current state of existence. Such a conceptualization includes symptoms, strengths, weaknesses, how the symptoms represent adaptation to environmental (internal and external) demands, how the maladaptation is manifesting, and what would constitute a more adaptive response to stressors within the cultural context of the client.

Treatment Planning

Of equal importance to diagnosis is the process of conceptualizing goals (i.e., how to help the client with the presenting problem) and being able to consider client characteristics (i.e., strengths and weaknesses) within the context of the counseling goals. Again referring to Figure 1.1, this purpose is represented by the lower-left section of the diagram, in which test data are used to inform the treatment process. For example, perhaps a client has verbally expressed in an intake session that she tends to be "a loner," meaning she does not enjoy the company of other people. A clinician could take that statement at face value, assuming the statement to be simply a description of personal preference or temperament, and not pursue further assessment of it. However, standardized testing might strongly suggest that the client has cognitive difficulty with processing words and oral communication. She may have subsequently developed anxiety about conversing in social situations, and her statement of being "a loner" might in fact be a description of how she attempts to adaptively respond to cognitive processing difficulties. Of greatest importance is that perhaps some of those processing difficulties could be addressed and remediated in cognitive rehabilitation. Thus, the information gleaned from a thorough assessment could be of great value to that client and perhaps dramatically improve her quality of life.

Self-Knowledge

The value of self-knowledge must not be underestimated as a goal for psychological, intellectual, or career testing. The process of assessment, evaluation, and feedback, as depicted in Figure 1.1, may be a pivotal point in the counseling process for some clients. Several authors (Finn & Tonsager, 1992; Spengler, 1998) have noted the potential positive effect that test feedback can have on favorable counseling outcomes. There are a number of possible reasons that receiving test feedback can be valuable to a client. In some cases, it might offer external validation for issues or problems about which the client has been aware for a period of time. In other cases, the test results might offer an explanation for difficulties the client has experienced. For the career client, increased self-knowledge may promote readiness for career exploration.

One of the current authors (K.M.) recollects evaluating an adult woman who was subsequently diagnosed with attention deficit disorder and a learning disability. The client burst into tears when the test results were shared with her because she had always attributed her learning difficulties to motivation and "stupidity." Another author (S.T.) recalls a client diagnosed with attention deficit disorder who woefully stated, at age 40, "I could have been a doctor," had she received appropriate diagnosis, treatment, and medication as a young adult. Consider the brief case example earlier of the woman who self-described as a "loner." Obtaining information from an objective instrument about her apparent challenge to process verbal-auditory stimuli could change her self-perception from "someone who isn't cut out to have friends" to someone whose neuropsychological composition makes it harder for her to participate in conversations with friends or to someone who scores "prefers to work with data or things" on a career interest assessment. The self-knowledge of her condition could have an impact on her self-evaluation, self-talk, or sense of career self-efficacy.

Developing skills in test score interpretation and application represents an advanced stage of clinical skill development because assessment and diagnosis are integrative, drawing on knowledge of psychopathology, development, and psychometrics. As noted earlier, in this context, diagnosis refers not only to a *DSM* (*Diagnostic and Statistical Manual of Mental Disorders*) (American Psychiatric Association, 2000) diagnosis but also to the broader process of understanding the complex interplay of cognitions, behaviors, and emotions of a client, with *cognizance* and understanding of the socio-cultural context that is relevant to that individual. Handler and Meyer (1998) noted that appropriate use of test data provides a clinician with understanding of many aspects of a client's existence, ranging from overt behavior, cognition, emotions, and conscious experience to self-representation.

Our emphasis is on integrating data from test scores into treatment planning and process. Interpretation and integration of test data into treatment are both an art and a science that involve incorporating the client's unique background data and observations of the client's behavior during the testing with test findings. This book is to be read with the caution that competence in using test data in practice requires two things: (a) knowledge of the psychometric properties of the test and (b) supervised experience in its use in the clinical setting.

The psychometric properties of the test refer to how the test was developed and normed, as well as the test's validity and reliability. As a very brief review, *validity* refers to whether the test measures what it purports to measure, and *reliability* refers to the consistency with which it measures the purported characteristic. Tests may vary considerably in their validity and reliability, and there may be differential validity and reliability across groups of people, across cultural groups, across developmental stages, or perhaps across gender. The term *differential validity* refers to the fact that although a test may accurately measure a characteristic for one type of person, it may provide an inaccurate measurement of that same characteristic for another type of person. A standardized academic aptitude test may accurately predict academic achievement of a middle-class Caucasian young adult, but it may inaccurately predict achievement for a middle-class young adult of color. A clinician needs to have an understanding of reliability, validity, and context and how those concepts apply in any given client case.

After acquiring the basic knowledge about the psychometric properties of an instrument, a clinician also needs to practice using the test in a clinical setting, under the supervision of a clinician who is already familiar with use of the instrument. For a novice clinician, looking at an actual profile of test data and then synthesizing that data into the treatment process can be a daunting prospect. Because knowledge and skill are required in the application of psychometrics, using test data in clinical practice without adequate training in theoretical and applied skills is unethical.

The Developmental Framework of This Text

Beginning in infancy, at any point that a child is not achieving developmental milestones on schedule, assessment could be indicated. There are developmental transitions in childhood that could warrant assessment, and we refer the reader to Sattler's *Assessment of Children: Behavioral and Clinical Applications, Fourth Edition* (2001a) and *Assessment of Children: Cognitive Applications, Fourth Edition* (2001b). The focus of this text is exclusively on adulthood. Within that context, it can be beneficial to be aware of the types of problems that motivate a client to seek professional mental health services.

For most people, external and internal events often occur throughout the adult years, some of which are perceived as positive or negative. Although some of those events may be perceived as positive, bear in mind the concept of *eustress* (i.e., events viewed as positive still require coping and emotional energy to accommodate the life changes). Furthermore, as sequelae of a positive life event, a situation can then evolve that creates subsequent problems. For example, perhaps an individual gets a promotion at work but then has the added responsibility to frequently travel overnight, thereby leaving his or her partner solely responsible for caring for an elderly parent. Another example would be the birth of a child, perceived by the parents as a joyous event. However, when both parents must return to work, stressors ensue when they have difficulty securing acceptable child care.

There are numerous developmental paradigms for conceptualizing life during the adult years. A description of this paradigmatic range is beyond our scope. One straightforward approach that lends itself to our current application is to consider life events and transitions as possible junctures at which concerns may evolve that lead a person into counseling. Hultsch and Plemons (1979) (as cited in Merriam & Caffarella, 1999) identified two types of life events (individual and cultural) and two types of circumstances (anticipated and unanticipated) under which those life events occur. Figure 1.2 offers a few examples of the types of life events that occur in adulthood, based on numerous theories and examples offered in Merriam and Caffarella (1999).

Bear in mind that the external, cultural events identified in Figure 1.2 are merely examples and are not intended to be inclusive of all current cultural events. At any given point in human history, those external cultural events vary dramatically and also may have a differential impact on individuals. For example, as a result of the terrorist attacks in New York, Pennsylvania, and Washington, D.C., on September 11, 2001, some people may feel that their perceptions of their life purpose or other core aspects of their existence have evolved dramatically, whereas other people may perceive little or no effect on their lives. Transposed over this paradigm is the concept of linear time and the fact that at a given chronological age, certain types of individual events are more likely to occur than others. For example, the issues of infertility and/or childbirth are likely to occur for a person in his or her 20s, 30s, and 40s. In contrast, although serious physical illness can occur at any age, probabilistically the chances of a serious illness increase with age, so that a person in his or her 60s has a greater likelihood of developing a serious chronic illness than a person in his or her 20s. This is a fact that is well recognized by the health insurance and life insurance companies.

Given the more narrow developmental scope of this text, though, the earliest developmental stage we will address is middle to late adolescence and young adulthood. At that stage, a client might benefit from career interest assessment to help him or her make decisions about what type of occupations to explore and, subsequently, what

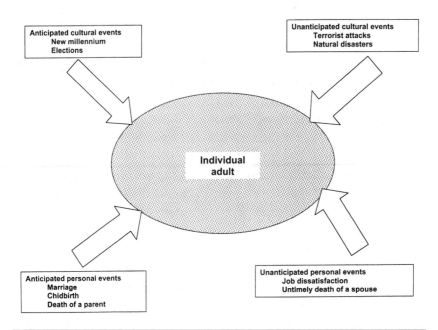

Figure 1.2   Categories of Events That Affect Adult Development and Functioning

type of training would be most appropriate. There may be ways in which intellectual and personality test data could possibly aid in the planning process. For example, testing might suggest that although a 19-year-old young woman expresses strong interest in becoming a hairdresser and generally does not enjoy being in academic environments, as could be indicated on the Learning Styles Scale of the Strong Interest Inventory, her visual-spatial coordination is not a particular strength for her in comparison to other aspects of her cognitive ability (Wechsler Adult Intelligence Scale—Third Revision [WAIS-III] data). Nevertheless, she tends to be quite extroverted and prefers activities and relating to people interpersonally in a traditional female gender role (Minnesota Multiphasic Personality Inventory–2 [MMPI-2]). The clinician might explore, with the client, how the test scores suggest that she might find the applied part of beauty school to be challenging. They could subsequently develop an alternative occupational goal and training plan that would meet the young woman's other needs and desires for interpersonal contact and traditional female occupations. In addition, an alternative goal and plan could broaden the client's career exploration of traditional female occupations in the event that the client is unable to satisfactorily complete the cosmetician training.

Another example of a need for assessment in a developmental context would be an adult college student, age 36, having academic difficulties despite "average" intelligence. It could be appropriate to assess her to determine whether there are developmental issues contributing, such as a learning disability (WAIS-III). Testing could also give some indication as to whether affective factors are impeding her academic performance, for example, either depression or anxiety (MMPI-2).

There is another means by which we can consider developmental information in the context of test interpretation. As opposed to testing being warranted as the *result* of a developmental crisis or delay in meeting expected milestones, we need to consider how to *interpret* the scores from a developmental viewpoint. The implications of any given test score are somewhat determined by the client's developmental stage, as well as by the referral questions. For example, consider a person who is 75 years old, living in an assisted-living apartment. Several family members and friends have noticed occasional disorientation and memory lapses. Perhaps the first avenue for assessment would be neuropsychological, to either rule in or out the presence of an organic impairment such as dementia. If, in fact, there is no evidence of organic involvement, personality and career interest testing could be quite helpful in identifying possible depression and what type of leisure, avocational, or volunteer activities might be good behavioral coping strategies for addressing the depression. However, intelligence test data would probably not have much clinical utility unless they were conducted in the context of evaluating neuropsychological functioning.

Justification for the Tests Presented in This Text

One common way tests are categorized is by the domains (or constructs) they purport to assess. Thus, entries in a publisher's catalogue of tests are typically organized around domains such as cognitive ability, personality characteristics, career interests, academic achievement, learning disabilities, and adaptive behavior. A newcomer to the field of psychometrics might be amazed by the number of different tests available to assess various individual characteristics. There are instruments developed to assess specific cognitive abilities, personality, career factors (e.g., self-efficacy, barriers, beliefs, or readiness), and specific diagnostic categories (e.g., anxiety, substance abuse, eating disorders, or affective disorders). This text covers three broad areas of assessment—intellectual functioning, personality, and career interest. We have chosen to focus on measures commonly administered in community mental health settings (Watkins, Campbell, & McGregor, 1988), college counseling center settings, and, to a lesser degree, secondary school settings. In each of the subsequent sections, we will present the tests used in this text, as well as rationales for selecting those particular instruments.

Before moving into specific domains of assessment, however, there is an aspect of test usage about which readers must be informed; this involves test publishers' restriction of access to products such as tests, answer forms, and test manuals. This restriction exists to protect the general public and was developed to ensure that only individuals with the proper education and training would be able to purchase and use psychological assessment instruments. The American Educational Research Association, the American Psychological Association, and the National Council on Measurement in Education (1999) jointly published a standard reference document titled *Standards for Psychological and Educational Tests*. In those standards, specific user qualifications were established. The user qualifications outline minimum training a person must have to purchase and use particular instruments. At Qualification Level A, there are no special qualifications needed. Qualification Level B requires a degree from an accredited 4-year college or university in psychology, counseling, or a closely related field as well as completion of coursework in test interpretation, psychometrics and measurement theory, educational statistics, or a closely related area *or* license/certification from an agency that requires appropriate training and experience in the ethical and competent use of psychological tests. Qualification Level C requires all the qualifications for Level B, plus an advanced professional degree that provides appropriate training in the administration and interpretation of psychological tests *or* license/certification from an agency that requires appropriate training and experience in the ethical and competent use of psychological tests.

Intellectual Assessment

The earliest intelligence tests were the Binet-Simon Scale, administered individually, and the Army Alpha and Beta tests, administered in a group format (Gregory, 2000). Interestingly, each of those tests was developed to aid in identifying optimal treatment or placement for the individuals being tested. In the case of the Binet-Simon Scale, in 1905 Alfred Binet devised his test to identify children in the Parisian public schools who were in need of special education services. The Army Alpha and Beta tests were developed to identify optimal assignment for enlisted Army personnel.

Diagnosis of special needs continues to be one reason for the use of an individual intelligence test. In addition to the current version of the Binet, now called the Stanford-Binet Intelligence Scale, Fourth Edition (Thorndike, Hagen, & Sattler, 1986), there are many other available individual intelligence tests for adults. Examples include the Kaufman Adolescent and Adult Intelligence Test (Kaufman & Kaufman, 1993), the WAIS-III (Wechsler, 1997), the Shipley Institute of Living Scale (Shipley & Zachary, 1986), and the Differential Abilities Scale (Elliott, 1990).

Certainly one traditional and valuable way that intelligence test results have been used is to help confirm a diagnosis. The WAIS-III (Wechsler, 1997) was chosen for this text for several reasons. First, the WAIS-III is a widely used individual intelligence test (Alfonso & Pratt, 1997). That means that if a clinician does encounter a client's intelligence test data, chances are high that those scores will be from a Wechsler Intelligence Scale for Children—Third Revision (WISC-III) (Wechsler, 1991) or from the WAIS-III (Wechsler, 1997). The WAIS-III offers several levels of standardized scores that enable a clinician to systematically quantify the extent to which attentional and affective factors may have influenced the client's test scores. In addition, the WAIS-III was normed with a stratified random sample that approximated the general population of the United States at the time of test revision (Wechsler, 1997). For psychometric reasons, the WAIS-III is most accurate when used with individuals whose level of intellectual functioning approximates "average" for their chronological age. When an individual is profoundly developmentally disabled or profoundly gifted, the WAIS-III is limited in the provision of a detailed, accurate picture of his or her strengths and weaknesses. However, probabilistically, many clients who will be seen in an outpatient community agency or college counseling center setting will likely be functioning intellectually somewhere in the "average" range, and the WAIS-III is certainly an appropriate instrument for individuals functioning at that level.

Individual intelligence test scores can also be used to augment counseling in a manner that does not emphasize formal diagnosis or classification. An alternative approach to classification is to describe a client's traits, abilities, and/or symptoms and to then consider those descriptions and preferences in the broader context of how to be most helpful to that person. Use of standard scores, scaled scores, and individual item analysis can sometimes shed substantial light on optimal environmental or situational conditions that will enable a person to think and process at his or her maximal level of ability. For those readers who may not recollect definitions of terms such as *scaled scores* or *item analysis*, definitions will be provided in subsequent chapters about specific instruments.

As an applied example, a client's WAIS-III scores might strongly suggest a relative strength in visual, nonverbal information processing and a weakness in auditory, verbal processing. This person is likely to encounter difficulty performing well in a traditional academic setting, which heavily emphasizes auditory, verbal functioning. That person's chances of excelling in an academic environment might be greatly enhanced by supplementation with materials that are visually based, such as textbooks with pictures and diagrams or films, to help with concept formation. Applied, hand-on examples and practice would also be especially important for him or her to consolidate the concepts and ideas. Chapters 2 and 3 will offer specific strategies for interpreting test scores, presenting test result information, and incorporating that information into the treatment planning process.

Personality Assessment

The U.S. military served as the midwife for the birth of objective personality assessment. How did this happen? After World War I, the military became interested in the development of a screening device that could help identify soldiers at risk for debilitating psychological problems when faced with combat. In 1920, Robert Woodworth developed the Personal Data Sheet, a test adopted by the military as a screening device. Needless to say, its reliability and validity were limited, but the military saw substantial potential in such devices and continued to fund personality assessment research over the next several decades with the goal of developing a psychologically sound cohort of recruits. Over the next decade, improvements in statistical techniques provided test developers with tools to better assess reliability and validity and resulted in more sophisticated personality tests. Projective personality instruments were developing on a parallel track, with little support or notice from any military organization. Rorschach published his famous Inkblot Test in 1921 and Murray his Thematic Apperception Test in 1943 (Murray, 1943; Rorschach, 1921/1941).

In 1942, Hathaway and McKinley published the original Minnesota Multiphasic Personality Inventory (MMPI). This test has become, by every measure, the most successful objective personality test ever developed. Not only is it the test the public recognizes most readily, but it is the most widely used by professionals in mental health settings (Watkins, Campbell, Niebirding, & Hallmark, 1995) and the best researched instrument ever developed (Walsh & Betz, 1995). Its success derives from three factors: the breadth of personality attributes it measures, the sophistication of its methods for assessing the test-taking attitude of the client, and the empirical basis for the inclusion of test items (Newmark & McCord, 1996). Before the MMPI, personality tests focused on single attributes and included no method to assess whether the client was understanding the items accurately and responding to them honestly. Starke and Hathaway also improved the reliability and validity of the test results substantially when they used the empirical method (called "empirical criterion keying") developed by Strong to determine test items (Newmark & McCord, 1996). In this method, test items were only included if they reliably differentiated between the norm group and the clinical (criterion) group on the attribute in question. For example, an item was retained on the depression scale only if those diagnosed with that disorder answered it significantly more frequently than the norm group.

The original MMPI remained in use for 46 years but was finally revised in 1989 (Butcher, Dahlstrom, Graham, Tellegen, & Kaemmer, 1989) to make the normative group more representative of the diversity of the population and the test items more relevant to new generations. The method for deriving standardized (in this case, T) scores from raw scores also changed, and a new group of scales, called the Content Scales, was added. Three years later, a separate adolescent version of the test was created to address longstanding problems in using the adult version with teenagers (Butcher et al., 1992).

Using the MMPI as a model along with advancements in the statistical analysis of results, other personality measures were subsequently published using a similar multiscale format. For example, in 1957 Harrison Gough produced the California Personality Inventory, which he referred to as the "sane man's MMPI" (see also Gough, 1975, 1987). Other well-known tests in this vein include the Sixteen Personality Factor Inventory (16PF) (Catell, Eber, & Tatsuoka, 1970, 1980), the Myers-Briggs Type Inventory (Myers, 1987), the Guilford-Zimmerman Temperament Survey (Guilford, Guilford, & Zimmerman, 1978), and the Millon Clinical Multiaxial Inventory (Millon, 1983, 1987).

The original thrust of each test was to provide clinicians and researchers with data about the personality attributes of test takers to gather assessment and diagnostic information. Starke and Hathaway, for instance, originally had as their exclusive aim the accurate and efficient assessment of the major forms of psychopathology. Subsequent research and clinical experience has demonstrated, however, that these tests have therapeutic as well as diagnostic value. Not only do they help clients and clinicians understand presenting and underlying issues more fully, but they can also enhance the therapeutic alliance, increase client motivation for change, and speed the pace of that change when used properly. To reach this level of effectiveness, clinicians not only need to know how to make sense of the findings of a test but also must understand how to orient the client to testing, how to present feedback to clients in ways that foster client self-disclosure, and how to integrate the data gained from the feedback session into an effective report of results. The strategies for achieving those goals are the focus of Chapters 4 and 5.

Career Interest

In 1993, Donald Super asked, "Career counseling, counseling, psychotherapy: are they essentially one, or are they really two, or three fields? Or is the answer 'none of these,' but rather a more complex intertwining, overlapping, interlocking combination that defies characterization?" (p. 132). In this text, we would like to suggest that the process of conceptualizing overlapping and intertwining qualities can also apply to career, intellectual, and personality assessment.

As was true for cognitive or intellectual measurement, vocational interest assessment was also introduced in the initial decades of the 20th century. Two of the early interest inventories that have stood the test of time will be addressed in this book. The first interest measurement, by E. K. Strong, Jr., appeared in 1927 as the Strong Vocational Interest Blank for Men and is currently published as the Strong Interest Inventory (Harmon, Hansen, Borgen, & Hammer, 1994). F. Kuder's interest assessment, the Kuder Preference Record, was published in 1934 and is now published as the Kuder Career Search (Zytowski, 2002). Both inventories have undergone considerable modifications over the past 70 years and now include technological advances in scoring and online capabilities. The various print and hard copy editions of the Strong and Kuder interest assessments have a long, extensive history. This text is grounded in that history but will also address the latest online editions of both vocational interest assessments. Even though it could be useful for practitioners to assess other vocational factors, such as abilities, beliefs, barriers, or readiness, a complete career battery is beyond the scope of this book. Interest assessments, most notably those initiated by Strong and Kuder, were included in this text because of their long history, consistent development, empirical support, and popularity.

As stated by Savickas (1999), "Given all they are and do, interests seem quite interesting" (p. 52). He further explained how interests contain elements of attention (what we are drawn to in the environment), induce affect or feelings, are behavioral motivators, and recur and endure. Others have also suggested that understanding one's interests would give us glimpses of one's personality (Holland, 1973; Roberti, Fox, & Tunick, 2001), abilities and values (Dawis & Lofquist, 1984), and, like personality and intellectual functioning, what one inherited (Gottfredson, 1999). Given all these potential elements contained within the domain of interests, clinicians obtain a wealth of information about their clients from interest assessment alone, yet they can acquire an even fuller view when interest assessment is combined with traditional intellectual and personality testing.

Increasing counselor understanding of the client is important, but of even greater value is assisting the client in learning more about himself or herself, one of the primary goals of vocational counseling since its origins (Parsons, 1909). Interest inventory explanation can be used as a catalyst to promote career exploration and to enhance career readiness (Toman & Savickas, 1997). Hoffman, Spokane, and Magoon (1981) provided evidence that interest inventories could influence students in seeking more occupational information and in achieving more goal attainment. Various researchers have investigated methods of delivering interest inventory explanations, from Bixler and Bixler's (1945) "how-to" recommendations, to those studies that considered group interpretation sessions (Swanson, 1964; Toman & Zytowski, 1997), to including technological advances in delivering interest inventory results (Gati, 1987; Gati & Blumberg, 1991). In later chapters of this text, the five principles of interest inventory interpretation proposed by Zytowski (1999, pp. 280-283) will be used in relationship to the use of the Strong Interest Inventory and the Kuder Career Search With Person Match. The five principles are as follows:

1. Prepare for the discussion of results

2. Involve clients in communicating results

3. Use simple, emphatic communication

4. Ask clients to recapitulate their results in their own words

5. Stimulate continuing career development

As one other preview of chapters to come, a comprehensive case study of an adult will be presented in Chapter 8. That case study offers a range of background information, behavioral observations, and test scores that might be typical for a client referred for assessment.

One caveat, of which readers need be aware, is that the use of a battery of tests might be considered a more valid source of data than the use of a single test. This approach would be consistent with a multiple baseline approach to assessment in which the behavior or problem of focus is being considered from several angles, as might be afforded by the use of two cognitive instruments and/or two or three personality instruments. Carrying this instance also into the career development realm, again data yielded from multiple instruments could be more helpful than data from a single instrument. The value of the battery approach is that it can offer an estimation of the concurrent validity of the test scores. A practical example of the concept of concurrent validity is that if one test identifies a client as being high on the trait of introversion, the introversion trait should be apparent in test scores across a number of instruments, ranging from behavioral observations on the WAIS-III, to scores on the MMPI and other personality measures, to scores on an interest inventory. The battery approach offers clinicians the opportunity to cross-validate test results.

Consideration of Diversity Issues in Testing

Having discussed the domains of assessment covered in this text, we now will turn our attention to a topic of critical importance in the mental health disciplines: cross-cultural and diversity issues. These issues and concerns transcend any particular assessment domain. They also transcend the arbitrary developmental stage boundaries imposed by this text. Diversity issues have tremendous implications for all people working in and being served by the mental health professions.

In the postmodern era, there seems to be an ever-increasing awareness of individual and cultural differences. The term *diversity* is a concept that is becoming increasingly recognized and valued not only in the mental health disciplines but also more broadly across contemporary culture. Diversity is being used here in a broad context, referring not only to ethnicity but also to any other ways in which a given individual differs from the majority group. The ways in which individuals may differ include sexual orientation, religious beliefs, medical conditions or disabilities, or ethnic or culturally based values and beliefs. So it is a major error to assume that if a client looks like a member of the majority, cultural influences have had negligible impact on his or her individuality. One author had a student in class discussing a community-based alcoholism support group, and in describing the group composition, the student commented, "There were no people attending who had an ethnic background." The student was probably referring to the fact that there were no group members of a visually recognizable ethnic group. In reality, though, to be human is to have some individual attributes and characteristics that are the direct result of cultural and ethnic context, regardless of whether one is a member of the majority or minority group in a community. Therefore, in assessing a client and interpreting the meaning of standardized test scores, the question should not be, "Are there cultural influences manifested in these scores?" but instead, "*How* are this person's cultural influences manifested in these scores?" By asking the question this way, adequate attention is being afforded the effect of culture in the person's demonstrated test scores.

The importance of cultural awareness in the mental health professions cannot be overemphasized. In referring to the misuse of test data with people from cultural minority groups, Gould (1981) said the following:

> We pass through this world but once. Few tragedies can be more extensive than the stunting of life, few injustices deeper than the denial of an opportunity to strive or even hope, by a limit imposed from without, but falsely identified as lying within. (p. 28)

The topic of diversity issues in assessment is very complex. This discussion will present information about the history of testing in the context of how members of minority groups were affected, as well as concerns and implications for the current use of tests with people of minority status.

Cuellar and Paniagua (2000) made the following observation:

> During the last half of the 20th century, researchers placed a great deal of importance on brain-behavior relations. Much knowledge and control were undeniably gained from such efforts, but unfortunately culture, the true roots of much of our behavior, was largely overlooked. (p. xxiii)

As psychometrics emerged as a movement in psychology, researchers and theorists may have first overlooked culture as a strong determinant of behavioral motivation, with *behavioral motivation* in this context translating as a factor both intrinsic and extrinsic to the individual that heavily influences the nature of his or her responses to test items. Ironically, testing is one clinical area in which cultural influence carries substantial implications because of the types of decisions made about people across the full range of human development based on test results, especially in regard to IQ and personality testing. Such decisions include whether to place a child in a talented and gifted program or whether to exclude someone from certain types of occupational training (e.g., police work), based primarily on assessment data. The test scores do not necessarily gain admittance for a person, but they represent a threshold variable in setting minimum standards for inclusion in, or exclusion from, certain academic or educational privileges. In other cases, the test scores might erroneously indicate that a person has special needs and that he or she should be in a special residential placement.

Helms (1997) very eloquently summarized the problem in the context of cognitive ability testing (CAT) as follows:

> When CAT construction and performance are concerned, America's nonWhite racial and continuously subjugated ethnic minorities—especially African, Asian, Latino/Latina, and Native Americans—are most likely to be multiply . . . disadvantaged because developers of CATs generally do not have intimate knowledge of these groups. Consequently, test developers may not be familiar enough with the differential racial, cultural, and/or socioeconomic socialization experiences of these groups to integrate their unique experiences of race, culture, and class into CATs or to remove them from such measures. Thus, CATs may not be culturally equivalent for VREGs [visually recognizable ethnic group] and/or people of disadvantaged economic status and/or cultural heterogeneity. (p. 518)

Some authors (Helms, 1997; Lopez, 1997) have observed that inappropriate interpretations of test scores of clients of minority status have resulted in misclassification and, in some cases, misdiagnosis. In the past, standardized test scores have been one means of maintaining dominant versus inferior social status of individuals. Other authors (e.g., Herrnstein & Murray, 1994) have argued that differential average test scores across cultural groups "prove" the superiority and inferiority of particular ethnic groups. However, it has also been reliably demonstrated that some cultural groups process information in a manner that is not necessarily inferior but instead qualitatively different from the majority (Helms, 1997). It is important for consumers of test data to acknowledge that test scores in and of themselves have no inherent meaning—the meaning of the test scores consists of that which is ascribed to the scores by the person interpreting or making sense of the data.

One issue commonly addressed in the context of multicultural sensitivity is having an awareness of the norms and values of a client's indigenous culture. Hinkle (1994) noted the need for practitioners doing assessments to be knowledgeable of culture-specific behaviors that could influence the diagnostic process. However, developing guidelines or a belief system about culture-specific behaviors may constitute further stereotyping. Arbona (1998) noted that research has proven that among groups of people who are minorities, there tends to be more variability *within* groups than *between* groups. Thus, a diagnostic paradox exists for clinicians: A given characteristic observed in a client may be expected from the client's culture yet that characteristic would not be expected of other members of the client's culture. It is virtually impossible to classify and categorize a specific client's beliefs, attitudes, values, and behaviors as cultural or not cultural. To do so seems to represent a dichotomizing that does not exist in reality.

Ridley et al. (1998) identified this as a possibility of making either a Type I or a Type II error by not considering the impact of culture. In a Type I error, there could be a diagnosis of pathology when none exists. In a Type II error, there could be a diagnosis of no pathology when in fact some does exist. Either type of error could be detrimental to a client, depending on the context in which the error is occurring. When that erroneous interpretation is then used to make decisions about classroom placement, qualification for special services, or diagnosis and psychotropic medication, the implications for incurring harm to the client seem obvious. This is clearly a situation to be avoided at all costs. The testing process itself does not seem to be as much of a problem as is the *reason* for testing and the manner in which test scores have been used.

On the other hand, if interpreted in a culturally sensitive manner, test data can help understand a client's functioning. To be maximally beneficial to a client, test data must always be considered in a culturally relevant context and be specific to that individual. It is not too far removed from stereotyping to assume that because a person is of a particular heritage, he or she will hold certain beliefs or values. A specific case example might clarify this statement.

For this discussion, let's say we are testing a 50-year-old man, Jacques, for whom English is a second language, learned by Jacques at the age of 44. If Jacques demonstrated sub-average scores on the verbal subtests of the WAIS-III, a range of possible interpretive statements could be made, some of which would be more culturally sensitive and clinically accurate than others. The example interpretations begin with the least culturally sensitive and appropriate and progress through increasingly sensitive and clinically sound statements:

- Jacques's receptive and expressive language functioning is inferior.
- Jacques is demonstrating a relative weakness in his auditory processing.
- Jacques's facility with the English language creates difficulty for him in oral communication.
- It is unclear whether Jacques's demonstrated oral communication problems are the result solely of language differences or of residual inefficiencies in his cognitive processing that would be apparent had he been evaluated in his native language.

In this example, the test score was the same in each case, but the meaning ascribed to the test score in the first example is inappropriately judgmental and clinically inaccurate, whereas the final statement is both culturally sensitive and clinically accurate.

When testing and interpreting test scores for any client, regardless of whether he or she is of a cultural minority group, it is absolutely essential that the test scores be considered in the sociocultural context of that client's learning history. To do any less is to potentially commit an egregious error in understanding what the scores mean and in providing services to that person. Mental health practitioners must promote culturally sensitive interpretation of test data to prevent the use of test data as a means of suppressing and discriminating against people who are members of minority groups.

The practitioner using test data in a culturally sensitive manner is faced with two key questions in terms of diagnostic and treatment implications (Arbona, 1998). First, to what extent does the client's presentation (including symptoms, strengths, affect, and mood) constitute state versus trait characteristics? In other words, to what extent is this current presentation a situational response to a temporally defined stressor versus a characteristic, predictable way of responding to any one of many types of stressors? Second, to what extent do the client's behaviors or symptoms facilitate an adaptive response to stressors in the context of the client's sociocultural environment?

Summary

This chapter has presented a paradigm for understanding the process through which a referral question comes into being, a client is assessed and evaluated, test data are interpreted, and results are disseminated to involved people (the client, client's family, and/or the referring professional). We also presented one paradigm for conceptualizing how presenting problems and referral questions evolve for clients.

There are a number of rationales offered for the selection of the particular instruments being used and discussed in this book. Readers will note that there are a vast number of other valid and reliable instruments in each of the three domains (cognitive, personality, and career interest) being covered in this book.

In addition, we have discussed multicultural and diversity issues in the context of assessment. It is imperative that any assessment data be interpreted through the filter of sociocultural variables relevant to the individual client. Finally, this text is intended to be used as a supplement to training and supervision in application of test data.

Resource List

Readers seeking a broader description of many different types of tests are referred to textbooks on assessment such as *The Handbook of Psychological Assessment* (Groth-Marnat, 1999), *Psychological Testing* (Anastasi & Urbina, 1997), or *Tests and Assessment*

(Walsh & Betz, 1995). In addition, many books are available that help readers learn the subtleties of test interpretation for particular instruments, such as *Intelligent Testing With the WAIS-III* (Kaufman, 1996) or, alternatively, *Essentials of WAIS-III Assessment* (Kaufman & Lichtenberger, 1999). The best sources besides the test manuals on the MMPI-2 and MMPI-A are Butcher and Williams (2000) and Graham (2000). A valuable resource for orienting clients to personality testing and structuring feedback sessions about test results to gain maximum therapeutic effect is Finn (1996). For assistance with interpreting results obtained from a Kuder Career Search, readers can go online at www.kuder.com and open the Kuder Tutorial.

For readers wishing to further hone their skills in test administration and interpretation, another good source of training and developing expertise is to attend workshops or seminars. There are often advertisements in professional publications such as the American Psychological Association's *Monitor* or the American Counseling Association's *Counseling Today* for training workshops, sometimes presented by the author of a test or sometimes presented by representatives of a test publishing company. Such workshops often offer an explanation and understanding of the theoretical underpinnings of the instrument and then experiential learning opportunities to apply new learning in theoretical client situations. This training might also help a clinician develop a degree of confidence about using the test data in a competent and benevolent manner, thus maximizing the benefit to one's clients.

Discussion Questions

1. How does the issue of testing clients from minority groups affect you and your practice, or how did it affect you in the past?

2. In your work with clients, have you ever had the opportunity to refer someone for assessment? What information did you hope to gain from that process?

3. Have you had any contact or experience with test data that was misused or misinterpreted? How might a future situation like that be avoided?

References

Alfonso, V. C., & Pratt, S. I. (1997). Issues and suggestions for training professionals in assessing intelligence. In D. P. Flanagan, J. L. Genshaft, & P. L. Harrison (Eds.), *Contemporary intellectual assessment: Theories, tests, and issues* (pp. 326-344). New York: Guilford.

American Educational Research Association, American Psychological Association, and National Council on Measurement in Education. (1999). *Standards for educational and psychological testing.* Washington, DC: Author.

American Psychiatric Association. (2000). *Diagnostic and statistical manual of mental disorders* (4th ed., text rev.). Washington, DC: Author.

Anastasi, A., & Urbina, S. (1997). *Psychological testing* (7th ed.). Upper Saddle River, NJ: Prentice Hall.

Arbona, C. (1998). Psychological assessment: Multicultural or universal? *The Counseling Psychologist, 26*, 911-921.

Bixler, R. H., & Bixler, V. H. (1945). Clinical counseling in vocational guidance. *Journal of Clinical Psychology, 1*, 186-192.

Butcher, J. N., Dahlstrom, W. G., Graham, J. R., Tellegen, A., & Kaemmer, B. (1989). *MMPI-2 (Minnesota Multiphasic Personality Inventory-2): Manual for administration and scoring.* Minneapolis: University of Minnesota Press.

Butcher, J. N., & Williams, C. L. (2000). *Essentials of MMPI-2 and MMPI-A interpretation* (2nd ed.). Minneapolis: University of Minnesota Press.

Butcher, J. N., Williams, C. L., Graham, J. R., Archer, R. P., Tellegen, A., Ben-Porath, Y. S., & Kaemmer, B. (1992). *MMPI-A (Minnesota Multiphasic Personality Inventory for Adolescents): Manual for administration, scoring and interpretation.* Minneapolis: University of Minnesota Press.

Catell, R. B., Eber, H., & Tatsuoka, M. M. (1970). *Handbook for the Sixteen PF.* Champaign, IL: Institute for Personality and Ability Testing.

Catell, R. B., Eber, H., & Tatsuoka, M. M. (1980). *Handbook for the Sixteen Personality Factor Questionnaire (16PF).* Champaign, IL: Institute for Personality and Ability Testing.

Cuellar, I., & Paniagua, F. A. (Eds.). (2000). *Handbook of multicultural mental health: Assessment and treatment of diverse populations.* San Diego, CA: Academic Press.

Dawis, R. V., & Lofquist, L. H. (1984). *A psychological theory of work adjustment.* Minneapolis: University of Minneapolis Press.

Draguns, J. G. (1996). Multicultural and cross-cultural assessment: Dilemmas and decisions. In G. R. Sodowsky & J. C. Impara (Eds.), *Multicultural assessment in counseling and clinical psychology* (pp. 37-84). Lincoln, NE: Buros Institute of Mental Measurements.

Elliott, C. D. (1990). *Differential Ability Scales: Administration and scoring manual.* San Antonio, TX: The Psychological Corporation.

Finn, S. E. (1996). *Manual for using the MMPI-2 as a therapeutic intervention.* Minneapolis: University of Minnesota Press.

Finn, S. E., & Tonsager, M. E. (1992). Therapeutic effects of providing MMPI-2 test feedback to college students awaiting therapy. *Psychological Assessment, 4,* 278-287.

Gati, I. (1987). Description and validation of a procedure for the interpretation of an interest inventory score profile. *Journal of Counseling Psychology, 34,* 141-148.

Gati, I., & Blumberg, D. (1991). Computer versus counselor interpretation of interest inventories: The case of the Self-Directed Search. *Journal of Counseling Psychology, 38,* 350-366.

Gottfredson, L. S. (1999). The nature and nurture of vocational interests. In M. L. Savickas & A. R. Spokane (Eds.), *Vocational interests: Meaning, measurement, and counseling use* (pp. 57-85). Palo Alto, CA: Davies-Black.

Gough, H. G. (1975). *California Psychological Inventory manual.* Palo Alto, CA: Consulting Psychologists Press.

Gough, H. G. (1975). *Manual for the California Personality Inventory.* Palo Alto, CA: Consulting Psychologists Press.

Gough, H. G. (1987). *California Personality Inventory administration guide.* Palo Alto, CA: Consulting Psychologists Press.

Gould, S. J. (1981). *The mismeasure of man.* New York: Norton.

Graham, J. R. (2000). *MMPI-2: Assessing personality and psychopathology* (3rd ed.). New York: Oxford University Press.

Gregory, R. J. (2000). *Psychological testing: History, principles, and applications* (3rd ed.). Boston: Allyn & Bacon.

Groth-Marnat, G. (1999). *The handbook of psychological assessment* (3rd ed.). New York: John Wiley.

Guilford, J. S., Guilford, J. P., & Zimmerman, W. S. (1978). *Interpretive system for the Guilford-Zimmerman Temperament Survey.* Orange, CA: Sheridan Psychological Services.

Handler, L., & Meyer, G. (1998). The importance of teaching and learning personality assessment. In L. Handler & M. Hilsenroth (Eds.), *Teaching and learning personality assessment* (pp. 3-30). Mahwah, NJ: Lawrence Erlbaum.

Harmon, L. W., Hansen, J. C., Borgen, F. H., & Hammer, A. L. (1994). *The Strong Interest Inventory: Applications and technical guide.* Palo Alto, CA: Consulting Psychologists Press.

Hathaway, S. R., & McKinley, J. C. (1942). *The Minnesota Multiphasic Personality Schedule.* Minneapolis: University of Minnesota Press.

Helms, J. E. (1997). The triple quandary of race, culture, and social class in standardized cognitive ability testing. In D. P. Flanagan, J. L. Genshaft, & P. L. Harrison (Eds.), *Contemporary intellectual assessment: Theories, tests, and issues* (pp. 517-532). New York: Guilford.

Herrnstein, R. J., & Murray, C. (1994). *The bell curve: Intelligence and class structure in American life.* New York: Free Press.

Hinkle, J. S. (1994). Practitioners and cross-cultural assessment: A practical guide to information and training. *Measurement and Evaluation in Counseling and Development, 27,* 103-115.

Hoffman, M. A., Spokane, A. R., & Magoon, T. M. (1981). Effects of feedback mode on counseling outcomes using the Strong-Campbell Interest Inventory: Does the counselor really matter? *Journal of Counseling Psychology, 28,* 119-125.

Holland, J. L. (1973). *Making vocational choices: A theory of careers.* Englewood Cliffs, NJ: Prentice Hall.

Kaufman, A. (1996). *Intelligent testing with the WAIS-III.* New York: John Wiley.

Kaufman, A. S., & Kaufman, N. L. (1993). *Kaufman Adolescent & Adult Intelligence Test.* Circle Pines, MN: American Guidance Service.

Kaufman, A. S., & Lichtenberger, E. O. (1999). *Essentials of WAIS-III assessment.* New York: John Wiley.

Lopez, E. C. (1997). The cognitive assessment of limited English proficient and bilingual children. In D. P. Flanagan, J. L. Genshaft, & P. L. Harrison (Eds.), *Contemporary intellectual assessment: Theories, tests, and issues* (pp. 503-516). New York: Guilford.

MacCluskie, K. C., & Ingersoll, R. E. (2001). *Becoming a 21st century agency counselor: Personal and professional explorations.* Pacific Grove, CA: Brooks/Cole.

Merriam, S. B., & Caffarella, K. S. (1999). *Learning in adulthood.* San Francisco: Jossey-Bass.

Millon, T. (1983). *Millon Clinical Multiaxial Inventory manual* (3rd ed.). Minneapolis, MN: Interpretive Scoring Systems.

Millon, T. (1987). *Millon Clinical Multiaxial Inventory II (MMCI-II) manual* (3rd ed.). Minneapolis, MN: Interpretive Scoring Systems.

Murray, H. A. (1943). *Thematic Apperception Test.* Cambridge, MA: Harvard University Press.

Myers, I. (1987). *Introduction to type.* Palo Alto, CA: Consulting Psychologists Press.

Newmark, C. S., & McCord, D. M. (1996). The Minnesota Multiphasic Personality Inventory-2 (MMPI-2). In C. S. Newmark (Ed.), *Major psychological assessment instruments* (2nd ed., pp. 1-58). Boston: Allyn & Bacon.

Parsons, F. (1909). *Choosing a vocation.* Boston: Houghton Mifflin.

Ridley, C. R., Li, L. C., & Hill, C. L. (1998). Multicultural assessment: Reexamination, reconceptualization, and practical application. *The Counseling Psychologist, 26,* 827-910.

Roberti, J. W., Fox, D. J., & Tunick, R. H. (2001, April). *Alternative personality variables and the relationship to Holland's personality types in college students.* Paper presented at the Great Lakes Conference, American Psychological Association Division 17 Conference, University of Akron, Akron, OH.

Rorschach, H. (1941). Psychodiagnostics (H. Huber Verlag, Trans.). Bern, Switzerland: Bircher. (Original work published 1921).

Sattler, J. M. (2001a). *Assessment of children: Behavior and clinical applications* (4th ed.). San Diego, CA: Author.

Sattler, J. M. (2001b). *Assessment of children: Cognitive applications* (4th ed.). San Diego, CA: Author.

Savickas, M. L. (1999). The psychology of interests. In M. L. Savickas & A. R. Spokane (Eds.), *Vocational interests: Meaning, measurement, and counseling use* (pp. 19-56). Palo Alto, CA: Davies-Black.

Shipley, W. C., & Zachary, R. A. (1986). *Shipley Institute of Living Scale.* Los Angeles: Western Psychological Services.

Spengler, P. M. (1998). Multicultural assessment and a scientist-practitioner model of psychological assessment. *The Counseling Psychologist, 26,* 930-939.

Super, D. E. (1993). The two faces of counseling: Or is it three? *The Career Development Quarterly, 42,* 132-136.

Swanson, R. A. (1964). A study of the factors related to the distortion of interest inventory information interpreted to individuals and to groups. *Dissertation Abstracts International, 64,* 4214.

Thorndike, R. L., Hagen, E., & Sattler, J. (1986). *Stanford-Binet Intelligence Scale* (4th ed.). Chicago: Riverside.

Toman, S. M., & Savickas, M. L. (1997). Career choice readiness moderates the effects of interest inventories. *Journal of Career Assessment, 5,* 275-291.

Toman, S. M., & Zytowski, D. (1997, January). *Interpreting interest inventories to groups.* Paper presented at the annual convention of the National Career Development Association, Daytona Beach, FL.

Walsh, W. B., & Betz, N. E. (1995). *Tests and assessment* (3rd ed.). Englewood Cliffs, NJ: Prentice Hall.

Watkins, C. E., Jr., Campbell, V. L., & McGregor, P. (1988). Counseling psychologists' uses of and opinions about psychological tests: A contemporary perspective. *The Counseling Psychologist, 16,* 476-486.

Watkins, C. E., Jr., Campbell, V. L., Niebirding, R., & Hallmark, R. (1995). Contemporary practice of psychological assessments by clinical psychologists. *Professional Psychology: Research and Practice, 26,* 54-60.

Wechsler, D. (1991). *Wechsler Intelligence Scale for Children* (3rd rev. ed.). San Antonio, TX: The Psychological Corporation.

Wechsler, D. (1997). *Wechsler Adult Intelligence Scale* (3rd rev. ed.). San Antonio, TX: The Psychological Corporation.

Woodworth, R. (1920). *Personal data sheet.* Chicago: Stoelting.

Zytowski, D. (1999). How to talk to people about their interest inventory results. In M. L. Savickas & A. R. Spokane (Eds.), *Vocational interests: Meaning, measurement, and counseling use* (pp. 277-293). Palo Alto, CA: Davies-Black.

Zytowski, D. (2002). *Kuder Career Search: User's manual.* Adel, IA: National Career Development Services.

2

The WAIS-III

Guidelines for Administration and Interpretation

This chapter covers the pragmatic aspects of using the Wechsler Adult Intelligence Scale—Third Revision (WAIS-III) in clinical practice, with emphasis on how to integrate the data into counseling goals. We begin with a description and explanation of the psychometric features of the WAIS-III. This explanation is geared toward conceptual understanding of the instrument, including cognitive domains being assessed and technical aspects of the WAIS-III—namely, mean, standard deviation, and standard error of measurement. The goal is to give readers some general information that can quickly be referenced and is not intended to replace the more detailed explanations offered in a comprehensive assessment text.

We then go on to present a strategy for interpreting test scores. This strategy represents an integration of several experts' recommendations about how to interpret WAIS-III scores. Finally, the chapter concludes with a case example that presents background and behavioral data with test scores and illustrates the interpretive process. One important note is that when we discuss interpretation in this chapter, we are referring to a clinician synthesizing the test data and arriving at some conclusions. The process of giving the client feedback and explaining test results should happen after the clinician has fully interpreted and accounted for the score configuration and other data.

The WAIS-III

The WAIS-III administration manual gives a specific script for testers to use as they are introducing the WAIS-III to a client. As the WAIS-III is administered, the tester alternates between performance and verbal subtests. However, the descriptions of the subtests that follow are organized into the six subtests that comprise the Verbal scale and the five subtests that comprise the Performance scale. Table 2.1 presents a description of the WAIS-III subtests and the ability areas they purport to assess.

Overview of Psychometric Features of the WAIS-III

There are three levels of scores yielded from a WAIS-III administration: full-scale (or overall) score, factor scores, and subtest scaled scores. Scores on each of these levels are expressed as transformed scores, meaning that the client's score reflects how well the client performed compared to her or his age peers in the standardization sample. The transformed score represents a comparison of the client's raw score on a subtest, or combination of subtests, to the raw scores of many individuals in the standardization sample who were the same chronological age as the client.

One helpful way to conceptualize the variety of standardized scores that can be obtained from the WAIS-III is to think of beginning with broad, inclusive scores that express broad ability domains, then moving to scores that express progressively more specific, circumscribed ability domains. The concept of using systematically progressive refinement in analyzing a person's profile is an approach well documented and widely established in assessment literature (Kamphaus, 1993; Kaufman, 1990, 1994; Kramer, 1993; Naglieri, 1993; Sattler, 2001).

The factor scales are presented below following a scheme that progresses from most general to most specific. All of the factor scales are expressed as a standard score with a mean of 100 and standard deviation of 15. As a brief review, a standard score of 100 refers to the mean score obtained by people in the standardization sample. The standard deviation is an expression of how other scores are dispersed around the mean. In a normal (bell-curve) distribution, 68% of

Table 2.1   Description of WAIS-III Subtests and Domains Assessed

Subtest	Task Description	Skill Domains Being Assessed
Vocabulary	The tester says one word at a time and asks the client to provide a definition of the word. For example, "What does *delete* mean?"	Verbal communication skills, overall level of intellectual functioning, ability to retain and produce material learned in a variety of settings
Similarities	The tester gives the client word pairs and the client must identify a category sufficiently broad to encompass both of the stimulus words. An example would be, "How are a doctor and dentist alike?"	Ability to deduce relationships and abstract verbal conceptualization
Arithmetic	The tester reads story problems in which the application of arithmetic skills is required to solve the task. An example would be, "If I had 16 apples I wanted to evenly distribute to four people, how many apples would each person get?"	Ability to apply computational skills; ability to attend and concentrate
Digit Span	There are two components to this subtest. In Digits Forward, the tester reads a string of digits, and the client must repeat the digits in the same order as they were read. In Digits Backward, the tester reads a string of digits and the client must reverse the order of the digits as he or she repeats them.	Attention, concentration, short-term auditory learning
Information	The tester asks the client a variety of general information questions in a variety of topic areas. For example, a question might be, "Who was Helen Keller?"	Degree of acculturation, awareness of one's environment, extent of cultural stimulation

(Continued)

33

Table 2.1 (Continued)

Subtest	Task Description	Skill Domains Being Assessed
Comprehension	The tester asks the client a variety of questions about rationales for commonly accepted social norms, rules, and laws. An example might be, "Why should people go to the dentist?"	Awareness of social norms, degree of moral judgment and development, awareness and understanding of common social conventions
Letter-Number Sequencing	The tester reads a string of digits and letters, alternating between a letter and a number, and the client must sort them into first digits in ascending order, then letters in alphabetic order, before repeating them back to the tester.	Auditory discrimination, attention and concentration, sequencing ability
Picture Completion	The client is presented with a series of color drawings of common items and must identify an important component of the item that is missing.	Visual scanning ability, ability to distinguish essential from nonessential details
Digit Symbol Coding	The client is shown nonsense symbols, with a unique symbol that corresponds with each of the digits 1 through 9. Then, he or she looks at a series of blocks with a digit in the top of the box and a blank below the digit and reproduces the nonsense symbol that corresponds with that particular digit.	Visual motor speed, manual dexterity, persistence, attention
Block Design	The testee is given a number of blocks that are all red on some sides, all white on other sides, and half red/half white on other sides. Then he or she is given a series of drawings of red and white designs, which must be re-created using the available blocks.	Nonverbal concept formation, spatial visualization, overall perceptual organization, motor speed

(Continued)

Table 2.1 (Continued)

Subtest	Task Description	Skill Domains Being Assessed
Matrix Reasoning	The testee is presented with a color drawing in which there is some type of recurrent pattern. Then, from a choice of four possibilities, he or she must identify the item that best completes the progression.	Fluid intelligence, flexible problem solving
Picture Arrangement	The testee is given a series of small cardboard squares that have related drawings on them. The cards are presented out of sequence, and the testee must move the cards into a logical sequence that tells a story, similar to a comic strip.	Sequential reasoning, awareness of social norms
Symbol Search	The testee is provided with two target abstract symbols on one side of a page and then must scan a string of several symbols and ascertain whether both of the target symbols are present in the string.	Cognitive processing speed, visual scanning ability
Object Assembly	The client is presented with puzzle pieces that, when properly constructed, form a familiar object. He or she must assemble the puzzle correctly, as quickly as possible.	Ability to quickly form visual concepts, motor speed, visual-motor integration

NOTE: The description of Object Assembly is being offered in the event that the reader is using a WAIS-R rather than a WAIS-III. In situations when a WAIS-R has been previously administered, it can be clinically useful to administer Object Assembly for comparison of the client's current performance with previous Object Assembly performance. On the WAIS-R, Object Assembly was routinely administered as part of the test and was one of the subtests included in calculating the Performance IQ. However, when the WAIS-R was revised to the WAIS-III, the factor loadings for Object Assembly were so low in comparison to the factor loadings of the other performance subtests that it was not included in any factor score on the WAIS-III.

scores are within one standard deviation of the mean, 95% of the scores are within two standard deviations of the mean, and 99% of the scores are within three standard deviations of the mean.

WAIS-III Factor Scales

Figure 2.1 presents a visual scheme with which readers can conceptualize the stair-step approach to the increasing refinement with which scores should be considered as a test interpretation progresses.

Full Scale Intelligence Quotient (FSIQ). This score reflects the client's overall performance on the entire WAIS-III, across all the subtests administered. In a single score, it suggests the overall level of intellectual functioning as measured by the WAIS-III.

Verbal Intelligence Quotient (VIQ). This score indicates, in a single score, the client's performance across all the subtests that comprise the Verbal scale. Ideally, it describes a client's facility with language, including receptive and expressive language, verbal reasoning, verbal conceptualization, and auditory attention/concentration. Applicable subtests are Vocabulary, Similarities, Arithmetic, Digit Span, Information, and Comprehension.

Performance Intelligence Quotient (PIQ). This score indicates the client's performance across all the nonverbal subtests that comprise the Performance scale. It describes a person's eye-hand coordination, visual perceptual ability, motor speed, and processing speed. The involved subtests are Picture Completion, Digit Symbol Coding, Block Design, Matrix Reasoning, and Picture Arrangement.

Verbal Comprehension Index (VCI). This score describes his or her performance on the verbal subtests not heavily reliant on the client's attention, concentration, or processing speed for demonstration of the skill domain. The subtests in this factor are Vocabulary, Similarities, and Comprehension.

Perceptual Organization Index (POI). This score describes the client's performance on the nonverbal tests less dependent on speed of response than the remaining Performance subtests.

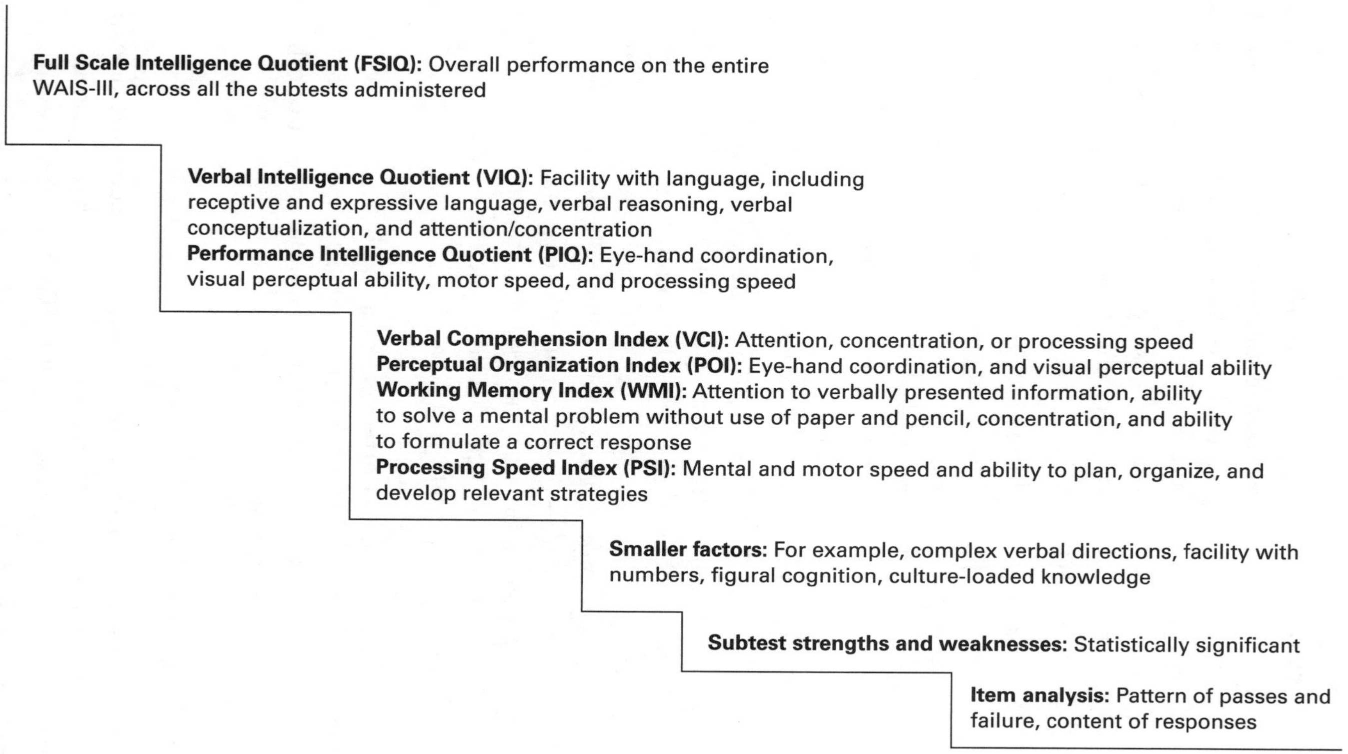

Full Scale Intelligence Quotient (FSIQ): Overall performance on the entire WAIS-III, across all the subtests administered

Verbal Intelligence Quotient (VIQ): Facility with language, including receptive and expressive language, verbal reasoning, verbal conceptualization, and attention/concentration

Performance Intelligence Quotient (PIQ): Eye-hand coordination, visual perceptual ability, motor speed, and processing speed

Verbal Comprehension Index (VCI): Attention, concentration, or processing speed

Perceptual Organization Index (POI): Eye-hand coordination, and visual perceptual ability

Working Memory Index (WMI): Attention to verbally presented information, ability to solve a mental problem without use of paper and pencil, concentration, and ability to formulate a correct response

Processing Speed Index (PSI): Mental and motor speed and ability to plan, organize, and develop relevant strategies

Smaller factors: For example, complex verbal directions, facility with numbers, figural cognition, culture-loaded knowledge

Subtest strengths and weaknesses: Statistically significant

Item analysis: Pattern of passes and failure, content of responses

Figure 2.1   The Stair-Step Approach to WAIS-III Interpretation

The subtests on the POI factor are Picture Completion, Block Design, and Matrix Reasoning.

Working Memory Index (WMI). This score integrates the client's performance on the subtests that require the most attention to verbally presented information, ability to solve a mental problem without use of paper and pencil, concentration, and ability to formulate a correct response. The subtests that comprise this factor are Arithmetic, Digit Span, and Letter-Number Sequencing.

Processing Speed Index (PSI). This score reflects the testee's performance on those subtests that are most dependent on speedy, yet accurate, performance. This factor estimates the testee's mental and motor speed and ability to plan, organize, and develop relevant strategies. This score can also be lowered by poor motivation. The subtests from which this factor are derived are Digit Symbol Coding and Symbol Search.

Subtest Scaled Scores. This score is the basic building block for each factor score (Verbal IQ, Performance IQ, Full Scale IQ, Verbal Comprehension Index, Perceptual Organization Index, Working Memory Index, and Processing Speed Index). Each of the subtests listed in Table 2.1 yields a raw score—the actual number of points for all the correct responses on that subtest. The tester then converts the raw score to a scaled score, which has a mean of 10 and a standard deviation of 3.

The following section offers definitions of common psychometric terms. Familiarity with these terms can be helpful not only in the context of cognitive assessment but also in the context of other types of psychological assessment.

Standard Deviation

As mentioned earlier in this chapter, the standard deviation is central to understanding the factor scores that constitute an IQ (also referred to as a deviation IQ). The standard deviation is an indication of how closely test scores are dispersed, or distributed, around the mean test score. In the norming process, test developers administer test items to a large number of people, and from all those test administrations they determine what raw score constitutes "average" performance. They are also able to determine, from that norming process, how wide the "spread" is—in other words, the frequency with which people in the norm group earned particular raw scores. On a "standardized" test, the test developers have established the frequency of raw scores for a given scale, and they then establish the mean and standard deviation values from those raw scores. A test with a small standard deviation is one on which many people obtained raw scores close in value; a larger standard deviation means that there was much variability or discrepancy between people's raw scores. On standardized tests available for purchase, the developers have already established the mean and standard deviation for users.

Standard Error of Measurement

In addition to standard deviation, one other statistical concept important for clinicians to understand in the interpretation process is standard error of measurement. The standard error of measurement is synonymous with the term *confidence band.* The test developers calculated standard error of measurement for each subtest as well as each factor scale. Standard error of measurement can be thought of as a normal distribution of raw scores obtained by the same person. Imagine the same subtest being administered to the same person many times (assuming that no practice effect improved his or her scores). The standard error of measurement is the distribution of scores he or she would obtain over all those administrations.

The administration manual provides standard error of measurement values for factor scales and subtests. On the factor scales, users can report either 90% or 95% confidence range, and on the subtests, scores can be reported at either the 85% or 95% confidence range. At the 85% confidence level, the range of scores will be smaller than at the 95% confidence level. For example, the standard error of measurement on the Vocabulary subtest is 1.99 at the .15 (85% confidence) and 2.30 at the .05 level (95% confidence). Thus, if a client obtained a scaled score of 11 on Vocabulary, in 85 out of 100 test administrations, his or her scaled score would fall between

9.01 and 12.99. In 95 out of 100 test administrations, his or her scaled score would fall between 8.7 and 13.3. In reality, scaled scores are always reported as whole numbers, not decimals. In this instance, the standard error of measurement of 1.99 versus 2.33 is a difference of .4, which is less than half a point. In this case, mathematical precision does not necessarily correlate directly with practical implications. However, the small differences in subtest standard error of measurement between the .15 and .05 confidence levels are evidence that the reliability of the WAIS-III is excellent, in that there is not much variability in a person's score that is the result of test construction.

Following the actual test administration, raw scores are used only for score conversion to scaled and standard scores. Raw scores are never reported as part of a final report because they have no utility beyond providing the raw data from which the standardized data are obtained. Conversion from raw to scaled and standard scores is part of the completion of the actual testing component of an evaluation.

Guidelines for Introducing and Administering the Wechsler Scales

The scope of this chapter will be limited to the WAIS-III because there are many constraints and conditions when testing children that differ from testing adults. The considerations and modifications for testing children are sufficiently extensive that many excellent texts have been written focusing solely on evaluating children. Interested readers might consider several such texts, listed at the end of the chapter.

Referral Sources

A client might be referred for testing by any one of a number of sources. Common referral sources include but are not limited to another mental health professional, a case worker in another human service agency, personnel in an educational setting, family members of the client, or the client himself or herself. A client is most likely to be referred for individual intelligence testing either because of awareness of some cognitive difficulty or because a decision is about to be made, and it is felt that intelligence test data will be helpful in making that decision. The following examples provide typical situations from which a referral question might evolve and the subsequent referral question as it would be appropriately worded:

- A client has been involved in an outpatient substance abuse treatment group and seems unable to track and follow the discussions in the treatment group.

  Referral question: Is this patient demonstrating evidence of organic impairment? Does his test performance offer any information as to the cause of his inability to stay on the topic?

- A client has applied for Social Security disability benefits, and the Social Security Disability Bureau requires an evaluation to determine whether the client is still capable of maintaining employment despite the disabling condition.

  Referral question: What is this person's current level of intellectual functioning? Would she be capable of maintaining employment and, if so, at what level of complexity?

- A client has begun attending college classes and is having difficulty passing tests despite strenuous studying and class preparation.

  Referral question: What are possible explanations for this client's apparent difficulty passing tests?

- An adolescent had been achieving at a slow average rate in school for several years and now is showing even less academic progress.

  Referral question: Why is this student achieving at such a slow rate?

Occasionally, a person might self-refer to find out "how smart" he or she is. However, the fees for testing are often high, and many third-party payers are disinclined to cover the cost of the evaluation. Therefore, demand for self-referred, self-paid evaluations is likely to be quite low. Nevertheless, it would be important for a clinician to discuss with the client what she or he hopes to gain by participating in testing. In some cases, the client's goals may not be best served by doing intelligence testing—perhaps some other type of assessment and/or evaluation would be more appropriate. Under these circumstances, either agreeing on alternative clinical activity or referring the client to someone who could offer the alternative clinical services would be appropriate.

Communicating Prior to Testing

It can be helpful for the tester to converse with the referral source to clarify the questions he or she hopes to have answered with the testing. Dialoguing with the referral source has several benefits.

First, it can help the tester determine whether individual intelligence testing is the best clinical activity to answer the referral question. There may be some other type of assessment that would be a more appropriate avenue for answering the question. Second, the referral source might be requesting testing because of observing problematic behaviors or possible symptoms of a disorder. Although one needs to be careful not to hold preconceived ideas about how the client's behaviors should be interpreted, it is also important to be alert to observe the types of behaviors that could be related to the reason for assessment. A clinician doing testing needs to find the balance between inappropriately pathologizing and minimizing or missing important behavioral clues to a possible disorder. Third, it can help the tester get feedback about previous reports that may have been done for that referral source. There may have been particular features or aspects of previous reports that were notably helpful to that person, which could be incorporated in the current report. Ensuring that the needs of the referral source are being met can increase the likelihood of additional future referrals. Fourth, it can inform the tester as to possible secondary gain the client may have for presenting with exaggerated symptoms. The emphasis here is on making an accurate observation and assessment of the client's abilities, and if the client is malingering, an accurate picture will be difficult to obtain. Finally, it can alert the tester that the client may have some special needs for which arrangements or accommodations can be made prior to when the client actually comes for his or her appointment (Kaufman & Lichtenberger, 2000). For example, the lighting arrangement may need to be modified for someone with poor vision.

Beginning the Evaluation

It is essential (Gregory, 1999; Katz, 1985; Kaufman & Lichtenberger, 2000) that the tester enter an assessment knowing what questions he or she is trying to answer and expecting to be as flexible as possible. For example, a tester needs to be able to know how to make flexible accommodations to assess the word knowledge and verbal conceptualization of a client with a hearing loss. It is possible that a client will present with some limitations of which even the referral source is unaware.

In every assessment, the tester is faced with a paradox—adhering to standardization guidelines yet maximizing testing conditions under which the client will optimally perform. On one hand, the Wechsler scales were normed under very consistent, standard testing conditions. The further away from standardization conditions one moves, the more one compromises the validity of the obtained scores. If the client's scores are not obtained under the same conditions as the scores of the norming population, then it will be inaccurate to compare the obtained scores to the scores of the norming group. However, it is impossible to exactly replicate standardization conditions. Although the WAIS-III administration manual describes ideal conditions, it may not always be possible for a tester to actually maintain those conditions throughout the testing. Nevertheless, it is important to at least try, knowing that absolute replication is an ideal goal to which testers strive but may not arrive.

Gathering Background Information

Katz (1985) suggested that the clinician conceptualize the testing process as parallel to the counseling process in terms of the value of relationship building and rapport, only with a more compressed time frame. It is also helpful at the beginning of the evaluation to discuss with the client his or her perception of the reason for referral. Surprisingly, a client may arrive for a testing appointment without a clear idea of why the referral source requested the evaluation. Taking the first few minutes of an assessment to explain the referral question can result in noticeable anxiety reduction for the client.

Having explained the referral question, it can also be helpful to then discuss the sequence of events that will occur over the course of the assessment.

It is advisable to do a clinical interview and mental status examination as a preliminary component of the evaluation. The clinical interview should be conducted with the client directly, and in some cases, it might also be valuable to interview a collateral such as an adult child, a relationship partner, or a parent. Gregory (1999) observed that "a thorough history is not just helpful—it is crucial to the proper interpretation of assessment results" (p. 7). Beyond the topic areas covered in a typical intake session, in the context of conducting an intellectual evaluation, additional points of discussion should be addressed. Helpful questions to ask might include the following:

How the reason for testing referral came about

The history of symptoms related to the reason for referral

Educational, occupational, social, medical, and cultural history

    Parents' educational history

    English as a first or second language?

    Is the United States the primary or secondary culture?

    History of head injury, seizures, high fevers, or substance abuse and, if so, awareness of any symptoms afterward

It is important to assess the extent to which organic impairment is contributing to a client's difficulties. Organic impairment refers to a physical or medical condition that causes either temporary or permanent deterioration of a client's psychological functioning. In the specialty field of neuropsychology, organic impairment can also refer to measurable impairment in a client's brain and brain stem, resulting in behavioral changes. Pollack, Levy, and Breitholtz (1999) noted that approximately 10% of the clients presenting for services at a mental health center present with symptoms entirely due to a medical illness. Nearly 25% have medical conditions that exacerbate their psychiatric condition. It follows that among clients referred for assessment, there could be an even higher likelihood of organic impairment. Thus, clinicians need to be aware of some hallmark indicators of organic disturbance. Pollack et al. (1999) offered readers a checklist of clinical presentations that can be indicators of an organic component in the diagnostic picture. They are as follows:

1. First episode of a major disorder with catatonic, psychotic, and severe mood symptoms

2. Acute or abrupt onset of symptoms, especially when the symptom onset is a drastic departure from the premorbid mood or behavior

3. Initial onset of symptoms after age 40

4. Psychiatric symptoms that emerge immediately before, during, or after a medical illness

5. Lack of identifiable situational or environmental stressors to account for the onset of symptoms

6. Symptoms that are disproportionately severe given identifiable psychosocial stressors

7. Cognitive complaints and vegetative symptoms that seem disproportionately severe given the other symptoms

8. Rapidly worsening change in mental status, involving level of consciousness, disorientation, attention deficits, short-term planning, language processing, or problem solving

9. Hallucinations involving senses other than auditory (tactile—touch, gustatory—taste, olfactory—smell, or visual—sight)

10. Changes in motor functioning such as tremor, slowed or uncoordinated gait, dysarthria (poor pronunciation of words), or simple, repetitive movements of the face and hands

11. Experiential phenomena such as déjà vu (sense of familiarity in a novel situation), jamais vu (sense of strangeness in a familiar situation), derealization, and depersonalization

12. Signs associated with possible brain dysfunction (e.g., language disturbance, difficulty coordinating motor movements

for complex tasks, and inability to recognize or name familiar objects)

13. History of illness that can be associated with mental status change

14. Symptoms of organ failure that can affect brain functioning (e.g., jaundice indicating hepatitis or dypsnea indicating cardiac or pulmonary disease)

15. New-onset headaches with no history of headaches

In the process of conducting the initial interview and/or collecting background information, patterns of symptoms or onset of the disorder that are consistent with the above listed indicators need to be further investigated. In some cases, this will mean further questioning and clarification; in other cases, it may mean referring the client to a physician for a thorough physical examination before proceeding. If the psychiatric symptoms are arising from a medical condition that is undiagnosed or untreated, the results of a psychological evaluation will not be a valid indication of the client's cognitive ability.

Beutler (1995) noted that one of the tasks of a clinician evaluating a client is to first establish a working hypothesis about levels of functioning and response to a variety of tasks and stressors and then to make an educated guest about the extent to which the test results are attributable to state versus trait characteristics. If the client's responses to you or the testing situation emanate from extreme anxiety, the anxious condition is a state not always characteristic of that person. A good evaluation should attempt to assess both state and trait components of the individual to generate a meaningful response to the referral questions.

At the same time the tester is gathering information related to the content of the client's responses to the above questions, he or she also must attend to mental status aspects of the interview information. Mental status aspects would include vocabulary, articulation, range of affect, ability to stay on a topic, hygiene, attention, and concentration. A tester should also look for the client's degree of engageability and rapport. It is essential to strive for maximum rapport. It also is important to keep awareness of how your preliminary interaction with the client can affect the client's test performance.

Intentional Misrepresentation
of Ability: " Faking Good" and " Faking Bad"

There may be circumstances surrounding an assessment referral that increase the chances a client will intentionally attempt to skew the results. On an objective personality instrument, the tester has the advantage of validity scales to inform him or her about client response sets and the likelihood of "faking good" (minimizing or underreporting symptoms) or "faking bad" (exaggerating or fabricating symptoms). On an intelligence test such as the WAIS-III, it is almost impossible to "fake good." In most cases, a client will be unable to present a misleadingly favorable impression of his or her level of intellectual functioning because of the nature of the test items and the manner in which the test is constructed. There are, however, some conditions under which a tester might obtain an *inflated* IQ score. One circumstance would be an administration of the WAIS-III too soon following a prior administration, although the WAIS-III administration manual states that practice effects on the Performance subtests can be minimized after a test-retest interval of 1 to 2 years. Surprisingly, the manual does not offer guidelines as to length of time that should elapse between WAIS-III administrations. There is some evidence (Gregory, 1999) that retesting a person of above-average functioning with the WAIS-R could result in scores higher than the first set of scores. This appears to be the result of practice effect and also the result of familiarity with test items. If the client is prompted or coached by the tester, obviously the resultant scores will be inflated and invalid. In other circumstances, an IQ score might not reflect impairment; for example, the client could have some type of neuropsychological or organic impairment that is not readily apparent on an intelligence test. The nature of the impairment could be such that there would be notable behavioral observations yet no notable deficits in terms of scaled scores. This would be particularly likely if the client was extremely bright prior to a neurological event and following the event was impaired yet still in the "average" range compared to his or her age peers.

A client can, however, intentionally give a false impression of limitations. It is also possible to obtain a depressed estimate of true ability level if motivation level is low. For a tester to obtain the most accurate estimate of intellectual ability level, the client needs to be trying as hard as he or she can.

Although a tester obviously cannot control a client's attitude, there are things a tester can do that maximize the chances the client will make a sincere attempt. Although these procedures were presented earlier in this chapter, in the context of what to do at the beginning of the evaluation, they are of sufficient importance that we will reiterate them here in the context of getting the most accurate results possible in the evaluation. First, explain the purpose of the testing to the client. It must be done in a manner that is not condescending to the client yet is phrased in language the client will understand, avoiding professional jargon. Following the explanation, allow an opportunity for the client to process his or her feelings about the reason for referral or referral question. Be prepared for the client to express any of a number of emotions, including anger, resentment, frustration, depression, discouragement, resignation, or enthusiasm. Then, explain that you will be presenting a number of tasks to complete, some being oral questions and some being manipulation of materials such as puzzles, and emphasize that the most important thing for the client to do is to try as hard as possible. State that guessing at an answer if the answer is not known is desirable and that he or she will probably find some of the tasks easy and other tasks difficult.

Perhaps the most important component in the rapport-building process is to give the client the opportunity to ask you any questions or express any concerns he or she may have. If a client is harboring unexpressed anger or resentment about being tested, those feelings could have a significantly detrimental effect on his or her test performance—a less-than-accurate profile of his or her true abilities will emerge.

Although there do need to be time boundaries as far as how long the tester can dialogue and process with the client, it is well worth the time investment to discuss and work through these types of issues with the client *prior to beginning* the testing. It offers the benefit of increasing the client's comfort level and also allows the clinician to have more accuracy in the interpretation process.

Gathering Behavioral Data During Testing

Kaufman and Lichtenberger (1999) offered excellent and highly detailed guidelines for specific behaviors, of which a tester should make note, on each specific subtest. Readers are referred to that text for a more detailed presentation of particular behavioral observations and diagnostic implications. For our purposes, there are some broad behavioral observations about a client's test-taking style that can be made across all the subtests. These observations may suggest a particular direction for a diagnosis or treatment recommendation. They include the following:

- Willingness to guess when unsure of an answer
- A general response style of impulsivity or reflectivity or a pattern of impulsiveness among subtests of a particular type (e.g., verbal or performance)
- Ability to generate alternatives when unable to readily solve a task (particularly on Block Design and Object Assembly)
- Response to being timed—higher concern for speed or for accuracy
- Willingness to announce when finished with a task (note that on Block Design and Picture Arrangement, the testee is instructed to state that he or she is finished)
- Ability to self-correct when appropriate
- Frequency with which the testee inquires about the accuracy of his or her responses
- Frequency with which the testee asks the tester for either the instructions or the stimulus item to be repeated
- Ability stay on task without redirection by the clinician to the task at hand

It is good clinical form to record these observations in the margins of the scoring protocol. Although the WAIS-III protocol offers space on the first page for recording behavioral observations, it has proven very helpful to record key observations in the margin adjacent to the subtest on which the behavior is being observed. A pattern sometimes emerges when reviewing the test responses and scoring that

was not readily apparent at the time of testing. For example, there may be distinct differences in tolerance of frustration on verbal versus nonverbal tasks. Such a pattern would be much easier to discern if the observations were recorded on the protocol beside the subtest on which they occurred.

The WAIS-III Interpretive Process

This section begins with the assumption that there now is a completed protocol with all raw scores transformed to scaled and standard scores. Some authors (Gregory, 1999; Kaufman & Lichtenberger, 2000) advise beginning test score interpretation with the broadest of scores, then moving systematically through the small factors. In a practical sense, clinicians need to bear in mind what the referral question is. In some cases, there will be a broad referral question inquiring as to the overall level of a client's intellectual functioning. When that is the case, looking at the Full Scale IQ, Verbal IQ, and Performance IQ might be sufficient to answer the referral question. However, even when the referral question is broad, it is advisable to thoroughly review all the data, including analysis of subtest strengths and weaknesses, to make sure there are no problems that have yet to be identified. It is important to work through all of the data offered by the test, ranging from the broad factors to individual subtests and, in some cases, an item analysis of particular items to support or refute a particular diagnostic hypothesis related to the referral question. Figure 2.2 offers a schematic representation of the test interpretation process.

The inverted triangle presents the approach of looking first at the broadest test scores, then moving to smaller factors, and so on. The items seen on the outside of the inverted triangle are on the outside because the information known about the client, in each of the identified categories, will have tremendous bearing on how the actual test scores are interpreted. A Full Scale IQ score of 89 tells us nothing about a person in the absence of background information pertaining to her or his medical history, educational history, racial and ethnic history, behavioral observations, and the reason for referral for testing. Truly competent test interpretation involves the clinician's ability to factor in

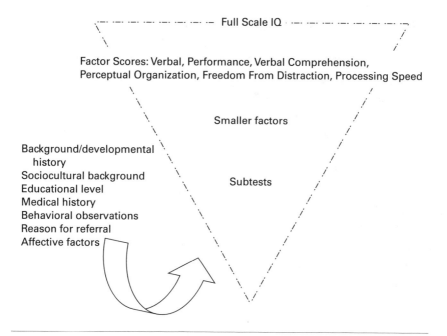

Full Scale IQ

Factor Scores: Verbal, Performance, Verbal Comprehension,
Perceptual Organization, Freedom From Distraction, Processing Speed

Smaller factors

Background/developmental
  history
Sociocultural background
Educational level
Medical history
Behavioral observations
Reason for referral
Affective factors

Subtests

Figure 2.2   The Process of Intelligence Test Interpretation

all of the above information and to use it as a frame of reference from which subsequent test score interpretation will be conducted.

This is where the *art* of test profile interpretation begins. It is an art because each client case will be different, with varying background data and a variety of diagnostic and treatment issues. An intelligence test profile *cannot* be meaningfully interpreted without the background information and behavioral data collected during the test administration (Sattler, 2001). The interpretive process actually represents a complex intertwining of systematic hypothesis generation, subsequent stepwise decision making, and creativity in considering possible etiologies as well as possible interpretations and treatment approaches. There is art involved in this process yet also certain key linear steps a tester must systematically take to begin constructing a relevant, accurate picture of the person's current intellectual functioning. Following a general description of the process, we will present specific steps. Finally, a case will be presented in which the following steps are followed to arrive at conclusions that will answer the referral question.

First, consider the reason for referral for the assessment. When you reflect on the problems inherent in the reason for referral, were those evident in the behavioral observations you made of the client during the assessment? Was there consistency between the two or lack thereof? Second, consider the manner in which social and cultural variables contribute to the reason for referral and to the behavioral observations. Also consider, before beginning to analyze the test scores, the extent to which sociocultural variables may have had a detrimental impact on the client's performance relative to the norming population.

After the tester has pondered these questions and arrived at some tentative, general hypotheses, he or she can move on to the next level of synthesis. The testing situation can be thought of as a microcosm of how the client relates to his or her environment in circumstances similar to the testing situation. The tester is offered valuable behavioral data about how the client deals with strangers, deals with people who are in a position of authority, and self-assesses his or her competence and capability, cognitive flexibility, and sensitivity and concern about time constraints. Such data are relevant to the process of understanding how the client relates to his or her environment; how he or she might be perceived by teachers, employers, or coworkers; how he or she might react to conditions of moderate stress; the client's degree of concern about performance; and the extent to which emotional factors might inhibit the client's functioning at optimal capacity. Remember that making an observation about such issues is entirely different from making a *judgment* about such issues, particularly when a client exhibits behaviors that deviate from White middle-class norms.

The best way for a clinician to make beneficent use of background and behavioral data is to put the observations in an environmental, sociocultural context. Ridley, Li, and Hill (1998) discussed the value of an emic versus etic approach to conceptualizing this data. An emic approach means conceptualizing these aspects of the client from the perspective of the client's indigenous culture rather than from external cultural standards (Dana, 1993; Ridley et al., 1998). Operationalizing this idea, the clinician would ask, "In this client's primary environment, what purpose does this behavior serve?" and "To what extent do these behaviors create difficulty for the client in his or her functioning and for others in the client's environment?" These questions represent a postmodern model for test interpretation, meaning that our realities, including our scientific realities, are culturally constructed (Marsella & Yamada, 2000). This approach was first advocated by Mercer (1979), who observed that a disproportionate number of students who were in minority groups scored in the "retarded" range on the Wechsler scales yet functioned quite adaptively in their primary environments.

The traditional psychometric interpretation of scores represents a more absolutistic interpretive, or etic, approach. The etic approach assumes certain universal human standards (Dana, 1993; Ridley et al., 1998). If a clinician departs from the client's primary environment as a frame of reference and instead thinks about majority culture, a different contextual definition is applied. It might be argued that although the client is being compared to others who are not part of the client's primary cultural identification, the client is going to be expected to function and contribute to a broad society and culture that consists of majority culture. So, regardless of the "fairness" of it, the client must go out, find a job, and, to maintain employment, subscribe to certain societal expectations such as reporting on time for work, treating customers and coworkers in a "socially accept-able" manner, and so on. In some cases, the client with a particular cultural or ethnic background might be able to live and work in an area heavily populated by others of similar cultural heritage. In these cases, beliefs, values, and subsequent verbal and nonverbal behaviors that deviate from the majority norm probably would not be a coun-seling issue of great import. For those clients whose cultural back-ground truly makes them a minority in their primary environment, however, these cultural concerns will have an impact on their ability to function in society. The fact that the client might not be familiar with or aware of majority cultural expectations may become a focus of treatment; many aspects of this dilemma will need to be worked through. A full discussion of minority identity development is beyond the scope of this book, but the importance of addressing cul-tural identity issues has relevance in the context of effectively using individual intelligence test data. Part of multicultural competence involves an understanding of theories of cultural identity development (Atkinson, Morten, & Sue, 1998).

Use With Diverse Populations

Care was taken with the WAIS-III standardization to get a strati-fied random sample, with corresponding numbers of Whites, African Americans, Hispanics, and other racial/ethnic groups based on the 1995 census (Wechsler, 1997). Nevertheless, when assessing clients who are members of minority groups, interpretation of the WAIS-III must be done with great caution. Some authors have expressed con-cerns about the appropriateness of the WAIS-III with minority popu-lations for a number of reasons:

- The most likely influence of ethnicity on test performance is in the realm of the meaning the testee ascribes to the test. For someone not of the majority culture, the relative importance of doing well on the WAIS-III might be diminished, resulting in "subtle and largely invisible differences in motivation" (Gregory, 1999, p. 124). The resulting effect is a score that underrepresents the client's true ability level.
- Any test will, by definition, favor those test takers who are from the same culture as the authors of the test (Helms, 1997). It is not yet known whether there is equal or differential predi-ctive validity for the WAIS-III when used with majority and minority group members. However, the Wechsler Intelligence Scale for Children—Revised (WISC-R) has been proven to be equally effective in predictive validity with majority and minority children.

Helms (1997) offered extensive observations about the use of cog-nitive ability tests with people in minority groups. She noted that all individuals have psychological attributes that are racial, cultural, and or socioeconomic in origin. Such attributes can be either an advantage or a disadvantage on a cognitive ability test. She further posited that people who are members of a visually recognizable ethnic group (VREG) may be multiply disadvantaged in that cultural and socioeconomic variables could preclude optimal test performance. The real issue, according to Helms, is whether a test has cultural equivalence for the testee. She provided readers with features that should be present for a cognitive ability test to be considered cultur-ally equivalent. There are seven: functional, conceptual, linguistic, psychometric, testing condition, contextual, and sampling. She observed that most cognitive ability tests currently in use with clients of minority groups have not met the criteria across all seven cultural equivalence characteristics.

To determine advisability of using the WAIS-III with a particular client who may be of minority group membership, one would need to go back to the referral question and the reason for referral. The primary point being emphasized here is that testers need to be aware of possibly questionable validity of the obtained scores with a minority client.

Step-by-Step Procedure for Interpretation

Readers are referred again to Figure 2.1, the stair-step approach to test interpretation.

1. Begin first with the Full Scale IQ. The Full Scale IQ is a number that attempts to summarize the client's overall performance on the test. It represents cumulative level of functioning across a broad number of cognitive areas. Groth-Marnat (1999) observed that for the purpose of interpretation to a client or a referral source untrained in psychometrics, percentile rank equivalent and descriptive classifications will probably mean more than the standard score. Remember that a percentile rank equivalent of 63, for example, means that the client did as well as or better than 63% of his or her age peers in the standardization sample.

2. Second, examine the factor scores. Look first at the two factor scores: Verbal IQ and Performance IQ. Determine the number of standard score points difference between the VIQ and PIQ. If there is a significant VIQ-PIQ discrepancy, it means that the FSIQ is not a particularly useful number because the FSIQ is essentially the average of the VIQ and PIQ. Thus, the FSIQ will give a false impression of the person's ability in that it will overestimate ability in his or her weak area and underestimate his or her strong area. The WAIS-III manual offers actuarial data for the relative frequency of score discrepancies in the general population in Table B.2. Authors agree (Gregory, 1999; Kaufman & Lichtenberger, 1999; Sattler, 2001)

that although a score discrepancy might be statistically significant, it is not necessarily indicative of pathology. Therefore, a factor score discrepancy must be both statistically significant and significantly atypical to consider the possibility of cognitive impairment. Nevertheless, a significant discrepancy between verbal and nonverbal abilities can offer implications for understanding a client and making recommendations, even in the absence of a "diagnosable" condition. However, there is some disagreement as to where the cutoff for considering pathology should occur; Kaufman and Lichtenberger (1999) recommend a discrepancy of 17 points because a difference of that magnitude occurs in only 15% of the population. In contrast, Gregory (1999) offers the following criteria:

- If there is a VIQ-PIQ difference of less than 10, just use the FSIQ and do not analyze Verbal and Performance differences at all.
- If there is a VIQ-PIQ difference of between 11 and 20, a moderate discrepancy, there are clinical implications but not diagnostic implications.
- If there is a VIQ-PIQ difference of greater than 20, an extreme discrepancy exists, with the probability of cognitive impairment increasing as the score difference gets larger.

Also at this level of interpretation, we can look at the index scores, which offer a more refined view of the verbal and nonverbal aspects of the client's functioning. Gregory (1999) suggested doing a multiple comparison of the index scales, comparing the Verbal Comprehension Index to the Perceptual Organization Index and the Verbal Comprehension Index to the Working Memory Index, then comparing the Perceptual Organization Index to the Processing Speed Index. The comparison between the Verbal Comprehension Index and the Perceptual Organization Index offers an estimate of strength or weakness in verbal abilities versus visual spatial ability.

The advantage of looking at the Verbal Comprehension Index and Perceptual Organization Index, in contrast to Verbal IQ and Performance IQ, is that it enables a clinician to ascertain the extent to which attention, concentration, and speed of processing exerted a maximum threshold on the client's test performance. If there is a Verbal Comprehension Index/Working Memory Index discrepancy greater than 10, there probably were some attention and concentration difficulties that impeded the client's performance, and the Verbal IQ is not a good indicator of the client's overall verbal capabilities. If there is a Perceptual Organization Index/Processing Speed Index discrepancy greater than 13, the Performance IQ is not a good indicator of the client's overall nonverbal abilities because there probably are some motor speed, motor skill, and attention concentration factors that put a maximum threshold on the PIQ.

3. Next, we go to individual subtest performance to identify significant strengths and weaknesses. It can be quite helpful to graph the subtest scaled scores on the grid on the protocol. Such a graphing enables the "intraocular" method of profile analysis—one "eyeballs" the data. One strategy would be to draw two dashed lines for comparison. One is a line across the scaled score value of 10, which represents average performance for the client's age peers. The other is a line across that client's average performance across all the Verbal or all the Performance subtests. There is a critical rule about using this technique: If the difference between the Verbal IQ and Performance IQ is less than 10, the clinician can calculate an overall mean scaled score and consider each scaled score in comparison to the overall mean. However, if there is a VIQ-PIQ split greater than 10, the clinician should calculate separate mean scaled scores for the Verbal and Performance scales. A clinician has the option of either consulting the WAIS-III administration manual (Table B.3) to get precise values for the amount of deviation from the mean that any scaled score must be to be statistically significant, or using a ballpark deviation figure of +3. If any subtest scaled score deviates from average performance by more than 3 (or by more than the critical value cited in Table B.3), then the abilities evaluated by that subtest can be considered to be a relative strength or a relative weakness. This information about relative strength or relative weakness is potentially far more helpful to treatment planning than just looking at relative standing compared to age peers, which is what is yielded in looking only at scaled scores.

4. Now that we have generated some broad hypotheses of the reason for referral, we can go back to the protocol and look at responses to individual test items. We will look at recorded behavioral

observations in the context of particular subtests to see if they do, in fact, support our interpretive hypotheses.

5. We look now to the background information to see what mitigating effect, if any, that data might have on our hypotheses.

6. We generate a response to the referral question and share our explanation of the test results with the client and the referral source.

A Case Example

George is a 17-year-old Caucasian male referred for testing because he applied for Social Security disability benefits at the suggestion of his caseworker. George lives in a very rural section of West Virginia and is the second of six children. His father had a seventh-grade education and worked in the coal mines until his death; his mother is a homemaker. His parents were second-generation American citizens; his grandparents were from Scotland and Wales.

Human Services became involved with George and his family because of allegations of physical abuse by their mother. Although the allegations were unfounded, there was a need for services. There is no history of head injury. Developmental milestones were reportedly met on schedule.

Behavioral Observations

George presented as a very tall, muscular young man, towering over the evaluator. Nevertheless, he did not seem to use his physical size in an overbearing manner; he was quite soft-spoken and retiring. He sat still in his chair; there was no extraneous movement. Likewise, there was no extraneous conversation. His demeanor was pleasant, yet he did not initiate conversation and offered perfunctory responses to inquiries from the tester.

At no time did he inquire as to the accuracy of his responses. He attended to the tasks presented to him in a businesslike fashion, demonstrating apparent concentration on the task at hand either until he had completed it or until the tester prompted him to put the task away. There was no obvious frustration on the more difficult performance items, and his persistence on difficult tasks was notable.

He seemed quite concerned with the quality of his responses, and despite being told to work as quickly as possible, he appeared to take his time. His approach to tasks was slow and methodical, and he seemed able to generate alternative problem solutions when it was necessary.

Test Results

George demonstrated the following scaled and standard scores on the WAIS-III:

Verbal		Performance	
Vocabulary	6	Picture Completion	7
Similarities	7	Picture Arrangement	7
Arithmetic	5	Block Design	6
Information	4	Matrix Reasoning	6
Comprehension	4	Coding	7
Digit Span	8	Symbol Search	6
Letter-Number Sequencing	8		

	Standard Score	Percentile	95% Confidence Band
VIQ	74	4	70–80
PIQ	78	7	73–86
FSIQ	74	4	70–79
VCI	76	5	71–83
POI	80	9	74–89
WMI	82	12	76–90
PSI	81	10	74–92

1. We will first apply the stair step analysis of standard scores. George's Full Scale IQ of 74 has a classification of borderline intellectual functioning.

2. We look next at the factor scores. His Verbal IQ and Performance IQ of 74 and 78 also place him in the borderline range. The difference in score between 74 and 78 is not a significant discrepancy. Therefore, we can conclude that the Full Scale IQ

is an accurate representation of George's overall test performance. George's secondary factor scores on the Verbal Comprehension Index, Perceptual Organization Index, Working Memory Index, and Processing Speed Index are all close to one another in value. The general conclusion from this profile of index scores indicates that he was reasonably motivated to perform on this test and that affective and motivational factors did not play a significant role in the scores we obtained in this evaluation.

3. Now we look at the individual subtests to see if additional light can be shed on strengths and weaknesses. It actually is unusual to see a profile in which all the ability areas are hanging together this closely. Translated into daily functioning, George is equally skilled in a variety of cognitive areas. His profile suggests that he will perform at approximately the same level regardless of whether he is presented with a verbal, auditory task or a visual-motor and spatial-processing task.

4. Our next step is to try to integrate the test data with the referral question, background information, and test scores to generate meaningful recommendations for counseling. First, look at George's Full Scale IQ of 74. Considering his economically impoverished home environment, we might initially hypothesize that his Full Scale IQ might be the result of minimal cultural, environmental, and sensory stimulation. If such were the case, we would expect to see somewhat higher scores on Vocabulary, Similarities, Block Design, and Matrix Reasoning. However, in George's case, when we look at those scores, we see that his scaled scores, in their percentile rank equivalents, correspond fairly closely with the percentile rank equivalent of the FSIQ. This poses a dilemma in interpretation. In the broadest sense, *everyone* is the product of his or her environment. Who can say how much higher George's scores would have been if he had lived in a more stimulating environment with parents who were focused on providing optimal learning conditions for their children? On the other hand, because George did score low on this traditional cognitive ability test, what we can say is that in a traditional, culturally mainstream environment with corresponding demands, George's performance will be substantially below "average." Because the Disability

Bureau is considering how employable George is, we can safely conclude that even in a job that did not require specific job training, George might encounter difficulty in performing to the employer's expectations. With his scores being where they are, he may very well qualify for some type of job training funded through a state or federal program.

Conclusions we can draw from George's profile analysis are that he is persistent, probably would be disinclined to waste time on the job chatting with coworkers, and is willing to see a job through to the end. In short, in the right work environment, he would probably be a great employee. Furthermore, one of George's strengths is that he is equally skilled and able across many aspects of cognitive functioning. This places him in the enviable position of looking at what he enjoys doing as a primary variable in job training. There also are the practical aspects of treatment planning that need to be integrated in his services. These include the training programs available, the job market in George's area, and George's level of interest in the training program.

There are two types of recommendations that can be made at the conclusion of an intellectual evaluation. One type is about suggestions related to the reason for referral. We discussed those types of recommendations that might be made for George in the preceding paragraph. The other type of recommendation focuses on additional types of evaluation that might be important or lend substantial information in some type of decision making. In George's case, career interest assessment might be exceedingly helpful. It would also be helpful to do an adaptive behavior assessment. We need to know whether George's deficits, as they seem to be represented by his WAIS-III scores, correspond with deficits in his day-to-day adaptive behavior. For example, his Arithmetic score was quite low. How well can he manage his money? His Vocabulary score was quite low. How comfortable will he be reading a work schedule posted on a bulletin board and how his wages are calculated? Is he capable of living independently? These are not questions that can be readily answered based solely on the data from the WAIS-III. An adaptive behavior rating or an in vivo observation would give substantially more information about these considerations and thus should be recommended at the conclusion of George's report.

Summary

In this chapter, we discussed a variety of issues—some pertaining to actual test administration and some pertaining to aspects surrounding test administration. Conducting a sound, competent evaluation involves administering a test accurately, with careful adherence to standardized procedures. Yet other facets of an evaluation are equally critical to obtain valid results. Some of those facets include communicating with the referral source to clarify the nature of the referral question, assessing for the likelihood of organic impairment, and communicating with collaterals to get additional information.

We also presented a sequential model for score interpretation, offering some guidelines for how to maximize the usefulness of the scores that were obtained. The interpretive process is far more difficult to master than test administration and requires extensive training and supervision. Nevertheless, we hope that application of the guidelines suggested can serve as a supplementation to other learning and training.

Resource List

Kaufman and Lichtenberger's (1999) *Essentials of WAIS-III Assessment* is very helpful in the interpretive process. The interpretive model used in that book is primarily Silver's (1993) information-processing model. Another good resource is Flanagan, McGrew, and Ortiz (2000), whose work is titled *The Wechsler Intelligence Scales and Gf-Gc Theory: A Contemporary Approach to Interpretation*. Finally, the *Handbook of Psychological Assessment* (Groth-Marnat, 1999) offers a comprehensive overview of the assessment process using the WAIS-III.

Discussion Questions

1. Think about your own style of learning and processing information. What are the optimum conditions under which you

can learn new information? If those optimum conditions are not present, how much does it affect your performance?

2. Which approach, etic or emic, is more useful in a client's score interpretation? What are some decision rules you might use about when to use each approach?

References

Atkinson, D. R., Morten, G., & Sue, D. W. (1998). *Counseling American minorities* (5th ed.). Boston: McGraw-Hill.

Beutler, L. E. (1995). Integrating and communicating findings. In L. E. Beutler & M. R. Berren (Eds.), *Integrative assessment of adult personality* (pp. 25-64). New York: Guilford.

Dana, R. H. (1993). *Multicultural assessment perspectives for professional psychology*. Boston: Allyn & Bacon.

Flanagan, D. P., McGrew, K. S., & Ortiz, S. O. (2000). *The Wechsler intelligence scales and Gf-Gc theory: A contemporary approach to interpretation*. Boston: Allyn & Bacon.

Gregory, R. J. (1999). *Foundations of intellectual assessment: The WAIS-III and other tests in clinical practice*. Boston: Allyn & Bacon.

Groth-Marnat, G. (1999). *Handbook of psychological assessment* (3rd ed.). New York: John Wiley.

Helms, J. E. (1997). The triple quandary of race, culture, and social class in standardized cognitive ability testing. In D. P. Flanagan, J. L. Genshaft, & P. L. Harrison (Eds.), *Contemporary intellectual assessment: Theories, tests, and issues* (pp. 517-532). New York: Guilford.

Kamphaus, R. W. (1993). *Clinical assessment of children's intelligence: A handbook for professional practice*. Boston: Allyn & Bacon.

Katz, L. (1985). *A practical guide to psychodiagnostic testing*. Springfield, IL: Charles C Thomas.

Kaufman, A. S. (1990). *Assessing adolescent and adult intelligence*. Boston: Allyn & Bacon.

Kaufman, A. S. (1994). *Intelligent testing with the WISC-III*. New York: John Wiley.

Kaufman, A. S., & Lichtenberger, E. O. (1999). *Essentials of WAIS-III assessment*. New York: John Wiley.

Kaufman, A. S., & Lichtenberger, E. O. (2000). *Essentials of WISC-III and WPPSI-R assessment*. New York: John Wiley.

64   Using Test Data in Clinical Practice

Kramer, J. H. (1993). Interpretation of individual subtest scores on the WISC-III IQ and index scores. *Psychological Assessment, 5*, 193-196.

Marsella, A. J., & Yamada, A. M. (2000). Culture and mental health: An introduction and overview of foundations, concepts, and issues. In I. Cuellar & F. A. Paniagua (Eds.), *Handbook of multicultural mental health: Assessment and treatment of diverse populations* (pp. 3-24). San Diego, CA: Academic Press.

Mercer, J. R. (1979). In defense of racially and culturally non-discriminatory assessment. *School Psychology Review, 8*, 89-115.

Naglieri, J. A. (1993). Pairwise and ipsative comparisons of WISC-III IQ and index scores. *Psychological Assessment, 5*, 113-116.

Pollack, J., Levy, S., & Breitholtz, T. (1999). Screening for medical and neurodevelopmental disorders for the professional counselor. *Journal of Counseling & Development, 77*, 350-358.

Ridley, C. R., Li, L. C., & Hill, C. L. (1998). Multicultural assessment: Reexamination, reconceptualization, and practical application. *The Counseling Psychologist, 26*, 827-910.

Sattler, J. M. (2001). *Assessment of children: Cognitive applications* (4th ed.). San Diego, CA: Author.

Silver, L. B. (1993). Introduction and overview to the clinical concepts of learning disabilities. *Child and Adolescent Psychiatric Clinics of North America: Learning Disabilities, 2*, 181-192.

Wechsler, D. (1997). *Wechsler Adult Intelligence Scale* (3rd rev. ed.). San Antonio, TX: The Psychological Corporation.

3

Presentation of WAIS-III
Findings in Reports and to Clients

This chapter begins with a reiteration of the assumption that the reason clients are referred for assessment is to answer some question(s) and that incorporating the information afforded by the evaluation into the treatment process represents an ideal culmination of the evaluation. Thus, interpreting test results and sharing those interpretations with the client and/or referral source are the ultimate outcome of an evaluation. Explaining those interpretations can take two forms—oral and written. If a clinician intends to share test results (either verbally or in a report) with a referral source, he or she must discuss that intention thoroughly with the client ahead of time. Even if the client has verbally agreed that the clinician can share test results with a third party, information should not be disclosed to the third party until a "Release of Information" form has been signed by the client, granting the clinician permission to do so (American Psychological Association, 1992; Committee on Psychological Tests and Assessment, 1996).

Guidelines for Giving Feedback

The term *test feedback* is actually quite broad and can refer to any of a number of situations in which evaluation results are interpreted

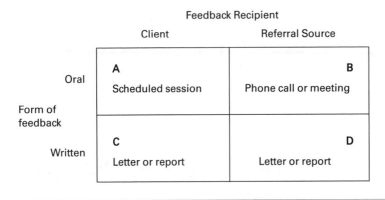

Figure 3.1   Forms That Feedback May Take Depending on Recipient of Information

and shared with interested others. To clarify the different forms feedback can take, consider the matrix in Figure 3.1.

Feedback to Clients Given Orally

This category of feedback is represented by Quadrant A in Figure 3.1. It is a tester's ethical obligation to offer clients feedback on their test results. The APA Ethical Guidelines (American Psychological Association, 1992, Section 2.09) state that

> unless the nature of the relationship is clearly explained to the person being assessed in advance and precludes provision of an explanation of results, psychologists ensure that an explanation of the results is provided using language that is reasonably understandable to the person assessed or to another legally authorized person on behalf of the client. Regardless of whether the scoring and interpretation are done by the psychologist, by assistants, or by automated or other outside services, psychologists take reasonable steps to ensure that appropriate explanations of results are given. (p. 1604)

Of particular relevance is the specification about giving the feedback in language the client will understand. In the lengthy training process of becoming a mental health professional, we become accustomed to conceptualizing and communicating about treatment issues using clinical terms. However, unless the client is also a mental health professional, use of clinical jargon in a feedback session may create a distance that is detrimental to the counseling process. Even more important in this context is the consideration of whether the client can comprehend what the clinician is attempting to communicate. Some clients who are sufficiently assertive might ask further questions about psychological terms they do not understand. Other clients, though, might be reticent to ask a clinician to explain a term. So, although the *clinician* may have a self-perception of having clearly explained the test results, it could be erroneous to assume that the message received by the client was indeed the message intended by the clinician.

One important component to explain as part of the feedback process is that intelligence and intellectual ability are *constructs*, meaning that they do not physically exist within an individual. What does exist is observable behavior that clinicians interpret as being *manifestations* of the construct in question (in this case, intelligence). So, in conceptualizing and understanding what intelligence is, there are competing theories and explanations, all of which attempt to account for the behaviors that are inferred to manifest "intelligence."

Some theories of intelligence are more complex than other theories. Regardless of the theory or models a clinician uses, part of the client feedback process will consist of educating consumers about those models, with emphasis on the fact that it is only a model or framework, not a real entity that exists within the person. Readers should note that we will touch very briefly on several commonly noted and used contemporary theories of intellectual functioning.

The Information-Processing Model

Kaufman (1994) stated that the information-processing model (Silver, 1993) has particular utility when assessing for a learning disability. Silver's (1993) model conceptualizes intellectual functioning as having four phases: input, integration, storage, and output. Input refers to data that enter the organism by way of one of the five senses. Integration consists of the brain organizing and synthesizing the data with other material already in the memory system. Storage refers to storing the information for later use, and output refers to expressing information behaviorally, either through speech or motoric activity.

The Triarchic Model

Another theory of intellectual functioning is Sternberg's (1986) triarchic theory of intelligence. In Sternberg's model, there are three types of cognitive components: metacomponents, which are the executive components that tell other components what and how to do something; performance components, which are the problem-solving strategies used to complete a task; and knowledge acquisition components, which are the processes used when learning new material. The knowledge acquisition components consist of selective encoding (identifying which are the relevant and salient aspects of a problem, as opposed to irrelevant detail), selective combinations (forming a new knowledge structure that combines new information with old information), and selective comparison (comparing the new knowledge structure to the previous knowledge structure).

Multiple Intelligences

Finally, Gardner's multiple intelligence theory (Gardner, 1983; Gardner, Kornhaber, & Wake, 1996) holds that people possess multiple capabilities cognitively, all of which exist somewhat independently of the others. Gardner has identified eight such competencies and postulated that there are at least an additional two:

1. Linguistic intelligence—capacity for using language

2. Musical intelligence—rhythmic and pitch abilities

3. Logical-mathematical intelligence—logical and quantitative thought ability

4. Spatial intelligence—perceiving the visual world, re-creating aspects of one's visual experience

5. Bodily-kinesthetic intelligence—athletics, physical ability

6. Intrapersonal intelligence—knowledge and awareness of self

7. Interpersonal intelligence—ability to accurately perceive others' feelings, beliefs, and intentions

8. Naturalist intelligence—ability to perceive and understand patterns in nature

9. Spiritual intelligence—concern with spiritual issues and awareness of the spiritual as the ultimate state of being

10. Existential intelligence—concern with ultimate "big-picture" issues

Beyond offering a basic explanation of how models enable clinicians to make sense of many divergent pieces of data, there are other steps a clinician might take to ensure that the feedback to a client is understandable. One easy technique is to find alternative, nonclinical ways to explain cognitive processes, possibly using analogies based on the client's daily life. For example, one analogy this author (K.M.) has used often in the feedback process is a computer. This particular analogy parallels the information-processing model of cognitive functioning (Silver, 1993). In a computer system analogy, the hardware would be brain tissue; software would be problem-solving strategy, cultural values, and beliefs; the keyboard for data input would represent visual and auditory stimuli and discrimination; the amount of memory in the central processing unit (CPU) would relate to processing speed; and so on. Another technique is to stop frequently to ask the client to explain his or her understanding of the points you just made, preferably in his or her own words. Finally, there must be ample opportunity throughout the feedback session for the client to process the effect of the content of the feedback. If the client is experiencing strong feelings in reaction to the test results and those feelings have not been processed, those feelings will prohibit the client from really hearing all of what is being said.

Students learning intelligence testing frequently comment that the hardest aspect of giving feedback to clients is finding lay terms to explain strengths and weaknesses. Beutler (1995) observed that tests serve as "analogue environments" (i.e., they create an environment)

that occur under controlled conditions, which simulate or resemble the client's actual living environment. This enables a clinician to take a client's test performance and extrapolate to likely ways the client reacts and performs in his or her day-to-day functioning. Consistent with this idea about the analogue environment, one challenge for a clinician is to find ways to liken the tasks performed during testing to daily tasks with which the client is presented in everyday functioning. A clinician can meet this challenge by thinking about day-to-day activities that involve the skill domains being assessed. Listed below are some common daily activity correlates to each of the Wechsler Adult Intelligence Scale—Third Revision (WAIS-III) subtests—there are likely to be others, and readers are encouraged to formulate their own corresponding daily activities that involve the subtest domains.

Vocabulary: Understanding and using a wide range of words in reading, speaking, and listening to others

Similarities: Understanding connections and relationships between things, events, and people

Arithmetic: Analyzing and computing situations and problems that involve math

Information: Storing and recollecting many isolated facts across broad topic areas (e.g., geography, history, science)

Comprehension: Understanding American culture and understanding complex concepts/problems that may have more than one solution

Digit Span: Short-term memory for things that are heard

Letter-Number Sequencing: Short-term memory, plus concentration (focused mental effort) and ability to move pieces of information into the correct order

Picture Completion: Identifying missing pieces; comparing what you see to your memory of how it should look

Picture Arrangement: Being able to anticipate, in the correct sequence, likely outcomes of a social situation

Block Design: Eye-hand coordination and speed, ability to problem-solve tasks that are not necessarily word based

Matrix Reasoning: Ability to understand relationships or connections between things by using the eyes

Coding: Eye-hand speed, attention, and concentration

Symbol Search: Eye-hand speed, attention, ability to quickly and accurately scan with the eyes

Verbal IQ (VIQ): Overall knowledge of and problem solving with words, language, and input through the ears

Performance IQ (PIQ): Overall ability and problem solving with eyes and hands

Full Scale IQ (FSIQ): A broad number that summarizes overall cognitive (brain and thought-based) activity across many skill areas

Readers are cautioned about careful differentiation between attention and concentration, which are sometimes incorrectly used as synonyms. *Attention* means sustained effort focusing on incoming stimuli, regardless of the sensory channel through which the stimuli are coming. *Concentration* means using some data or information that has come in and performing some mental operation or manipulation to it. On the Digit Span subtest, in Digits Forward, the testee must repeat the digits heard in the same order. This is primarily dependent on *auditory attention*. On Digits Backward, the testee must repeat the digits in reverse order to that which was heard. There is additional concentration required beyond the initial attention. Digits Backward thus involves two steps: auditory attention to first correctly hear the numbers, then mental reversal of the sequence. Concentration requires attention, plus additional mental exertion.

Clients may conceptualize tests in the context to which they were exposed in a school setting, in terms of the number right or wrong out of the total number possible. Some people may not have had exposure to the concepts of standard error of measurement, age norms, stratified random samples, and other psychometric characteristics that are integral components of understanding standardized test scores. It is a clinician's responsibility to explain these basic psychometric principles, preferably at the beginning of the feedback session.

It is also advisable to explain the two ways of considering test scores—normative and idiographic. Again, a layperson, especially one who wishes to know how "smart" he or she is, probably thinks only about the normative approach—how he or she "stacks up" against other people he or she knows. However, unless the purpose of testing is only to determine broad diagnosis, such as Full Scale IQ score to determine a client's eligibility for services, the idiographic approach can be more helpful in terms of integration of data into the treatment process. The idiographic approach was described in the "stair-step" approach in Chapter 2 (see Figure 2.1). It entails considering the client's strengths and weaknesses relative to one another—it is essentially a within-subject rather than a between-subject comparison. Again in the spirit of the client having a clear understanding of what the test scores mean, clinicians should emphasize to the client that when a skill is identified as a significant strength or weakness, it means that the client's ability in that domain (as reflected by that particular subtest scaled score) varies significantly from his or her abilities assessed on other subtests (and, theoretically, in other cognitive domains).

The between-subject comparison is already done in the process of converting raw to standard and scaled scores, and standard or scaled scores always have percentile rank equivalents. By knowing the transformed scores, then, a tester already knows the relative standing of the client's test performance in comparison to the standardization sample, which approximates the general population.

After explaining the standardization process and giving a comparative definition of the normative and idiographic approaches to test interpretation, the clinician will have prepared the client for a description of the client's scores. Some instructors and supervisors have admonished their supervisees not to share with a client his or her actual test scores. The rationale for withholding test scores is that clients lack the sophistication to understand the concepts behind the numbers and that only knowing the numbers without understanding is potentially damaging. There are some problems with this position, though. The client is the holder of the privilege. This means that he or she is entitled to a copy of all his or her records, including reports. So, in getting a copy of the report, he or she would have access to the actual numbers anyhow.

The clients with whom this author (K.M.) has worked seem to be most interested in the Full Scale IQ score as an indication of whether they are "smart." The extent to which a client is interested in an IQ score may depend somewhat on the reason for referral. If a person is being tested to determine presence of a learning disability or attention deficit disorder, he or she might not be as focused on the overall test performance. On the other hand, if a person is trying to join Mensa (an organization for very bright people) or is being tested to determine the degree of decline secondary to an illness, then perhaps overall test performance will, in fact, be heavily emphasized.

If the clinician is going to disclose actual numeric scores, there must be a corresponding explanation and emphasis on the standard error of measurement and its correlate, the confidence interval. The confidence interval must be part of the feedback process, primarily to underscore the idea that test scores are stable yet somewhat imprecise.

Confidence interval can be simply explained as follows: On any given day, a person's test performance is going to be the result of three things—true ability, conditions within the person at that moment in time, and conditions outside the person at that moment in time. True ability level is what we are attempting to measure, and we will only be able to do that when the effects of the within- and outside-person variables are minimized. Examples of within-person variables that could affect test performance include anxiety, depression, headache or other physical discomfort, or dislike for the examiner. There are many other possible variables; these are just a few examples. Conditions outside the person that might affect test performance include an inexperienced tester, distracting noises in the test environment, or uncomfortable seating arrangements.

Because the internal and external circumstances vary continually, there is a degree of error inherent in a test score. This is a somewhat abstract concept to grasp, and some clients may have difficulty understanding it. If they do, perhaps that is a diagnostic indicator that disclosing the actual test scores might do that person more harm than good. Perhaps one decision rule about when to disclose numbers is when the clinician is able to explain the confidence interval and the client is able to paraphrase back to the therapist an accurate understanding of the concept.

The order in which test scores should be discussed should go from broad to narrow, following a similar sequence to the stair-step analysis and hypothesis generation as discussed in Chapter 2. Begin with the most broad, general score, the Full Scale IQ score, talking generally about what range of functioning the client is in by using the verbal descriptors from the WAIS-III test protocol. The breakdown of descriptors by range (Wechsler, 1997) is as follows:

≤ 69 = extremely low

70-79 = borderline

80-89 = low average

90-109 = average

110-119 = high average

120-129 = superior

≥ 130 = very superior

Before reporting a numeric score to a client, it may be helpful to process what it is about knowing the actual score that is important to the client. Sometimes there can be grist for the therapeutic mill by discussing and processing the relevance of the numbers to the client's life. For some people, the Full Scale IQ or other IQ scores can be intertwined with self-concept, self-efficacy, identification with one or the other parent, or other psychological issues that could bear on the therapy process. If these types of circumstances are the case, processing those components and issues before discussing the numbers is essential.

As one moves away from the Full Scale IQ, the natural progression is to go to the broadest factor scores first, the Verbal IQ and Performance IQ. Kaufman and Lichtenberger (1999) and Gregory (1999) recommend not reviewing index scores unless the discrepancies between Verbal Comprehension Index and Working Memory Index, or Perceptual Organization Index and Processing Speed Index, are sufficiently large to suggest doing it. Then, following factor scores, move into scaled scores on individual subtests, de-emphasizing names of the subtests and favoring concrete descriptions of the *tasks* he or she was asked to do on that subtest. Offering examples (not actual test items but sample test questions *closely similar to* the subtest) and descriptions of subtests can help the client recall the subtest because he or she was probably unaware of subtest names in the first place.

Again, this discussion should focus primarily on the relative ease or difficulty with which she or he does activities related to those subtests in daily life. Sometimes it can be helpful to tie subtest-related life experiences in with his or her academic history (e.g., "So, remembering trivial facts is hard for you. Did you find history tough in high school?" or "Does it seem like these descriptions of how you did fit with your day-to-day experiences?").

Giving oral feedback to another involved party (referral source or family member) constitutes Quadrant B of the Figure 3.1 matrix. Many of the same principles identified in giving client feedback are applicable here. One of the most critical principles is the necessity of avoiding jargon in favor of more behavioral or descriptive terms. Another important principle is to de-emphasize subtest names, or factor names, instead focusing on the functional aspects of the domain in question. The following is an example of inappropriate jargon and an appropriate explanation of functional correlates:

> Inappropriate jargon: "Sally's Verbal IQ of 117 means that her verbal functioning is one standard deviation above average and her crystallized ability is well developed."

> Appropriate explanation: "Sally's ability with language appears to be quite a bit above average. This means that in school-related tasks like note-taking, reading, and remembering what she read, she will do very well."

Integration of Test Data Into the Counseling Process

We touched on this topic earlier in suggesting discussing with clients what the test scores mean to them. One way to explore that meaning is to ask, "How will your life be different when you learn about your test scores?" The client may have some very specific expectations about the test scores, which may or may not be based on realistic outcomes of the testing. For example, in the case of George, a decision was being made about whether he qualified for Social Security disability income, with the test scores being a primary variable in the decision. For George, the test process itself, though not the *test scores*, from *his* perspective, had some very real and practical implications about how his life would be affected. For other people, there might be similarly broad implications, either in terms of possible disorders for which they are being tested or in terms of positive response to some treatment or educational programming.

There are a number of ways in which test results may be incorporated in the counseling process. The following are three broad considerations of how test data could augment therapy.

1. *How the client feels and what meaning the client ascribes to the testing process.* For some people, the testing will stir up myriad feelings about any of a number of things. Examples of possible emotional issues include feelings about being evaluated, intellectual adequacy, general adequacy and self-acceptance, and self-perceived ability to control or respond adaptively to the environment. Each of these issues potentially has a very strong emotional valence. The clinician needs to informally assess and discuss with the client the extent to which feelings about testing relate to current treatment goals. Even if there is no apparent relationship, the possibility of a connection should also be discussed and considered. Here is an example:

Qizhi is a 21-year-old woman of Asian descent, an engineering major at a university. She has had three counseling sessions over the past 3 weeks and was referred for counseling by her academic advisor due to low grades in her math courses. The advisor referred her for evaluation and possible counseling to rule out a learning disability. However, she revealed to the counselor that she has panic attacks. As the counselor is discussing test scores with her, she begins to cry. Further exploration reveals that Qizhi experiences extreme anxiety in the context of evaluation, and she fears she will bring dishonor to her family by not being at the top of everything she does.

Qizhi's concerns may be related to cultural values, and her test scores may very well have a dynamic connection to the panic attacks that brought her to counseling. The nature of that connection and what to do about the connection need to be the focus of discussion between Qizhi and her therapist. In fact, the test scores might become a concrete example of the prevailing striving for excellence that, although intangible, represents a real-life goal for Qizhi. With something as concrete as psychological test data from which to work, she might increase her insight about how striving for excellence affects her life choices and, secondarily, the extent to which she wishes to continue to make decisions based on that criterion.

2. *Identifying treatment strategies or techniques geared toward a client's strengths.* Some clients will demonstrate a significant discrepancy ("split") between the Verbal IQ and Performance IQ scores. For those individuals, the clinician's use of intervention strategies that are based on the client's area of strength can accomplish two things. First, it increases likelihood that the client will successfully follow through with assignments and suggestions. Second, resulting from the follow-through, the client may experience an increased sense of self-efficacy and achievement that can help the forward momentum of the therapy process.

In general, a client who has a demonstrated strength in the Performance realm is one who has strength in visual processing and visual-motor skills and abilities. Therefore, participating in experiential activities such as some of the Gestalt techniques or some of the behavioral techniques such as role-play and modeling will probably be appealing.

In contrast, with a client whose strength is in the Verbal realm, there might be a preference for auditory-based interventions such as insight-oriented talk therapy or bibliotherapy. This suggestion is not meant to imply that strength-based strategies should be done to the exclusion of other strategies. As possible treatment strategies are explored, there is a wealth of other information a therapist needs to also consider, such as outcome data about treatment approaches for certain disorders. However, an intervention congruent with a strength will probably have appeal to the client, thereby increasing the likelihood that he or she will follow through with the assignment.

3. *Identifying the types of pursuits vocationally or avocationally that would be most ecological for the client.* A counselor would do this by looking first at the client's areas of strength on the factor and index scales and then looking at the subtest scores. There may be some areas of strength or ability of which the client was unaware.

For example, perhaps a person has a significant strength in visual discrimination and also enjoys the outdoors yet never considered bird watching as a possible leisure activity. The test data could help generate ideas for areas of development or growth.

The following case example offers a scenario in which a client is making some vocational decisions. The client and counselor agree that an evaluation, including an intellectual assessment, might facilitate the decision-making process. Readers will note that Silver's (1993) information-processing model will be the framework from which test scores are understood and from which recommendations will originate. Here is the case example:

Robert is an African American male, 35 years old, who has decided he needs to get some additional job training. He has worked for the past 15 years for a cable company, installing and repairing cable lines. He is frustrated by his lack of progress in company promotions and believes he needs more formal education. He is requesting some assistance in deciding whether to get training in management or in some more technical aspects of cable and software/hardware interfacing. To put tests to use in answering his questions, we would consider two types of instruments. First, a career interest inventory could help him clarify whether training in working with people or working with things would be a better fit for him. Second, an individual intelligence test might help evaluate likely ease with which he would pursue either of those vocational tracks. Robert's WAIS-III evaluation yielded the following scaled and standard scores:

Verbal Subtests		Performance Subtests	
Vocabulary	12	Picture Completion	9
Similarities	9	Digit Symbol	6
Arithmetic	10	Block Design	13
Digit Span	7	Picture Arrangement	15
Information	11	Matrix Reasoning	11
Comprehension	10	Symbol Search	11
Letter-Number Sequencing	6		

Factor	Standard Score	Percentile	95% Confidence Band
Full Scale	102	55	99-107
Verbal IQ	100	50	102-112
Performance IQ	105	63	104-117
Verbal Comprehension	114	82	108-119
Perceptual Organization	116	86	108-122
Working Memory	99	47	92-106
Processing Speed	99	47	90-108

As we consider Robert's factor scores, we note that the VIQ and PIQ are within 4 points, suggesting that his verbal and nonverbal abilities have developed at approximately the same rate. However, there is a magnitude of difference between his (a) Verbal Comprehension and Perceptual Organization and his (b) Working Memory and Processing Speed, which suggests that some variables such as anxiety or depression may have suppressed his overall test performance. Nevertheless, his scaled scores on Block Design and Matrix Reasoning reveal efficiency in abstract conceptualization ability. His high Picture Arrangement score suggests strong ability in sequencing when the stimuli are visual. His lower scores on Digit Span and Letter-Number Sequencing are statistically significant weaknesses. It is unclear whether they are the result of anxiety or a relative weakness in auditory input. However, his relative strength in visual sequencing and conceptualization suggests that he would do best in an academic curriculum not exclusively auditory/verbal. So, if he chose to pursue management training, which is primarily verbal/auditory (lecture), he would likely find it more difficult to excel than if he went for technical training involving schematics, computerized training, or other more visually based training approaches. Occupational goals that would offer opportunities for problem solving, especially abstract problem solving, might be quite rewarding to him. Training goals that might be contraindicated would be those that would require acquisition and retrieval of many pieces of information or data, especially when the primary mode of input is auditory.

Report Writing

Report writing constitutes Quadrants C and D in the Figure 3.1 matrix, those being written forms of feedback. Some referral sources prefer that a report be written in the form of a letter, whereas other referral sources may prefer a report written in more standard format, labeled "Psychological Report," "Cognitive Evaluation," "Psycho-educational Evaluation," or some other title. We mentioned earlier the importance of communicating with the referral source prior to beginning the evaluation. One topic of discussion in that communication might be the report form preferred by the referring person. There may be some specific requirements for format stipulated by the referring person or agency as an extension of his or her own documentation requirements.

There are two aspects of report writing that will be addressed—format for the report and style of communication. Because *style* refers to the overall tone of the written report, the discussion will begin there. Sattler (2001) and Harvey (1997) identified several purposes for a written report of test results and interpretation. Those purposes are as follows:

1. To provide information yielded from the evaluation to the referral source

2. To become a basis for clinical hypotheses

3. To serve as a basis for selection of particular treatment strategies

4. To establish a baseline against which progress (or deterioration) can be measured

5. To serve as a legal document

As we discussed in Chapter 2, when a client is referred for an evaluation or diagnostic assessment, the referral often is the result of some difficulty he or she has been experiencing. The range of severity of those possible difficulties could be very broad. (*Severity* in this context refers to either the degree of subjective distress being experienced by the client or the extent of the negative effects as a result of the symptoms.) In some cases, the client's concerns will have a minimal impact on his or her daily functioning. In other cases, the client's concerns will be extensive and will create a negative impact on multiple aspects of his or her functioning. For example, one client may be expressing curiosity about career exploration, with no notable symptoms evident in his current functioning level. In contrast, after being evaluated as part of a pending disability evaluation, another client might experience significant anxiety and some disruption in daily functioning secondary to having been diagnosed with bipolar affective disorder.

As is the case with oral feedback, the written report needs to be directed toward the person who made the referral, meaning it should be written with an awareness that the reader may not be familiar with technical terms. Once again, this means the writer must avoid jargon and instead use lay terms to explain cognitive functions, tasks, and the client's abilities. Harvey (1997) noted emphatically that test results need to be communicated in language understandable to the client.

In addition to writing in user-friendly terminology, prompt turnaround from the time of testing to the time of interpretation and feedback is important (Sattler, 2001). There are multiple justifications for this statement. First and foremost, the client may be in distress, and the data interpretation may offer some clues about how to diminish his or her discomfort. In addition, the referral source may be awaiting the information from the assessment to help the client with significant treatment or placement decisions. Also, recollection of behavioral observations and impressions about the testing situation are freshest in one's memory shortly after the evaluation. Thus, it will be easier to accomplish a meaningful and accurate synthesis of the test data within a few days following testing, rather than waiting days or weeks to write the report. Finally, the referral source will likely be very pleased with a short turnaround and be more likely to make future testing referrals.

The reason for referral, as well as the subsequent referral question, is one driving force behind the decision about how much or how little detail a report writer needs to include. Another important consideration, as mentioned by Katz (1985), is the need of the referral source—how the test data are going to be used. Sometimes a client will be referred to determine whether she or he meets criteria for some services. For example, some clients applying for Social Security Disability Income (SSDI) benefits for psychiatric reasons are referred for an evaluation. Those evaluations often specifically require an individual intelligence test and an objective personality test. There probably are some specific configurations of data the SSDI determination bureau is looking for in determining whether the client meets the criteria to receive disability benefits. Such a report might be somewhat more succinct because the reason and referral questions will typically be quite specific.

In this author's (K.M.) work in a neuropsychology clinic at a psychiatric hospital, there were frequent patient referrals for cognitive evaluation. Patients referred for testing were often elderly people with psychiatric symptoms due to a wide variety of disorders. A typical referral question would be, "Is this elderly patient demented or is she suffering from pseudodementia (depression with symptoms that mimic dementia)?" There was also an inpatient substance abuse treatment unit. Frequently, patients would first be detoxified, and after detoxification they showed impairment in attention and concentration. A typical referral question for one of those patients was, "Can this person concentrate sufficiently to benefit from the treatment program?" These types of evaluations typically involved two to three instruments, yet the final report was never longer than one page!

A very different report would be warranted under different referral circumstances. For example, perhaps a client is referred for testing by an academic counselor at a community college due to poor grades and achievement despite extensive effort in studying and course preparation. The referral question under these circumstances might be along the lines of, "Does this student suffer from ADHD? A learning disability? Will he or she be able to achieve satisfactorily in a community college setting? What can we do to help him or her achieve at maximum potential? If community college is not the appropriate place for training, where is?" Given the breadth of these questions, it seems that extensive detail in profile analysis and subsequent recommendations will be more likely to meet the needs of the referral source than a report of one or two pages would be.

Some test publishers offer software that makes it possible to administer, score, interpret, and generate reports in a completely automated format. Examples of such publishers include Psychological Corporation and Psychological Assessment Resources. One concern about relying on a computer-generated report is that it is exceedingly difficult to write a computer program for report generation that adequately accounts for the multitude of individual variables that comprise a human being. Consequently, there may be bits and pieces, or perhaps large pieces, of the computer-generated interpretation that are applicable to the client. Nevertheless, it is not advisable to simply accept those interpretations at face value. Some readers may have encountered a client record in which there was a computer-generated test interpretation that a clinician had signed and placed in the client's record without an accompanying clinician-generated interpretation. This is poor professional form. The responsibility remains on the *clinician*, not a computer program, to accurately interpret and use test scores.

One advantage for a novice test user in scoring, interpreting, and writing a report without computerized assistance is that it may help the test user develop a better conceptualization of the whole assessment process. An analogy would be learning to calculate standard deviation by hand rather than having a statistics program do it. The process of doing the subtractions, summing, and dividing by hand makes it easy to see how the final number was derived and subsequently to have a very clear conceptualization of exactly what the standard deviation means. The same principle seems to hold true for test scoring and interpretation. After the initial learning has taken place, moving to computerized testing, score interpretation, and report writing can be quite efficient.

There seems to be consensus across authors that the format of a report will vary based on the needs of the referral source or the purpose of the evaluation. A report needs to thoroughly answer the referral question, but it is acceptable to keep the background information and other data confined to that which is germane to the referral question. The following are the categories of information that authors consistently advise for a standard report format:

Identifying Information. Name, date of birth, date of evaluation, referral source.

Reason for Referral. What questions are being attempted to answer.

Background Information. Start with the history behind the referral question, then go to a brief developmental history, noting those historical events that pertain to the evolution of the referral question.

Instruments Used. Although some clinicians title this section "Tests Administered," the term *instruments* is more appropriate because some of the procedures a clinician may have done with a client are technically not tests. For example, a clinical interview conducted as part of the assessment constitutes a procedure or instrument but is not a test. Likewise, behavioral rating scales would not be considered "tests," yet it would be appropriate to list them here. Therefore, "Instruments Used" is a more appropriate section title. List the clinical interview and, if applicable, also list any collateral interviews that may have been conducted, who the collateral was, and how they are connected to the client. Also in this section of the report, you need to list the full name of each test administered, followed on the same line by the abbreviation for that test.

Behavioral Observations. In Chapter 2, we discussed nine key behaviors to observe during testing. In this section of the report, each of those observations is put into sentence form. The behavioral observation data are presented as one basis for the subsequent conclusion that the evaluation either (a) yielded a probably accurate estimation of maximal effort and capacity or (b) revealed affective, cultural, behavior, and/or environmental factors that may have resulted in test scores that underestimated the person's true intellectual potential. Sattler (2001) emphasized that only behavioral descriptions, not interpretations, should be included here. It can be helpful to readers if the writer includes verbatim material expressed by the client to illustrate broad behavioral descriptions. Consider the following two examples:

1. Jocelyn was nervous about being tested.

2. Jocelyn frequently wrung her hands and shuffled her feet, and on several occasions she exclaimed, "Oh, I don't think I'll be able to do that!"

The second example offers a clearer description of the client's behavior and creates a basis for making data-based interpretations about the validity and generalizability of her test results.

Test Results. There are several ways test results can be presented. One method is to discuss scores and interpretations by test. Another technique is to discuss interpretations by domains such as intellectual/ cognitive functioning, personality, and career interest. It would be most applicable to discuss results by domain if a battery of tests was given. For example, in the cognitive domain, results could be given on an intelligence test and an achievement test; in the personality domain, multiple personality tests such as one objective and one projective would be presented; and in the vocational domain, multiple career interest and career readiness inventories would be presented.

The present discussion focuses only on the reporting of intelligence test scores. (In Chapter 8, we will present a comprehensive case study that will include composition of a report covering the three domains of cognitive and personality functioning and career concerns.) First, present the scaled and standard scores in a chart format. Note the method of presentation of test scores in the case example on Robert (presented earlier). Once again following the stair-step scheme, go from broad to specific in your interpretation of the numbers. Begin with Full Scale IQ; then go to Verbal and Performance IQ; then secondary factor scores of Verbal Comprehension, Perceptual Organization, Working Memory, and Processing Speed; then, finally, subtest scores.

When you begin the text interpreting the scores, try to keep two things in mind. First, the title of the factor or subtest will probably mean much less to the reader than a description of the skills in that domain. For example, rather than saying, "Betsy's Verbal IQ is in the high range," it will mean more to the reader to say, "Betsy's overall ability with hearing and using language is quite highly developed in comparison to other people." Second, interpret the test data with continuous awareness of how they pertain to answering the referral question. Once again, we approach the proverbial fork in the road, determined by the nature of the referral question. If the question is broad, the reader might be looking for anything of clinical note. However, when there is a very specific question to be answered, just answer the question. The one exception would be if the evaluator had observed some remarkable findings, especially if additional assessment or evaluation is indicated. For example, if there was some suggestion of a visual-spatial reversal problem, it would be crucial to make a recommendation for more precise evaluation, even though the referral question might be something unrelated (e.g., "Does she have attention deficit disorder?"). Another important objective to be accomplished in this section of the report is the integration and synthesis of background information (socioeconomic, cultural variables, history of the problem, behavioral observations) and test scores, again in the direction of answering the referral question. In some cases, the concluding paragraphs of the Test Results section can begin with a reiteration of the question, then your response to the question.

Summary and Recommendations. Some recipients of reports do not read the results but instead go directly to the Summary and Recommendations. The summary should be just what the heading implies— succinctly reviewing major findings. Information should never be presented for the first time in the Summary section. The recommendations may be, for some clients, the most important information to come out of the evaluation. Making recommendations involves looking at the referral questions and test data and then making specific suggestions about what could be done to help the client with the problem. This might take the form of referring the client for additional testing because the configuration of data may actually raise more questions than it answers. However, even when it is necessary to make a referral for additional services or testing elsewhere, it may be quite valuable to the referral source and to the client if the tester can also offer ideas for activities that would help address or ameliorate whatever difficulties prompted the referral for testing. Sattler (2001) noted that "the intent is not to look for a 'cure' or 'label,' but to offer a flexible approach for intervention and appropriate placement" (p. 687).

A Case Example

We will now refer to Robert's test data, reported earlier in this chapter. Because Robert is a self-referral and he will be the only recipient of the report, it will be a good example of how to write a succinct document for a layperson. Robert is self-referred for an evaluation focusing on career decision making. It would be appropriate, given his question, to administer a career interest inventory in conjunction with the individual intelligence test. The results of both of those tests would go in the report. However, because a comprehensive case example will be presented in Chapter 8, this specimen report will only interpret Robert's WAIS-III test data:

Intellectual Evaluation

    Name: Robert Simpson

    Date of Evaluation: 10/15/2000

    Date of Birth: 10/1/1965

    Chronological Age: 35 years, 6 months

Reason for Referral

Mr. Simpson was self-referred for an evaluation to explore possible career options. Mr. Simpson was referred to the career development specialist, Dr. Toman, in this group practice to complete the career interest portion of this evaluation.

Background Information

Mr. Simpson reported that he had experienced frustration in not earning a promotion at City Cable Media Centre, where he has been employed for the past 15 years. He hypothesized that the reason for his lack of upward movement in the company was due to insufficient training and work experience in jobs related to those he was trying to get promoted into.

Historically, Mr. Simpson reported being the second of four children in his family of origin. His father was a laborer, and mother was a homemaker. Education was heavily emphasized in the family, and academics were always placed as a higher priority in the household than either chores or fun. Mr. Simpson's developmental history was reportedly unremarkable.

He states his academic history was also unremarkable. He earned Bs and Cs in school, enjoying math and the sciences. He was in the general education track. Upon graduation from high school, he chose to work rather than pursue a college education. At the age of 20, he decided to attend classes at the community college but then was offered a job laying cable at City Cable. Because the hourly wage and benefits package were extremely attractive, he took the job. Since then, however, he has become somewhat dissatisfied with the job. There have been multiple opportunities for promotions, and despite applying for the promotions, he has yet to move up in the company. In discussing this matter with several coworker friends and immediate supervisor, he has concluded that the reason has been lack of adequate formal education beyond high school. Thus, he has renewed his commitment to get the necessary education to get promoted.

Mr. Simpson's main question when he requested this evaluation was whether he should pursue training in management and supervision or in some other technical aspect of cable work such as cable hardware/software interfacing.

Mr. Simpson resides alone, stating definitively that he is a "confirmed bachelor." In his leisure, he is in a bowling league and an intramural basketball team, and he is active in his church. Mr. Simpson denied any history of head injury. He also denied substance abuse or any significant medical problems.

Instruments Used

Clinical interview

Wechsler Adult Intelligence Scale—Third Revision (WAIS-III)

Behavioral Observations

Mr. Simpson is a 35-year-old African American male who appeared to be somewhat younger than his stated age. He demonstrated a broad, situationally appropriate range of affect. He had a good sense of humor, smiling and laughing often. His social skills were engaging, and there was no visible anxiety. During the WAIS-III administration, Mr. Simpson was quite willing to guess when unsure of an answer. He demonstrated excellent tolerance for frustration, as well as persistence. In addition, there were multiple instances when he exhibited cognitive flexibility in generating alternative solutions to tasks. He appeared to be somewhat concerned about time constraints but not at the expense of accuracy. He was a reflective responder, taking time to consider his responses before offering them. This evaluation is thought to have yielded an accurate estimate of Mr. Simpson's intellectual abilities as they currently exist.

Test Results and Interpretation

Factor	Standard Score	Percentile	95% Confidence Band
Verbal IQ	100	50	102-112
Performance IQ	105	63	104-117
Full Scale	102	55	99-107
Verbal Comprehension Index	114	82	108-119
Perceptual Organization Index	116	86	108-122
Working Memory Index	99	47	92-106
Processing Speed Index	99	47	90-108

Verbal Subtests		Performance Subtests	
Vocabulary	12	Picture Completion	9
Similarities	9	Digit Symbol	6
Arithmetic	10	Block Design	13
Digit Span	7	Picture Arrangement	15
Information	11	Matrix Reasoning	11
Comprehension	10	Symbol Search	11
Letter-Number Sequencing	6		

Mr. Simpson obtained a Full Scale IQ of 102, indicating that there is a 95% probability his true IQ lies between 99 and 107. This places him in the average range of intellectual functioning in comparison to the standardization group that is roughly representative of the U.S. population. Examining the Verbal and Performance IQ scores, there is only a 5-point discrepancy, suggesting that his verbal/auditory and nonverbal/visual-motor abilities have developed at approximately the same rate. Thus, the Full Scale IQ is, for Mr. Simpson, a useful number in describing his cognitive ability as a unitary factor.

In considering the secondary factor (index) scores, Mr. Simpson's Verbal Comprehension and Perceptual Organization are both higher than his Working Memory and Processing Speed. This suggests that the VIQ and PIQ may be underestimates of his true ability because the Working Memory and Processing Speed Index scores are particularly sensitive to anxiety, depression, carelessness, distractibility, or slow mental processing. Mr. Simpson did not disclose any past symptoms or problems as the result of anxiety or depression, nor was there any indication in behavioral observations of carelessness or impersistence. Therefore, we can tentatively conclude that Mr. Simpson's general cognitive style might be very slow and deliberate. The pattern of factor scores reveals a very small difference in index scores between Perceptual Organization and Verbal Comprehension, again indicating evenly developed verbal and nonverbal abilities.

Mr. Simpson did demonstrate statistically significant strengths and weaknesses among the subtests. Mr. Simpson demonstrated a strength on the Picture Arrangement subtest, which is thought to assess ability to differentiate relevant from irrelevant stimuli, ability to think sequentially, and social awareness. He also demonstrated a significant strength on the Block Design subtest, which assesses nonverbal abstract reasoning and visual-spatial problem solving. His visual-motor skills, particularly in sequencing and abstract problem solving, are very efficient. Matrix Reasoning might be considered a somewhat more abstract set of tasks than Block Design.

It may be helpful to consider the information-processing model of cognitive functioning. According to that model, intellectual functioning is seen as having four phases: input, integration, storage, and output. Input refers to data that the person acquires by way of one of the five senses. Integration consists of the brain organizing and synthesizing the data with other material already in the memory system. Storage refers to storing the information for later use, and output refers to expressing information behaviorally, either through speech or motoric activity.

All of Mr. Simpson's statistically significant weaknesses occurred on subtests that require short-term memory—Digit Span and Letter-Number Sequencing, both of which are auditory tasks, and Digit Symbol Coding, which is visual and motoric. The fact that he performed in the average range on Vocabulary and Comprehension indicates that short-term memory, as well as the transfer of information into long-term memory, has not historically been a problem for him. When one considers his constellation of weaknesses in the context of the information-processing model, it is unclear whether these weaknesses are arising from the input, storage, or retrieval phases. A vulnerability or inefficiency in any one of those three phases might account for Mr. Simpson's pattern of scores. This raises several possible explanations that will require further assessment.

First, there may be a possible organic, or biological, component inhibiting his learning. It is also necessary to investigate any awareness Mr. Simpson has had of memory problems in the recent past. There may be some physical condition or contribution to his memory impairment. Possibilities could include a metabolic imbalance or current or past substance abuse. Second, it is possible that some other type of affective process, such as anxiety or depression, could be contributing to his difficulty. Despite the fact that there were no observable symptoms of either anxiety or depression, presence of anxiety or depression could significantly hamper his ability to store and retrieve information from his short-term memory.

Summary and Recommendations

Mr. Simpson is a 35-year-old African American male who currently is functioning in the average range intellectually. He demonstrated strength in visual-motor processing, particularly sequential reasoning, and abstract problem solving when the correct response involved construction. There was some suggestion of difficulty with short-term auditory and visual memory. This difficulty is inconsistent with his average performance in other areas that require long-term memory, of which short-term memory is a precursor. Therefore, the memory difficulty appears to be of recent origin. Effort needs to be made to determine the source of the demonstrated memory difficulty. Therefore, before career counseling continues, the following concerns need to be addressed:

1. Rule out organic etiology, arising from medication, substance abuse, recent head injury, or disease process

2. Rule out affective disorders that could be impeding his cognitive functioning (e.g., anxiety or depressive disorder)

3. Pursue personality and career interest assessment

If each of the differential diagnoses identified in numbers 1 and 2 is ruled out, there is evidence supporting Mr. Simpson pursuing training either in management and supervisory skills or in a more technical direction. He has strength in abstract problem solving, suggesting that a technical course of study such as hardware/software interfacing might be quite manageable and enjoyable for him. Given his current short-term memory weakness, especially auditory, an auditory/verbal curriculum such as a management course might pose more of a learning challenge for him and require more effort in studying and learning. The results of an interest inventory and a personality inventory might assist Mr. Simpson in making a decision about which direction would be more enjoyable for him. Nevertheless, with regard to his cognitive functioning, either course of study and occup-ation would be well within his capability to achieve and perform.

James T. Counselor, M.Ed.
Counselor, Ohio License Number 1234

Summary

In this chapter, we have examined many aspects of the feedback process. Although the scenario for referrals varies, based on the referral source and referral question, certain aspects remain constant. Those aspects are accountability and precision in analysis of all client data and clear communication of the results and one's conclusions. The value of an assessment is directly proportional to the extent to which it answers the referral question. If an assessment has not enabled the clinician to answer the referral question or at least refine the direction for further evaluation, the assessment has been an exercise in futility—a waste of valuable time and resources.

The feedback process is an opportunity to explore with the client how to apply the information afforded by the test data—to actualize and justify the time the client and clinician have spent in the assessment. The feedback process is ideally the time to initiate steps that can somehow improve the client's condition or reduce his or her suffering. It is imperative that a clinician make conclusions based on diverse sources of data gathered throughout the assessment and be able to facilitate the client's and referral source's understanding of those conclusions.

Here is a suggested outline for the sequence giving verbal feedback to clients:

1. Explain the concepts of standard and scaled scores, norming, and your model for conceptualizing cognitive process and ability

2. Review the reason for referral

3. Ask the client if he or she has any sense of how the testing went

4. Discuss test scores, moving from the broadest factor scores to smaller factors and subtests—stick with functional explanations of the subtests rather than referring to the subtests by name

5. Discuss the implications of the test results in light of the reason for referral

6. Discuss rationales for any additional recommendations that may have arisen

7. Make plans for follow-up with you, by referral to another practitioner, or with the client's original referral source

Resource List

A thorough and outstanding presentation of the history of intelligence theory and explanation of contemporary theories is offered in Sattler's (2001) *Assessment of Children: Cognitive Applications*. This is a presentation of theories independent of developmental theory, and even for those clinicians working exclusively with adults, the presentation of theories is exemplary. The same Sattler text provides good report examples. Two additional sources readers may consult for report writing are Kaufman and Lichtenberger's *Essentials of WISC-III and WPPSI-R Assessment* (2000) and *Essentials of WAIS-III Assessment* (1999).

Discussion Questions

1. Role-play giving test feedback to one another. If you have not done any testing, use the data presented from Robert's case (this chapter) or Anna's case (Chapter 8).

2. Discuss the theories of intellectual functioning, comparing Gardner's (1983) multiple intelligences theory with Silver's (1993) information-processing model and Sternberg's (1986) triarchic theory. Which of those theories is most closely aligned with your own thoughts about cognitive functioning?

3. Which of those theories is most applicable cross-culturally? Generate some cross-cultural examples that support cross-cultural generalizability and also some examples that suggest that the theories are culture bound.

References

American Psychological Association. (1992). Ethical principles of psychologists and code of conduct. *American Psychologist, 47,* 1597-1611.

Beutler, L. E. (1995). Integrating and communicating findings. In L. E. Beutler & M. R. Berren (Eds.), *Integrative assessment of adult personality* (pp. 25-64). New York: Guilford.

Committee on Psychological Tests and Assessment. (1996). Statement on the disclosure of test data. *American Psychologist, 51,* 644-648.

Gardner, H. (1983). *Frames of mind: The theory of multiple intelligences.* New York: Basic Books.

Gardner, H., Kornhaber, M. L., & Wake, W. K. (1996). *Intelligence: Multiple perspectives.* Fort Worth, TX: Harcourt Brace College.

Gregory, R. J. (1999). *Foundations of intellectual assessment: The WAIS-III and other tests in clinical practice.* Boston: Allyn & Bacon.

Harvey, V. F. (1997). Improving readability of psychological reports. *Professional Psychology: Research & Practice, 28,* 271-274.

Katz, L. (1985). *A practical guide to psychodiagnostic testing.* Springfield, IL: Charles C Thomas.

Kaufman, A. S. (1994). *Intelligent testing with the WISC-III.* New York: John Wiley.

Kaufman, A. S., & Lichtenberger, E. O. (1999). *Essentials of WAIS-III assessment.* New York: John Wiley.

Kaufman, A. S., & Lichtenberger, E. O. (2000). *Essentials of WISC-III and WPPSI-R assessment.* New York: John Wiley.

Sattler, J. M. (2001). *Assessment of children: Cognitive applications* (4th ed.). San Diego, CA: Author.

Silver, L. B. (1993). Introduction and overview to the clinical concepts of learning disabilities. *Child and Adolescent Psychiatric Clinics of North America: Learning Disabilities, 2,* 181-192.

Sternberg, R. J. (1986). *Intelligence applied: Understanding and increasing your intellectual skills.* New York: Harcourt Brace.

Wechsler, D. (1997). *Wechsler Adult Intelligence Scale* (3rd rev. ed.). San Antonio, TX: The Psychological Corporation.

4

The MMPI-2 and the MMPI-A

Guidelines for Administration and Interpretation

The Minnesota Multiphasic Personality Inventory (MMPI) (Hathaway & McKinley, 1942) is the most widely used psychological test in the world (Butcher & Williams, 2000), having been translated into more than 150 languages. The MMPI also qualifies as the most extensively researched psychological test in existence (Butcher & Rouse, 1996) and is the first choice of mental health practitioners in clinical settings to assess the personality characteristics of their clients (Watkins, Campbell, Niebirding, & Hallmark, 1995). Since its publication, the MMPI has been revised only once (Butcher, Dahlstrom, Graham, Tellegen, & Kaemmer, 1989), and the new adult version is referred to as the MMPI-2. (Publication of the original MMPI was discontinued in 1999.) The MMPI-A (Butcher et al., 1992) is a modified version of the MMPI-2 aimed at assessing adolescent personality.

People taking the MMPI-2 are asked to give one of three responses to each of the 567 items: true, false, or cannot say. Reponses are scored on seven validity scales and a variety of clinical scales subdivided into three major categories: Basic Scales (10), Content Scales (15), and Supplemental or Special Scales (varying number). The test is scored by transforming raw scores into uniform T scores with a mean of 50 and a standard deviation of 10. Typically, T scores of 60 or greater on clinical scales are of concern to the clinician. T scores of 65 or greater are considered elevated and representative of psychological distress and dysfunction. The original MMPI used a linear T score format rather than the uniform T score and set the cutoff point for psychopathology at $T = 70$. A T score of 65 translates into a percentile rank of 92 for Basic Scales 1 to 4 and 6 to 9 and for all the Content Scales. In other words, on those scales when a respondent scores at $T = 65$, that person's score is higher than 92% of the norm group.

Several features of the MMPI have made it uniquely valuable to clinicians. First, it is comprehensive, assessing a wide range of aspects of personality and interpersonal behavior. Second, it focuses on dysfunctional aspects of the personality, the dimensions to which clinicians need to be especially attentive if they are to be helpful to their clients. Third, it provides detailed information about the test-taking attitude of the client, allowing the clinician to evaluate whether the clinical findings of the test are likely to be accurate and honest representations of functioning. Fourth, it has a large number of special scales to assess problems such as substance abuse, posttraumatic stress, and hostility. Fifth, the huge research base provides extensive evidence of the test's reliability and validity, giving clinicians more confidence in the meaning of its results. Finally, its scores have both diagnostic value and therapeutic value. On one hand, its findings help confirm or refute the diagnostic judgments clinicians have drawn from interview and behavior data and offer additional diagnostic possibilities to consider. On the other hand, the process of discussing test results with clients helps clients understand themselves and their problems better and, if done properly, seems to enhance the therapeutic alliance and to move the treatment forward (Finn, 1996; Newman & Greenway, 1997). The insights clients gain often motivate them to engage more fully in the difficult therapeutic work before them, give them confidence in the ability of the clinician to understand their problems, and provide them with hope for change. The process also highlights in a very concrete way the value of client's own expertise about themselves when clinicians integrate their clients' reactions to test findings into their ultimate report.

This chapter identifies the circumstances under which the MMPI-2 and MMPI-A can be helpful resources to clinicians in assessing and treating client problems. We also include practical suggestions for the administration of the test in clinical settings, with special emphasis on orienting clients to the test so that the results obtained are meaningful. Finally, the chapter offers a step-by-step guide to interpretation of results. Readers who are not familiar with the psychometric features of these tests should familiarize themselves with that information through other sources, such as Butcher and Williams (2000) and the test manual (Butcher et al., 1989), because those features will not be reviewed in the pages that follow. Use of the MMPI-2 or MMPI-A is limited to those with sufficient education, training, and supervised experience in the administration, scoring, and interpretation of these instruments. Clinicians who attempt to employ these tests without such background are acting in violation of the ethical standards of the profession (American Psychological Association, 1992). (For more detailed information on the ethics of using psychological tests responsibly, see Chapter 9.)

Screening Clients for MMPI-2 Use

The MMPI-2 contains 567 items, requires at least a fifth-grade reading level, takes approximately 1.5 hours to complete, and asks respondents to provide honest answers about highly personal and often socially undesirable behaviors. The MMPI-A is nearly as long, containing 468 items. Moreover, for reliability reasons, items are sometimes repeated and other similar items appear throughout the test, leaving test takers with the impression that they are being repeatedly asked virtually identical questions about personal content. Obviously, then, not all clients are suitable for such testing. Who should be selected, and under what conditions should the test be given? The following criteria identify the client characteristics and environments needed to obtain an interpretable test:

- The availability of a suitable quiet space for test taking under controlled conditions so that the clinician can be assured that the results obtained are from the client himself or herself, with as few distractions as possible

- Careful instruction in completing the answer sheet or using an electronic version so that inadvertent errors do not invalidate the test
- Access to a knowledgeable person to whom clients can address questions about procedures as they arise during the administration
- The capacity to read at a sixth-grade level in the language of the test. Butcher et al. (1989) recommend at least 8 years of formal education for the MMPI-2. Clinicians with access to tape-recorded versions of the tests may substitute these as needed. A test in a language in which the client is a native speaker is ideal for use. Butcher and Williams (2000) provide a list of translators and translations for a variety of languages
- The ability to concentrate sufficiently to complete a lengthy paper-and-pencil test either in one sitting or in a limited number of briefer sittings under controlled conditions. Both acute psychological distress and physical illness may make administration contraindicated until the distress subsides or the illness improves
- A basic level of self-knowledge to answer a wide range of questions about one's functioning and personal history, along with a willingness to give truthful answers to highly personal questions
- A personal investment in the test results so that when clients get weary or uncomfortable with the test procedures, they will have adequate motivation to continue with the process
- An understanding that they will be informed about the test results and have control over how they are used

When considering the administration of the adolescent version of the test, the clinician should add the following guidelines to the process:

- A focused assessment of reading level (sixth grade minimum), sampling complex words used in the instrument and reviewing them with the client prior to the test to ensure that the client understands their meaning. Special attention should be given to items that use "double negatives" because adolescents are more vulnerable to misinterpreting the meaning of such items (Butcher & Williams, 2000). The following sentence includes a double negative: "It is not unimportant that test takers get enough sleep the night before a test."

- The inclusion of a short break in the middle of testing or a division of the testing into separate time periods to account for the more limited attention span of many young people. More mature adolescents may have no need for such a break and may actually prefer to work without interruption, but the option for a break should be available.

- An understanding of how much information from the test will be disclosed to parents, teachers, or other professionals. Adolescents who have confidence that they will have some privacy in the process or trust in the adults involved are more likely to provide honest responses to items.

Even when these conditions are met, clinicians are well advised to use the test prudently and prepare clients carefully. MMPI scores are of greatest value when the problems clients are describing seem complex, subtle, or confusing; when they are not able or willing to articulate their experience very well; or when the current problems appear embedded in a longer history of dysfunction or distress. The MMPI-2, for example, is less likely to be fruitful for an otherwise well-functioning client who has experienced a sexual assault and needs crisis counseling than for a quiet, withdrawn client who describes a pattern of disabling anxiety and depression interspersed with periods of explosive anger. The latter set of symptoms does not readily fit into a common diagnostic category, nor can the client discuss the symptoms with ease and in detail. Clinicians may also find the MMPI-2 or MMPI-A useful to confirm an evaluation of client functioning derived from interview and behavioral data. For instance, clients with personality disorders often present for counseling with an acute problem such as a depressive episode. Under these circumstances, counseling often focuses on management of the acute depressive episode, and clients are often unwilling or unable to give a full verbal description of their history and longstanding problems. Nevertheless, this client's responsiveness to treatment of depression is likely to be different from that of someone with otherwise normal functioning. The MMPI-2 acts as a reliable tool in gaining additional information about the whole constellation of personality characteristics and problems in functioning in which the depressive episode is embedded.

In situations in which the clinician is uncertain whether the administration of the MMPI-2 or MMPI-A will be fruitful, he or she may opt to administer a symptom checklist as an initial step as a basic screening related to the presenting issues. The brevity and focus on these instruments make them easy to administer and score, and the responses to their items can serve as a jumping-off place for in-depth discussion of the presenting problems. The Beck Depression Inventory (Beck, Steer, & Brown, 1996), the Trauma Symptom Inventory (Briere, 1995), and the Eating Disorders Inventory (Garner, 1991) are three examples of the many symptom-oriented measures currently available. Clinicians should note, however, that such tests tend to have lower levels of reliability and validity than the MMPI-2 and, therefore, are more vulnerable to error.

Scoring MMPI Results

Once a client has completed the items, the first step in scoring is to review the printed answer sheet for errors, multiple omissions, and other indications of invalidity. Ideally, this task should be completed before the client leaves the testing area so that minor problems in responding can be remedied immediately. If more than 10 omissions have occurred, the client should be asked to try again to give responses to most of those items. If the client fails to complete items at the end of the test or marks those items as all true or all false, the client can be asked to redo that portion of the test so that it can be scored. When such events occur, clinicians should approach clients in a nonjudgmental way, avoiding inducing guilt and expressing empathy with their fatigue or distraction on this long test. If the bubble items are not darkened sufficiently, a staff person can make the responses more readable.

When obvious problems with the answer sheet have been ruled out or corrected, the test is ready for scoring and the clinician must choose among several options for this task. The test can be computer scored or hand scored, a task that takes approximately 1 hour for an experienced person. When the computer is used, the answer sheet is usually sent to a scoring service that performs the task for a fee. (A computer-generated report of results may also be available for an additional fee; the value of such reports will be discussed in the next chapter.) Some professionals own computer programs that allow them to score on-site. Procedures for scoring are delineated in the test manuals, and readers should refer to them for specific guidelines in that task (Butcher et al., 1989; Butcher et al., 1992).

Interpreting MMPI Results: Understanding the Scales

The task of interpreting MMPI results is a complex one because of the multiple sources of data and the need to integrate all that data into a coherent assessment of the client's personality characteristics. Clinicians new to this enterprise should allot several hours to the task and should consult with senior colleagues about their understanding of the results prior to discussing those results with clients or including a report in a client's chart. The test manuals and related resources (e.g., Butcher & Williams, 2000; Graham, 2000) should be thoroughly consulted in this process. If such resources do not become well worn and dog-eared quickly, then they are being underused. The central features of interpretation include the following:

1. Verifying that the test results are valid

2. Determining the client's approach to the test-taking process

3. Describing the major features of the client's personality and interpersonal functioning using the Basic, Content, and Supplemental Scales

4. Exploring the implications of results on Critical Items and Research Scales

5. Identifying points of confusion or contradiction that need to be explored in session with a client

Verifying the Validity of Results

The MMPI does a masterful job of assessing whether the pattern of results obtained is likely to represent an honest and accurate view of the client's current problems and functioning. Clinicians who review these results carefully can glean an enormous amount of information from them, not only about the tendency of the client to "fake" results but also about the client's personality characteristics. Needless to say, though, the validity scores are not foolproof and must be interpreted with awareness of the client's social and cultural background. Moreover, the line at which a score reaches the level of questionable validity is not absolute (Table 4.1 and 4.2). For example, a Lie scale score of $T = 67$ may not invalidate the scores on the clinical scales for a person with a very strict religious upbringing and belief system. (Sometimes clients raised in an Amish or Mennonite tradition, for example, score in this range on the Lie scale.) Those people should not be seen as trying to fake a good score—they can be honestly responding even at that level, so that the rest of the test is not invalid. Seven major validity scales are routinely scored on the MMPI-2.

If a test is judged to be sufficiently valid to interpret, clinicians can then evaluate the scales that deal with personality features. There are four groups of such scales: Basic Scales, Content Scales, Supplemental Scales, and Critical Items.

Interpreting Basic Scales

Ten Basic Scales comprise this section of the MMPI-2 and MMPI-A. These scales were formed when the test was first developed, and they have proven to be the core of the test. Because the terms used to designate these scales do not fully represent the personality characteristics found to be associated with elevations, the recommended strategy is to refer to the scales by number or by abbreviation (see Table 4.3). Using the names of the scales, such as Psychasthenia for Scale 7 or Psychopathic Deviate for Scale 4, can also unnecessarily worry or offend clients. Scales 1 to 4 and 6 to 9 deal with distress and dysfunction, but Scales 5 and 10 are not considered clinical scales. Scale 10 (Si) measures introversion/extroversion, and Scale 5 (Mf) has little interpretive value. Originally designed as an attempt to measure latent homosexuality, Scale 5 never reliably assessed that, and it currently has few reliable descriptors associated with it. When the MMPI was being revised, the authors even discussed eliminating Scale 5 from the instrument but ultimately decided that changing the physical

Table 4.1   Standard Validity Scales for the MMPI-2

Scale Name	Purpose	Score of Suspected Invalidity
Cannot Say	Identify omitted items	30 omissions
Lie scale	Identify faking good	T score = 65 or higher
F scale	Identify deviant responding	T score = 81 or higher
Fb scale	Deviant responding in second half of test	T score = 89 or higher
VRIN	Identify inconsistent responses	T score = 80 or higher
TRIN	Identify tendency to yea-say or nay-say	T score = 80 or higher
K scale	Identify defensive responding	T score = 65 or higher

Table 4.2   Newer Validity Scales for the MMPI-2

Scale Name	Purpose	Score of Suspected Invalidity
Fp	Detect true psychopathy	T score = 80
S	Detect superlative self-descriptions	T score = 65

layout of the test in that way would be too significant a departure from accepted form. For Scales 1 to 4 and 6 to 9, T scores over 65 are considered clinically significant, and, with the exception of Scale 6, T scores on those scales between 60 and 64 are viewed as moderately elevated. For a full explanation of the descriptors associated with elevations on each scale, see Butcher and Williams (2000).

Six of the Basic Scales (Scales 2, 3, 4, 6, 8, and 9) contain heterogeneous content, so subscale scores, called Harris-Lingoes subscales after their developers, are used to understand these findings more fully. Harris-Lingoes scores become meaningful only when the Basic Scale T score is 60 or higher and the Harris-Lingo score is at least $T = 65$.

Interpreting Content Scales

The 15 Content Scales are new with the MMPI-2, but research thus far indicates that they show high levels of reliability and validity and are of substantial value to the clinician (Butcher, 1990; Butcher & Williams, 2000). Paralleling the Basic Scales, T scores become of concern to the clinician when they reach $T = 60$ or higher, and the criterion for a full elevation is $T = 65$ or greater. The content of these

Table 4.3   Features Associated With MMPI-2 Basic Scales

Scale Number	Basic Features Assessed With Elevated Scores
1 (Hs)	Tendency to worry excessively about physical illness and to insist on physical rather than psychological explanations of distress
2 (D)	Tendency to feel depressed, unhappy, fatigued, unfocused, guilty, hopeless, helpless, suicidal, and generally overwhelmed by life at the moment
3 (Hy)	Tendency to react to stress with physical complaints, lack insight into their problems, and be overly needy of affection and approval from others but superficial in interpersonal relations
4 (Pd)	Tendency to describe family circumstances as conflict ridden, have problems with authority and possible illegal actions, have loose moral standards, and act in immature and self-interested ways that make intimacy difficult
5 (Mf)	Tendency to have social and occupational interests and patterns atypical of one's gender
6 (Pa)	Tendency to be suspicious of others and to feel persecuted and be overly sensitive to criticism, rigid in thinking, and externalizing blame for their problems
7 (Pt)	Tendency to be anxious, tense, self-critical, uncomfortable in interpersonal situations, obsessive-compulsive, and perfectionistic
8 (Sc)	Tendency to feel alienated from others and from self, have difficulty coping with the demands of life, worry that they are losing their minds, and have inappropriate affect and bizarre sensory experiences, including hallucinations or delusions
9 (Ma)	Tendency to be agitated and impulsive, seek risky and thrilling activity, be self-interested and unrealistic in positive views of self, and be easily frustrated by others
10 (Si)	Tendency to be shy, introverted, socially withdrawn, and apprehensive in groups when score is elevated and a tendency to be extroverted, seeking out groups and feeling comfortable with others and possibly uncomfortable when alone if the score is low

scales overlaps with that of the Basic Scales, but what these scales measure are the problems that the client readily admits to. The interpretive meaning of the Basic Scale items is not obvious from their wording, but the personality features associated with the wording of the Content Scale items are obvious to clients. Fundamental descriptors associated with elevations on each scale are presented in Table 4.4.

Interpreting Supplemental Scales

The list of Supplemental Scales available for the MMPI-2 is quite lengthy, and readers who seek to become acquainted with the full range of such scales should consult Butcher and Williams (2000) or Graham (2000). The following Supplemental Scales are most commonly used and most strongly supported by research evidence.

Substance Use and Abuse Scales. In the MMPI-2, three scales directly address this topic. These are (a) the MacAndrew Alcoholism scale (Mac-R), a scale composed of items that statistically differentiate people with alcohol abuse problems from those with psychiatric problems; (b) the Addiction Potential scale (APS), which measures the personality characteristics associated with addictions; and (c) the Addiction Acknowledgment scale (AAS), which assesses a client's willingness to admit problems with drugs or alcohol. The Mac-R and the APS include items that are associated with the more subtle and behavioral features associated with substance abuse, and the AAS is composed of items that ask direct questions about substance abuse.

Marital Distress Scale (MDS). This scale examines a person's acknowledgment of relationship problems and is composed of items that distinguish couples in conflict-ridden and unhappy relationships from those in healthier relationships.

Posttraumatic Stress Disorder Scale (PK). The PK scale is the newest of this group of Supplemental Scales, and it was developed to measure the presence of posttraumatic stress disorder (PTSD) symptoms using a sample of combat veterans. High scores on this scale do not mean that a diagnosis of PTSD is justified. They indicate that a person acknowledges a set of symptoms that are part of the PTSD diagnosis. Additional data are necessary to determine whether a past trauma occurred and whether the diagnosis of PTSD is warranted.

Other Supplemental Scales. The MMPI-2 also includes scales that assess dominance, social responsibility, overcontrolled hostility, ego strength, anxiety, and repression.

Table 4.4   Features Associated With MMPI-2 Content Scales

MMPI-2 Content Scale	Descriptors Associated With Elevated Scores
Anxiety (ANX)	Symptoms of worry, tension, heart pounding, sleep problems, indecision, difficulty concentrating, fear of losing their mind
Fears (FRS)	Symptoms of specific fears and phobias in contrast to generalized anxiety
Obsessiveness (OBS)	Symptoms of rumination and obsessive thinking, distress by change, difficulty with decision making, compulsive behavior, strain in interpersonal relations when others get impatient with them, easily overwhelmed
Depression (DEP)	Symptoms of depression, sadness, brooding, worry about the future, hopelessness, possible suicidal ideation, frequent crying, and feelings of distance from other people
Health Concerns (HEA)	Symptoms of multiple physical problems across several body systems; worry about health more than most people
Bizarre Mentation (BIZ)	Symptoms of thought disorder, including hallucinations, paranoid ideation, or delusions
Anger (ANG)	Symptoms of being hotheaded, easily irritated, and some loss of control with anger, including verbal aggression and urges toward physical aggression
Cynicism (CYN)	Symptoms of distrust of others, suspicion of others' motives, negative feelings even toward those close to them, misanthropic attitudes
Antisocial Practices (ASP)	Symptoms of problem behaviors in school, illegal actions, enjoyment of the antics of criminals
Type A Personality (TPA)	Symptoms of a driven, perfectionistic, and hostile personality who is work oriented and competitive and is easily frustrated and viewed as overly aggressive and blunt in interpersonal relationships
Low Self-Esteem (LSE)	Symptoms of a low opinion of self separate from feelings of depression, a belief that others dislike them, and a sense of being overwhelmed by their own faults
Social Discomfort (SOD)	Symptoms of uneasiness in social situations, shyness, and a preference for solo activities

(Continued)

Table 4.4 (Continued)

MMPI-2 Content Scale	Descriptors Associated With Elevated Scores
Family Problems (FAM)	Symptoms of substantial family discord, alienation from family, hate toward family members, and a sense of being unloved by family
Work Interference (WRK)	Symptoms of negative attitudes toward work, problems with work performance, lack of perseverance in work tasks, lack of family support for career, and difficulties with coworkers
Negative Treatment Indicators (TRT)	Symptoms of negative attitudes toward health are and mental health professionals and skepticism about their ability to understand or be helpful, unwillingness to share personal information in treatment, resistance to change, and avoidance of crisis

Using Critical Items

Some MMPI items are more obviously tied to psychological dys-function than others, and these items have particular value in suggesting hypotheses that clinicians should explore in more detail with the client. Clinicians can obtain groupings of Critical Items that deal with psychopathology ranging from acute anxiety to persecutory ideas and threatened assault. Although these items are not scales and do not have the same explanatory power as formal scales, they can alert clinicians to particular issues that need to be discussed in future sessions. (See the test manual or Butcher and Williams [2000] for example of Critical Items.)

Using Code Types

When Hathaway and McKinley first developed the MMPI, they expected clients diagnosed with depression or clients with schizophrenia to have elevations only on the Basic Scales that deal with those problems. However, much more often clients with psychological problems produced results with two or more elevations. Over time, researchers came to understand that a subset of descriptors was uniquely applicable to many of those combinations of elevations. Currently, whenever a client's results show elevations on more than one scale, clinicians should explore whether that particular combination of elevations is better described by a 2- or 3-point code type than by the descriptors used with each elevation. The most common 2-point code types are 1-3 or 3-1, 2-7 or 7-2, 4-9 or 9-4, and 6-8 or 8-6. The unique descriptors associated with them and the other validated code types are presented in the test manual and comprehensive textbooks. Butcher and Williams (2000) identified 20 different 2-point code types and 3 common 3-point code types (1-2-3, 2-7-4, and 2-7-8). A code-type interpretation is most helpful when the two or three relevant scales are the only elevated clinical scales, are within 5 to 10 T score points of each other, and are at least 5 T score points higher than any other clinical Basic Scale (Butcher & Williams, 2000).

Interpreting MMPI Results: Developing Meaningful Client Descriptors

Once a clinician has scored the test and reviewed the results in each of the above sections of the MMPI-2, he or she has the daunting task of organizing all that data into coherent preliminary notes to be discussed with the client. Clients in therapeutic settings commonly show results with multiple and conflicting elevations. This section of the chapter presents a strategy for making sense of those findings so that a meaningful feedback session with the client can take place. To do that, we will turn to the test results of Margot, a 23-year-old graduate student who is feeling depressed and anxious and is experiencing increasing levels of conflict with her spouse of 18 months. Margot came to therapy 2 months ago because her symptoms were interfering with her progress on her degree and her pleasure from her marriage. Margot agreed to take the MMPI-2 to get more insight into her unhappiness and her role in the marital conflict. The review of Margot's test results takes place in eight major steps:

Step 1: Review the scores on the validity scales to ensure that the client cooperated with testing.

Step 2: Review the Basic Scale scores to identify elevations and moderate elevations and relevant descriptors either from individually elevated scales or from a 2- or 3-point code if present. Eliminate descriptors inconsistent with behavioral or other data. Review relevant Harris-Lingoes subscale descriptors to identify additional meaningful descriptors.

Step 3: Note descriptors inconsistent with other data that need additional evaluation at a later point. For example, a test may show an elevation on the substance abuse scales, but interview and family data do not reveal a history of such problems.

Step 4: Review Content Scale elevations and moderate elevations to reveal additional relevant descriptors and potential inconsistencies.

Step 5: Review Supplemental Scale elevations and moderate elevations to reveal additional relevant descriptors and potential inconsistencies.

Step 6: Review Critical Items to clarify findings.

Step 7: Reconcile inconsistencies and identify questions to ask client to gather more information.

Step 8: Write up preliminary findings to discuss with the client.

The first step in understanding Margot's results, shown in Figure 4.1, is to ascertain whether those results are likely to be valid representations of her current functioning. In reviewing the validity scales of this MMPI-2, we can deduce that Margot cooperated with the testing by answering nearly all the questions (Cannot Say score) in a way that showed she understood and consistently paid attention to the content of the items (VRIN and TRIN scores). The validity scales also show that she did not respond defensively (K and S scores), and she did not try to present herself as being exceptionally virtuous (L score). Nor did she significantly exaggerate her problems (F scale scores), although her scores are in the range that show that she is experiencing symptoms and is willing to acknowledge problems. In short, this pattern of validity scores reveals a person who is likely to be honestly presenting herself and her current level of distress.

With evidence that the clinical findings of the test are likely to be meaningful, we can move on to review the Basic Scale scores and

Validity Scales	Raw Score	T Score
Cannot Say	1	Not applicable
L scale	2	43
F	7	66
Fb	5	62
TRIN	7(T)	65
VRIN	6	54
K	13	46
S	11	43

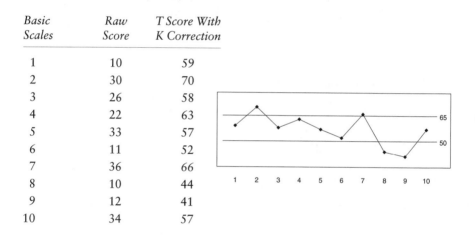

Basic Scales	Raw Score	T Score With K Correction
1	10	59
2	30	70
3	26	58
4	22	63
5	33	57
6	11	52
7	36	66
8	10	44
9	12	41
10	34	57

Relevant Harris-Lingoes Scores

D_1	16	70
D_2	8	62
D_3	4	56
D_4	5	61
D_5	6	68
Pd_1	6	74
Pd_2	3	53
Pd_3	4	47
Pd_4	6	60
Pd_5	7	68

Figure 4.1   The Case of Margot: MMPI-2 Scores

Figure 4.1 (Continued)

Content Scales	Raw Score	T Score
ANX	17	74
FRS	8	56
OBS	6	50
DEP	23	80
HEA	12	63
BIZ	5	47
ANG	10	64
CYN	7	52
ASP	4	41
TPA	8	55
LSE	10	60
SOD	13	60
FAM	9	57
WRK	6	46
TRT	5	51

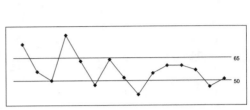

Supplemental Scales	Raw Score	T Score
Mac-R	20	53
APS	25	55
AAS	3	56
MDS	7	68
PK	14	58

Harris-Lingoes scores. This process starts with a listing of the scales that are elevated and moderately elevated. In Margot's case, the elevated scales are Scales 2 ($T = 70$) and 7 ($T = 66$), and the moderately elevated scale is Scale 4 ($T = 63$). Because the two elevated scales comprise a 2-point code, the descriptors for that code are used in lieu of combining the descriptors for each scale. These descriptors identify the following personality characteristics (Butcher & Williams, 2000):

- Anxious, tense, nervous, and depressed
- Unhappy, sad, and tending to worry excessively
- Feels vulnerable to real and imagined threats
- Anticipates problems before they occur and may overreact to minor stress
- Reports symptoms of fatigue, exhaustion, weight loss, slowed speech, and retarded thinking
- Broods and ruminates often
- Shows great indecisiveness
- Reports sleep disturbance
- Feels guilty when personal goals are not met
- Perfectionistic and conscientious
- Excessively religious or moralistic
- Docile, passive-dependent, and nonassertive in relationships
- Capable of forming deep emotional ties but leans on people excessively
- Feels inadequate, insecure, and inferior
- Tends to be intropunitive
- May be diagnosed as depressive, obsessive-compulsive, or anxiety disordered
- Pessimistic about overcoming problems and rigid in thinking
- Usually motivated for psychotherapy and counseling

At this point, the clinician begins sorting through this long list of symptoms to identify those that are incompatible with behavioral or other test data about the client. Because Margot has revealed that she does not belong to a religious organization, is not sure about whether she believes in God, and is accepting of other people's ways of living their lives, the descriptor "excessively religious or moralistic" can be eliminated. She also denies any weight loss and shows no evidence of slowed speech or rigidity in thinking in her interactions with the clinician, so those descriptors are also eliminated. Next, the moderate elevation ($T = 63$) on Scale 4 should be evaluated. Because this scale has such heterogeneous content and the list of possible descriptors is so extensive, clinicians should examine the pattern of elevations on the Harris-Lingoes subscales to see whether the moderate elevation cuts across many of the heterogeneous descriptors or whether it is focused in one or two subsets of those descriptors. In Margot's case, only two elevations appear—on Pd_1 (Family Conflict) and on Pd_5 (Self-Alienation). (It is important to remember that H-L scores are only considered meaningful when they reach a level of $T = 65$.) These elevations are associated with the following descriptors (Butcher & Williams, 2000):

- View their home situation as lacking in love, support, and understanding
- View their family as critical and controlling
- Indicate a desire to leave home
- Deny feeling happy
- Report that life is not worth living
- Easily hurt by criticism
- Feel they are losing control of their thought processes
- Feel useless
- Feel uncomfortable and unhappy with themselves
- Have problems concentrating
- Find life uninteresting or unrewarding
- Have difficulty settling down
- May use alcohol excessively

Next the clinician should identify the descriptors associated with the H-L subscales for Scale 2, the only other elevated Basic Scale with H-L subscales. Margot's results show interpretable findings for D_1 (Subjective Depression) and D_5 (Brooding), revealing the following descriptors:

- Feel depressed, unhappy, nervous
- Lack energy

- Have few interests
- Feel they are not coping well with problems
- Have difficulty concentrating and attending to daily tasks
- Feel inferior and lack self-confidence
- Are often shy and uneasy in social situations
- Tend to brood and ruminate a great deal

A preliminary review of these descriptors indicates that the majority either are identical with some of the 2-point code descriptors (e.g., depressed, unhappy, nervous, tends to brood and ruminate) or are consistent with them (e.g., finds life uninteresting, feels useless). Two are not indicated from the 2-point code or the moderate elevation on Scale 4 and should be explored further to determine their appropriateness in this case—"possible excessive use of alcohol" and "feel they are losing control of their thought processes." The fit between these descriptors and the client's personality is uncertain until other evidence from the test and interview data is evaluated.

As a final part of the review of the Basic Scales, clinicians should note the client's score on Scale 10 that measures introversion/extroversion. Its score is important regardless of the level of elevation insofar as it provides information about the person's tendency toward introversion or extroversion. In Margot's case, her score on this scale is within one standard deviation of the norm group ($T = 57$), indicating that her typical pattern is a mix of introversion and extroversion and that extreme shyness and social discomfort are probably not longstanding issues for Margot. Persons with scores in this range tend to have the requisite social skills and temperament to function adequately in social settings.

At this point, the clinician has already begun to gather a clear view of the client's symptoms and interpersonal functioning, but an analysis of the Content Scales and Supplemental Scales can clarify that picture further. Margot's MMPI-2 reveals elevations on two Content Scales, ANX and DEP, findings consistent with her endorsements on the Basic Scales. A review of the descriptors in the manual and Butcher and Williams (2000) produces the following set of descriptors:

- Symptoms of anxiety, worry, and tension
- Somatic problems, such as heart pounding and shortness of breath

- Sleep difficulties
- Decision-making difficulties
- Poor concentration
- Fear of losing their mind
- Indecision
- Finding life a strain
- An awareness of these symptoms and problems
- A willingness to admit to anxiety-related problems
- Significant depressive thoughts
- Feeling blue and uncertain about their future
- Uninterested in their life
- Likely to brood, be unhappy, and cry easily
- Feeling hopeless and empty much of the time
- Possible thoughts of suicide or wishing they were dead
- Beliefs that they are condemned or have committed unpardonable sins
- Feeling that other people are not supportive

All of these are consistent with what the clinician has already learned from the interpretation of the Basic Scales, but they also include a few new descriptors that are important. Primary among these is the consideration of suicide and the thoughts about death. Because the Content Scale items include content that is obviously related to the scale on which the items are scored, these findings also tell the clinician that Margot is aware of these symptoms and ready to reveal them to the clinician, although discussion of them may be more difficult than admission of them on an objective test.

The four moderately elevated Content Scales are Health, Anger, Low Self-Esteem, and Social Discomfort. The following descriptors are associated with these scales:

- Many physical symptoms across several body systems
- Worries about their health
- Feeling sicker than the average person
- Anger control problems
- Feeling irritable, grouchy, and impatient
- Being hotheaded, annoyed, and stubborn
- Sometimes feeling like swearing or smashing things

- Concern over losing self-control
- Having been physically abusive toward people and objects
- Low opinion of self
- Disbelieving that others like them
- Feeling unimportant
- Holding many negative attitudes towards self and believing themselves to be unattractive, awkward, clumsy, useless, and a burden to others
- Lacking self-confidence
- Difficulty accepting compliments from others
- Feeling overwhelmed by their own faults
- Very introverted and distant from others
- Very uneasy around others, preferring to be alone
- Likely to sit alone rather than join the group
- Shy and disliking parties and group events

This group of descriptors is more diverse than any prior group. In addition to the reflection of themes of discomfort with self that were evident in earlier elevations, they also suggest more problems with anger, interpersonal discomfort, and health than seen before. The clinician cannot help but note that some of them seem internally inconsistent; the picture of someone with explosive anger does not fit with the pattern of self-criticism, depression, and high anxiety already noted. Similarly, although the client notes health concerns on this Content Scale, those concerns were not significant enough to elevate Scale 1, which also assesses excessive concern about physical health. The clinician should note these contradictions and generate hypotheses about their cause. One plausible explanation is that the items endorsed on the Anger scale reflect irritability and impatience, a by-product of the depression and anxiety, rather than physical or verbal aggression. Another plausible hypothesis is that Margot endorsed items about being hotheaded because in her depressive state, her memory of her behavior is distorted so that isolated events of angry words and impulses appear to her as an ongoing pattern. In parallel fashion, her endorsements of health concerns on the Content Scales may be a reflection of her current depressed and anxious state rather than an ongoing pattern for Margot. All possible explanations can be tested by reference to Supplemental Scales and Critical Items and, most important, by discussion of the results with Margot. Finally, the moderate elevations on the Social Discomfort scale are inconsistent with her score on Scale 10. Because research shows that the score on Scale 10 is one of the most stable (Butcher & Williams, 2000), it is possible that the score on SOD is primarily a function of Margot's current distress, although this inconsistency should be explored further with the client. Finally, her score on Negative Treatment Indicators ($T = 51$) is consistent with descriptors for the Basic Scales and other Content Scales that show no negative attitudes toward psychotherapy or psychotherapists. It also bodes well for her responsiveness to treatment.

Next, the Supplemental Scales reveal only one elevation on the Marital Distress scale ($T = 68$), a finding consistent with the client's reports about the conflict in her marriage. All of the scales dealing with possible substance abuse show no evidence that Margot is misusing substances at this point, nor does she show a potential for future substance abuse in the patterns of her responses. This finding conflicts with one of the descriptors for her moderate elevation on Scale 4. If interview data and Critical Items do not support substance abuse as a problem, then the clinician can safely eliminate "possible excessive use of alcohol" from the list of relevant descriptors in this case.

Finally, a review of Margot's Critical Items confirms the pattern of high anxiety and depression and further supports the notion that she has considered suicide. They do not suggest a pervasive problem with explosive anger. As a whole, then, the findings support the clinician's interview data but underscore the seriousness of the depression and anxiety this client is experiencing and the need for a thorough suicide assessment.

Based on all these data, in Step 7 of the interpretation process, the clinician identifies the following issues that need clarification in the feedback session with the client before the final report of results is written:

- How frequently have you thought of suicide, and what means of committing suicide have you considered?
- How would you characterize your typical response to angry feelings toward other people? How much irritability and impatience are you currently showing in your relationship with your

spouse and with other people you are close to? Have you ever acted in a physically aggressive way toward others?

- You express some social discomfort in your pattern of test results but do not show a longstanding pattern of shyness and social withdrawal. Have the feelings of social discomfort arisen in tandem with the feelings of depression and anxiety?

- When was your last physical examination, and what health problems, if any, did it reveal? To what degree do you see the current health problems you identify as tied to the depression and anxiety or do you see them as persistent regardless of feelings of depression or anxiety?

- Your responses suggest high levels of marital distress and conflict. What is your view of the reasons for this distress and your expectation for the future of your marriage? Would you and your spouse be open to couples' counseling for these problems?

- The results suggest significant problems with concentration and focus on the task at hand. Does this finding fit for you? If so, how much risk do you think these emotional problems have meant for your performance in your graduate courses? (Client has reported passing all her graduate courses thus far.)

The clinician is now ready to organize these data into *preliminary* notes about findings that can be finalized into a report only after discussion of the results with the client. MMPI scholars recommend a variety of formats for reports, but we favor the structure offered by Butcher and Williams (2000) that divides the report into six sections: Validity Considerations, Symptomatic Behavior, Interpersonal Behavior, Behavioral Stability, Diagnostic Considerations, and Treatment Considerations. The following questions are addressed in each section.

Validity Considerations

- Did the client cooperate with the testing by answering questions completely and honestly and show acceptable levels of consistency in his or her pattern of responding?

- Was the client able to admit problems and weaknesses without exaggeration, on one hand, or defensiveness, on the other?

- To what extent did the cultural and social background of the client influence scores on these scales?
- Are there any confusing or conflicting results on the validity scales that need to be clarified with the client?

Symptomatic Behavior

- What cognitive, affective, and behavioral symptoms of internal distress are associated with the elevations and moderate elevations on the test?
- What evidence is there that the client is using dysfunctional means to cope with that distress (e.g., using substances to self-medicate)?
- To what extent did the cultural and social background of the client influence scores on these scales?
- Are there any confusing or conflicting results on these scales that need to be clarified with the client?

Interpersonal Behavior

- What do the scores reveal about the client's current pattern of interacting with other people?
- What do the scores reveal about the client's typical pattern of interpersonal behavior and level of extroversion or introversion?
- How does the client experience other people's behavior toward him or her?
- To what extent did the cultural and social background of the client influence scores on these scales?
- Are there any confusing or conflicting results on these scales that need to be clarified with the client?

Behavioral Stability

- What does research show about the stability of the pattern of elevations on this profile?

Diagnostic Considerations

- Keeping in mind that a clinician cannot come to a diagnosis solely on the basis of test results, what diagnostic possibilities arise from these findings?
- To what extent may the cultural and social background of the client influence the possible diagnoses that emerge from test results?

Treatment Considerations

- What do these symptoms and interpersonal behaviors identified in the results suggest about the client's willingness to disclose personal information in therapy and engage in the process of therapeutic change?
- What does this pattern suggest about the likelihood of talk therapy to be immediately helpful to this client?
- What modifications in therapeutic approach do these results suggest for the clinician?

Ideally, clinicians should bring to the feedback session notes that respond to each section with special attention to the descriptors that seem most likely to fit the test results. The clinician should prepare a written set of questions about internally conflicting results or results inconsistent with behavioral data so that the client can offer clarifying information about those findings. In Margot's case (in addition to the questions already listed here), the clinician would bring the following notes to the session.

Validity Notes

These include complete, cooperative, and consistent responses that show an open and nondefensive attitude toward the test, an understanding of test items, and a willingness to admit a variety of symptoms of distress.

Notes on Symptoms

Because Margot shows several sets of symptoms, the notes should be organized into primary and secondary symptoms. Then the symptoms that the test results seem to rule out should be noted along with the strengths the test indicates. Her primary symptoms relate to depression and anxiety. In the affective domain, they include feeling sad, overwhelmed, hopeless, guilty, tense, worried, vulnerable, and inadequate. The cognitions associated with these symptoms are likely to be brooding, rumination, difficulty concentrating and making decisions, perfectionistic thinking, pessimism, loss of interest in formerly pleasurable activities, and a tendency to be highly self-critical. Behaviorally, Margot is likely to be experiencing fatigue, sleep disturbance, appetite problems, social withdrawal, and difficulty in carrying out her usual life and work tasks. She is likely to have suicidal ideation and may have a recent history of a suicidal gesture or attempt.

Her secondary symptoms revolve around concerns about marital and family conflict, her current health, and her ability to be comfortable in social relationships at present. The test results are inconsistent with any concerns about substance abuse or dependency, psychotic processes, sociopathic behavior, or mania and show potential strengths in forming close relationships with people, making a commitment to psychotherapy, and taking responsibility for self.

Notes on Interpersonal Behavior

Although Margot is not typically an introvert, at this point she is not enjoying interpersonal contact, may tend to withdraw from others, and may act nonassertively and passively in relationships. She may feel particularly sensitive to criticism by others. Conflict and dissatisfaction mark her current relationship with her spouse. Her other family relationships may also be unsatisfying to her, but in general, Margot seems capable of establishing deep emotional ties with other people and shows no evidence of acting in narcissistic or self-interested ways in interpersonal relationships.

Behavioral Stability Notes

The scores in this profile do not show high elevations and high definition, so they are likely to change with therapy or environmental changes in Margot's life. Her tendency to worry about herself and her own flaws rather than deflecting responsibility for her problems onto others is more likely to be a stable characteristic, as is her score on social introversion.

Notes on Diagnostic Considerations

The diagnostic categories that merit further investigation based on these results are depressive disorders and anxiety disorders. Margot may be experiencing an episode of major depression or generalized anxiety, or these symptoms may be secondary to her relationship problems. The profile shows no consistent suggestion of substance abuse problems, sociopathic behavior, or thought disorder.

Notes on Treatment Implications

Individuals with the elevations shown in Margot's profile tend to be motivated for therapy, have hope that therapists can help them, and be capable of insight and behavior change. The depressive symptoms that appear on the profile suggest that, initially, it may be difficult for Margot to muster the energy she needs for behavior change and to hear negative feedback, but in the long run she is likely to be responsive to therapy. Her therapist should probably be cautious about confrontation and about Margot's tendency to be passive, dependent, and nonassertive in relationships, behaviors that may also be exhibited in the therapeutic relationship.

The final report on Margot's MMPI-2 responses is included in the next chapter, which focuses on integrating client feedback into the interpretation of test results.

Using the MMPI-A With Adolescents

The original MMPI was widely used with adolescents, but their scores were more difficult to interpret accurately in light of the adult norm group (Butcher & Williams, 2000). The MMPI-A was designed in 1992 to include a more appropriate adolescent norm group and a number of new items and Content Scales directly relevant to adolescent experience. It also is briefer than the MMPI-2 (468 items instead of 567) and omits those items likely to be applicable only to adults. Its Basic Scales are unchanged from the adult version, although Butcher and Williams (2000) presented some additional

Table 4.5   Features Associated With MMPI-A Content Scales

Scale Name	Basic Features Assessed With Elevations
A-Anxiety	Identical with MMPI-2
A-Obsessiveness	Identical with MMPI-2
A-Depression	Identical with MMPI-2
A-Health	Identical with MMPI-2
A-Alienation	A feeling of emotional distance from others, of being misunderstood and not liked by others, of getting a raw deal from life, and of having less fun than others
A-Bizarre Mentation	Identical with MMPI-2
A-Anger	Identical with MMPI-2
A-Cynicism	Identical with MMPI-2
A-Conduct	A variety of behavior problems, oppositional attitudes, legal problems, and negative peer group influences
A-Low Self-Esteem	Identical with MMPI-2
A-Low Aspirations	Disinterest in studying, academic success, or going to college; avoidance of reading or tasks that require attention and persistence; low confidence in ability to succeed
A-Social Discomfort	Identical with MMPI-2
A-Family	Identical with MMPI-2
A-School Problems	Numerous difficulties in school, including poor grades and behavior problems, lack of involvement in school activities, and a tendency to be easily upset about things at school
A-Negative Treatment Indicators	Identical with MMPI-2

descriptors based on research with adolescents. In contrast to the adult version, when the MMPI-A is scored, the K correction is not used because the research evidence does not support its value in this case. The validity scales differ slightly—instead of an Fb scale, the F scores on each half of the test are labeled F1 and F2. The most noticeable divergence for the adult form appears in the Content Scales, four of which are unique to this version. A list of the adolescent Content Scales is presented in Table 4.5.

As with the MMPI-2, scores of $T = 65$ or more are considered elevated on the Content Scales, and scores of $T = 60\text{-}64$ are considered moderately elevated. Clinicians who have clients with a history of delinquency or who are undergoing inpatient treatment should consult Butcher and Williams (2000) for additional descriptors relevant to elevations for these populations. For example, Butcher and Williams pointed out that for inpatient boys, an elevation on Scale 7 suggests that an evaluation for a possible history of sexual abuse is in order.

There are some variations in the most important Supplemental Scales on the MMPI-A as well. The Mac-R is identical with the adult version, but the other two substance-related scales have different names. The Addiction Acknowledgment scale (AAS) on the MMPI-2 is called the Alcohol and Drug Problem Acknowledgment scale (ACK) on the adolescent version, and the Addiction Potential scale (APS) has been renamed the Alcohol and Drug Problem Proneness scale (PRO) on the adolescent version. The descriptors are consistent with the MMPI-2, however. One unique Supplemental Scale is included on the MMPI-A, the Immaturity scale (IMM). Research supporting the descriptors for this scale is still in the preliminary stage, but an elevation on this scale signals that the client is likely to be less mature than other adolescents and be vulnerable to low self-esteem, externalization of blame, and lack of insight.

Case Example of MMPI-A Interpretation

Peter is a 14-year-old boy living in an apartment with his father and younger sister. His parents are divorced, and his mother has remarried and lives in another city. His parents are first-generation immigrants from South Africa who have been in the United States for a decade. Peter was referred to counseling by the school counselor who noticed that Peter was beginning to get into trouble in school, that his grades were falling, and that he was spending time with older high school students who had histories of alienation from school and behavior problems. Peter was willing to enter outpatient treatment because he was really frustrated about the increasing level of conflict he was experiencing with his father.

Interpretation of Peter's Test Scores. Because the clinician prepared Peter well for the MMPI-A and helped him have a personal investment in a meaningful result, the validity scales show a cooperative client who answered all the questions honestly, nondefensively, and consistently. Moreover, Peter admitted the problems he had without exaggeration or distortion.

Validity Scales	Raw Score	T Score
Cannot Say	1	Not applicable
L scale	4	55
F	21	64
F1	9	63
F2	12	64
TRIN	3(T)	45
VRIN	9	51
K	18	61
	TRIN	
S	Not reported	

Basic Scales	Raw Score	T Score
1	8	50
2	24	58
3	19	46
4	29	70
5	20	47
6	16	57
7	14	45
8	29	55
9	29	68
10	20	42

Harris-Lingoes	Raw Score	T Score
Pd_1	7	66
Pd_2	5	65
Pd_3	5	61
Pd_4	7	57
Pd_5	8	63
Ma_1	4	63
Ma_2	10	65
Ma_3	5	64
Ma_4	7	64

Figure 4.2   The Case of Peter: MMPI-A Scores

Figure 4.2 (Continued)

Content Scales	Raw Score	T Score
A-ANX	8	49
A-OBS	5	44
A-DEP	13	61
A-HEA	5	46
A-ALN	10	62
A-BIZ	2	45
A-ANG	12	64
A-CYN	16	57
A-CON	16	68
A-LSE	8	58
A-LAS	9	62
A-SOD	10	53
A-FAM	18	62
A-SCH	10	60
A-TRT	11	52

Supplemental Scales	Raw Score	T Score
Mac-R	25	59
ACK	7	63
PRO	22	62
IMM	18	57

Notes on Peter's Symptoms. The Basic Scales reveal two elevations, on 4 and 9, and a tendency not to be socially introverted. With the MMPI-A, scholars recommend a scale-by-scale interpretation instead of a code-type interpretation because code types are less reliable with this population. Thus, we refer to the descriptors for Scales 4 and 9 along with the elevated Harris-Lingoes subscale elevations to obtain a picture of this young man's functioning. The following descriptors appear applicable:

- Behavior problems
- Family difficulties, including quarrelsome family life
- Fault-finding family members
- Little love and companionship from home
- Desire to leave home
- Parental disapproval of peer group and future career plans
- Poor school adjustment
- Dislike of school
- Poor school performance
- Risk of suspensions, failure, or dropping out of school
- Use of alcohol or drugs
- Possible difficulties with the law and illegal behaviors
- Easily influenced by others
- Enjoyment of risk-taking and exciting activities
- Possible sexual acting out
- Restlessness
- Racing thoughts possible

Peter's Content Scale scores show one elevation on Conduct Problems and several moderate elevations on Depression, Alienation, Anger, and Low Aspirations. Taken together, these scores suggest the same behavior problems as the Basic Scales and point to a young man likely to be engaging in activities that put him at risk for trouble with authorities. None of these findings is obviously inconsistent with the results on the Basic Scales, although they do suggest more internal distress and additional concerns than were suggested by prior elevations. These include the following:

- Feelings of sadness and hopelessness
- Feeling that life is not really interesting or worthwhile right now
- Feeling uncared for, misunderstood, and lonely
- Thinking that others are happier than he
- Keeping emotional distance from others
- Feeling unliked by others and having difficulty getting along with others
- Feeling that life has been unfair and that others may be out to get him
- Having some anger control problems
- Reporting dislike of school and disinterest in studying
- Having low expectations of success
- Giving up easily when problems arise

Finally, the Supplemental Scales show that Peter has moderate elevations on both ACK and PRO, scales that assess the adolescent's admission of drug and alcohol use and his risk for substance abuse problems. In his case, it appears that he acknowledges some problematic substance use and is at risk for the development of a substance abuse disorder. The Critical Items support the prior findings and focus attention on family and school issues as crucial concerns for Peter.

Notes on Diagnostic Considerations. The diagnoses to be explored based on this profile are in the category of behavior problems, such as conduct disorder, oppositional defiant disorder, or adjustment disorder with mixed disturbance of emotion and conduct.

Notes on Responsiveness to Therapy. The findings do not suggest strong resistance to therapy or suspicion of therapists, but they do offer slightly conflicting findings relating to Peter's receptiveness to engagement in the therapeutic process. On one hand, his internal distress and family problems suggest that he may be motivated to participate, but on the other, his tendency to act out and blame others for his problems may make it difficult for him to take responsibility for the part of his problems that he owns.

Questions to Be Addressed in the Feedback Session With Peter. Taken as a whole, the profile suggests that the following questions need to be addressed in the feedback session prior to the final completion of the report:

- Is the level of tension and conflict at home with his father as high as the profile seems to suggest?
- To what extent do cultural differences between his father's experience in South Africa and his own experience in the United States influence the level of family conflict and Peter's sense of alienation from his family and his school?
- Has the conflict with his father ever erupted into physical aggression or even physical abuse by the father?
- When Peter reports being absent from his home, is he in a safe place?
- How extensive exactly is Peter's use of alcohol and drugs?
- How depressed and hopeless does he feel, and how seriously has he considered suicide?
- What is his current status in school, including grades, academic potential, and behavior status?
- What are his attitudes toward therapy at this time, and how willing is he to engage in both individual counseling and family therapy, if appropriate?

MMPI-2 Practice Case

Jerome is a 45-year-old carpenter who enters counseling at the mandate of the court because he has been arrested for stalking a woman whom he had dated. After she ended the relationship, Jerome began to call her many times a day, watch her at her workplace, follow her around on weekends, and send her letters, as many as four or five per day. Jerome has no prior history of trouble with the law. He has been in psychotherapy before for problems with depression and with posttraumatic stress after a house fire nearly killed him in 1988. Jerome recognizes that he needs to "get on with his life" but is not sure about how to do that, so he did not resist the court's insistence on counseling. His MMPI-2 results are presented in Figure 4.3.

Using the model below and with reference to Butcher and Williams (2000), Graham (2000), or the MMPI-2 manual, develop preliminary notes on Jerome's test findings.

Step 1: Review the scores on the validity scales to ensure that the client cooperated with testing.

Step 2: Review the Basic Scale scores to identify elevations and moderate elevations and relevant descriptors either from individually elevated scales or from a 2- or 3-point code if present. Eliminate descriptors inconsistent with behavioral or other data. Review relevant Harris-Lingoes subscale descriptors to identify additional meaningful descriptors.

Step 3: Note descriptors inconsistent with other data for evaluation at a later point.

Step 4: Review Content Scale elevations and moderate elevations to reveal additional relevant descriptors and potential inconsistencies.

Step 5: Review Supplemental Scale elevations and moderate elevations to reveal additional relevant descriptors and potential inconsistencies.

Step 6: Review Critical Items to clarify findings.

Step 7: Reconcile inconsistencies and identify questions to ask client to gather more information.

Step 8: Write up preliminary findings to discuss with the client.

When you are finished, you can compare your notes with those of the authors in the appendix.

Validity Scales	Raw Score	T Score
Cannot Say	0	Not applicable
L scale	6	61
F	11	70
Fb	7	71
TRIN	8(T)	57
VRIN	6	54
K	19	58
S	Not available	

Basic Scales	Raw Score	T Score With K Correction
1	15	57
2	22	59
3	23	54
4	26	57
5	23	45
6	12	57
7	30	57
8	34	66
9	23	56
10	35	62

Relevant Harris-Lingoes Scores

Sc_1	17	65
Sc_2	3	67
Sc_3	2	55
Sc_4	3	59
Sc_5	4	65
D_5	2	50

Figure 4.3   The Case of Jerome: MMPI-2 Scores

Figure 4.3 (Continued)

Content Scale	Raw Score	T Score
ANX	6	52
FRS	5	54
OBS	8	59
DEP	10	61
HEA	5	51
BIZ	4	57
ANG	10	63
CYN	15	59
ASP	12	58
TPA	10	53
LSE	10	64
SOD	14	63
FAM	10	63
WRK	10	56
TRT	8	59

Supplemental Scale	Raw Score	T Score
Mac-R	26	62
APS	26	57
AAS	6	65
MDS	Not applicable	
PK	17	65

Summary

The MMPI-2 and MMPI-A are the most widely used personality tests in mental health practice today and are particularly useful for assessing the problems a client may have in interpersonal functioning and in coping with stress. These tests can help clarify confusing data gathered from interviews, can help inarticulate clients reveal the difficulties they are experiencing but do not have the words to discuss, and can provide clinicians with a structure for exploring a breadth of issues not obviously related to a client's presenting problem. Clients need to be properly prepared to take the test because it is lengthy and deals with highly personal content. That preparation includes explanation about the testing process, the uses to which the results will be put, and an exploration of the client's goals and hopes for testing. The aim here is to ensure that the client gives a fully informed consent to testing and that he or she develops an investment in a reliable and meaningful outcome. When both things occur, the chances of a valid result with an honest report of problems increase.

When interpreting test results, clinicians must first check that the client has produced a valid result, and then they should develop a set of descriptors from the manual and other resources that appear consistent throughout the test, based on all the clinical scales. Clinicians should integrate interview data and take cultural and social variables into account in applying the descriptors identified in the manual. Professional ethics requires that clinicians always approach test findings as hypotheses about client functioning, rather than truths, because no test is infallible and no conclusions about client problems should be drawn on the basis of test results alone. See Butcher, Nezami, and Exner (1998) for a concise summary of the influence of culture on personality test scores.

Discussion Questions

1. What advantages and disadvantages may appear when the administration of the MMPI-2 is divided over several sessions? How should clinicians respond to minimize the risks of such an approach when an uninterrupted session is not feasible?

2. Often, MMPIs need to be administered when clients are in substantial distress. What criteria should be used to determine whether a given client is in too much distress to make testing meaningful?

3. As the demographics of the population of the United States change and an increasing proportion of clients will be individuals older than age 50 years, what accommodations should be made in the administration and interpretation of MMPI scores for older clients?

4. Adolescents are often eager to keep personal information private from their parents; conversely, worried parents are often desirous of more information about their teenager's mental health. How can a clinician who is proposing the administration of an MMPI-A with an adolescent help each party approach the test with a frame of reference that maximizes the possibility of a valid result?

References

American Psychological Association. (1992). *Ethical principles of psychologists and code of conduct.* Washington, DC: Author. Available at www.apa.org/ethics/code.html

Beck, A. T., Steer, R. A., & Brown, G. (1996). *Beck Depression Inventory* (2nd ed.). San Antonio, TX: The Psychological Corporation.

Briere, J. (1995). *Trauma Symptom Inventory professional manual.* Odessa, FL: Psychological Assessment Resources.

Butcher, J. N. (1990). *The MMPI-2 in psychological treatment.* New York: Oxford University Press.

Butcher, J. N., Dahlstrom, W. G., Graham, J. R., Tellegen, A., & Kaemmer, B. (1989). *MMPI-2 (Minnesota Multiphasic Personality Inventory-2): Manual for administration and scoring.* Minneapolis: University of Minnesota Press.

Butcher, J. N., Nezami, E., & Exner, J. (1998). Psychological assessment of people of diverse cultures. In S. S. Kazarian & D. R. Evans (Eds.), *Cultural and clinical psychology: Theory, research and practice* (pp. 61-105). New York: Oxford University Press.

Butcher, J. N., & Rouse, S. V. (1996). Personality: Individual differences and clinical assessment. *Annual Review of Psychology, 47,* 87-111.

Butcher, J. N., & Williams, C. L. (2000). *Essentials of MMPI-2 and MMPI-A interpretation* (2nd ed.). Minneapolis: University of Minnesota Press.

Butcher, J. N., Williams, C. L., Graham, J. R., Archer, R. P., Tellegen, A., Ben-Porath, Y. S., & Kaemmer, B. (1992). *MMPI-A (Minnesota Multiphasic Personality Inventory for Adolescents): Manual for administration, scoring and interpretation.* Minneapolis: University of Minnesota Press.

Finn, S. E. (1996). *Manual for using the MMPI-2 as a therapeutic intervention.* Minneapolis: University of Minnesota Press.

Garner, D. M. (1991). *Eating Disorders Inventory-2.* Odessa, FL: Psychological Assessment Resources.

Graham, J. R. (2000). *MMPI-2: Assessing personality and psychopathology.* New York: Oxford University Press.

Hathaway, S. R., & McKinley, J. C. (1942). *The Minnesota Multiphasic Personality Schedule.* Minneapolis: University of Minnesota Press.

Newman, M. L., & Greenway, P. (1997). Therapeutic effects of providing MMPI-2 feedback to clients at a university counseling center: A collaborative approach. *Psychological Assessment, 9,* 122-131.

Watkins, C. E., Jr., Campbell, V. L., Niebirding, R., & Hallmark, R. (1995). Contemporary practice of psychological assessments by clinical psychologists. *Professional Psychology: Research and Practice, 26,* 54-60.

5

Effective MMPI Feedback Sessions and Written Reports

Providing clients with feedback about the results of psychological testing is not only an ethical responsibility of clinicians (American Counseling Association, 1995; American Psychological Association, 1992; Pope, 1992), but it is also a process with substantial diagnostic and therapeutic value. A competent feedback session can improve the accuracy of diagnosis, the quality of the final report of results, the strength of the therapeutic alliance, and the readiness of the client for change. This chapter presents a model for preparing and conducting that feedback session and for integrating the knowledge gained from the session into the final test report and the client's treatment plan.

Preparing for the Feedback Session

As discussed in Chapter 4, a clinician should have completed the interpretation of the Minnesota Multiphasic Personality Inventory–2 (MMPI-2) scores, developed a series of crucial questions to explore in the feedback session, and written a set of preliminary notes about test findings prior to any discussion of results with a client. In most cases, the clinician should bring a copy of the MMPI-2 profile for the client to see at the session. Having the profile plotted on the graph helps the client absorb the feedback, keeps the clinician from inadvertently omitting important findings, and communicates that the clinician is committed to a full and frank discussion of results. The exception to that procedure comes into play when the profile is highly elevated and the client is likely to be surprised and highly distressed by those elevations. In the majority of situations with high elevations, however, sharing the profile with the client is not problematic because most clients in severe distress and with longstanding dysfunction are not surprised by their scores. However, on occasion, a client is in a particularly vulnerable state, is very resistant to acknowledgment of the scope of his or her problems, or is unusually naive about their severity. In that relatively rare instance, it is preferable to bring a set of descriptors into the room rather than the plotted scores on the profile sheet.

The length of a feedback session varies with several factors, the most important of which is the complexity of the findings. In situations in which a valid and elevation-free profile occurs, feedback may last only a few minutes and is limited to exploring whether the client and clinician believe the results to be accurate. However, when multiple elevations appear or when a confusing pattern of findings happens, feedback usually occupies a full counseling session. We have experienced clients for whom the test findings were so rich and provocative of important insights that we devoted several sessions to this task. Needless to say, when financial considerations influence the length of test feedback, devoting more than one session may be impractical, so clinicians should plan feedback with cost considerations in mind.

Structure of the Feedback Session

The feedback session has six major parts:

- Assessment of the client's experience of test taking and review of client's interests and concerns about test results
- Review of the history and use of the MMPI in mental health settings and the organization of the findings on the profile sheets
- Discussion of the client's validity scales and attitude toward testing

- Discussion of clinical findings on Basic, Content, and Supplemental Scales, with attention to the relationship between those findings and the presenting problems
- Reference to the Critical Items as appropriate
- Exploration of the emotional and intellectual impact of these findings on the client and his or her understanding of the problems
- Discussion of the implications of the test results for treatment

We will discuss each step in sequence.

The feedback session should begin with an exploration of the client's reaction to the test administration using questions such as, "What was it like for you while you were taking the test?" or "What concerns did you have about the test results while you were answering the items?" Clients often disclose how tedious the test taking was, how they noticed repeated items, and (if they trust the clinician) how they hypothesized about the purpose of some of the items. This question can serve as a backdrop for explaining the validity scales and can provide useful information for interpreting scores of questionable validity. Clinicians can also use this discussion to reinforce a cooperative client for persevering in a difficult and anxiety-provoking task or to tactfully disclose elevations that may have occurred in the validity scales. The clinician should then describe the process for discussing the test findings, emphasizing that the goal is for this session to be a two-way interaction, with the client offering comments about the fit between the descriptors identified by the test and his or her personal experience. Clinicians should give clients explicit permission to disagree with findings, ask questions about findings they do not understand, express their emotional reaction to the results, and slow down or stop the session if they feel overwhelmed by the feedback. In addition, clinicians should inform clients that they may have a summary of test results once the report is written if they wish to have that for their files. This information can be repeated throughout the feedback session as needed.

It is important to note that a feedback session should be conducted even if the testing produced an invalid result. Obviously, in that situation no review of clinical findings can take place, but an exploration of the issues and concerns that interfered with honest or consistent responses to the test items can still be productive. The client may be willing to retake the test, or the discussion may unveil problems not yet identified in therapy, such as poor reading ability, difficulty trusting the clinician to use the information wisely, or an unreported medical or psychological problem.

Next, assuming that the test profile forms are being shared with the client, the clinician should explain the graph and the meaning of the scores, with special attention to the norm group and the meaning of elevated and moderately elevated scores. Such an explanation is best placed in the context of the history and widespread use of the instrument. When clients know that the MMPI-2 is the most widely used and strongly researched instrument in mental health, they tend to have more confidence in the meaning of the results. Clinicians should then discuss the findings on the validity scales. They may organize this process with general comments on the level of cooperation and honest disclosure that clients showed during testing, or if they have questions about the findings for particular scales, they may discuss each scale separately. Clients are typically quite surprised that the MMPI can reveal anything about their test-taking attitude. This surprise has both benefits and drawbacks. On one hand, assuming the test's hypotheses are correct, it inspires confidence in the power of the test to "read their attitudes." On the other hand, if they were less than forthcoming, it embarrasses and worries them about what other secrets the test may have revealed. Clinicians, therefore, should be alert for both verbal and nonverbal reactions of discomfort. A frank discussion of client worries is the best strategy both at this point and throughout the feedback session.

When they first see their profile, clients' eyes sometimes go directly to the peak elevations on the Basic or Content Scales. If this happens, clinicians should reassure clients that those scores will be fully discussed but will make more sense if they first review the validity scale results.

As soon as the client and clinician questions about validity findings are sufficiently addressed, the attention focuses on the clinical findings. The clinician should have developed a plan for the feedback session that includes an assessment of likely client reactions to the findings. Although there are many acceptable ways to organize this portion of the feedback, Finn (1996) has developed a particularly well-structured approach that takes into account the ability of the client to hear findings that may be unpleasant or unsettling. He recommends organizing the findings into three levels. The first level includes information that the client would probably experience as obvious and nonthreatening. An example of such information is a person's tendency toward introversion or extroversion. Most people already know that about themselves. Similarly, a person who has already acknowledged feeling quite depressed and has sought treatment for that distress is also unlikely to be surprised by elevations on Scale 2 and DEP (Depression). Finn recommends opening the feedback session with such information to help the client feel more comfortable with the process and to encourage a dialogue about the test results.

The second level of feedback includes findings that are within the client's awareness but that are more uncomfortable to hear about. A client who acknowledges a history of depression, for example, may also be aware of problems with anger control or a tendency toward obsessive-compulsive behaviors but may feel that discussion of the latter issues is less safe than depression. Similarly, another client may readily acknowledge a tendency to be hotheaded and quick to act before thinking but may be uncomfortable when discussing the implications of those tendencies for his or her sexual behavior. That client may be aware that he or she has acted out inappropriately in regard to sexual relationships but may wish to deny or minimize the role of this problem in his or her general unhappiness or distress. Finn advises that clinicians explore content at the second level after they have evidence that the client has responded well to Level 1 feedback and has developed sufficient rapport with the clinician to tolerate such stress to the therapeutic relationship. Clinicians should explore such material tactfully and at a slow pace, using a few descriptors and then asking for client reactions, rather than listing many descriptors in a row. Clients should be encouraged to express disagreement with the findings at this point if they believe them erroneous. In that event, clinicians should gauge whether continued confrontation about that finding is advisable or whether such an approach would negatively influence the client's response to therapy. Sometimes clients need time to absorb a Level 2 finding and will be more receptive to discussion at a later session or even a later point in the current session.

Level 3 feedback deals with highly sensitive topics about which the client may have little conscious awareness. According to Finn (1996), these include findings "so novel or discrepant from clients' usual ways of thinking about themselves that they are likely to be rejected in feedback sessions" (p. 35). In addition, the content of these findings may threaten a client's defenses and cause a client to withdraw from therapeutic interaction. An example of such information is an elevation of Scale 6 showing paranoia, suspicion, and possible paranoid delusions in persons whose conscious awareness tells them that they are victims of other people's real malicious intent toward them. Hearing that their perceptions of others may be distorted can be psychologically unacceptable. Needless to say, when clinicians identify findings as fitting into this category, they must be especially cautious about the manner and timing in which they convey these results. The most gentle and tactful descriptors that are accurate should be presented first, and the client should be given leeway to deny their applicability and to express the emotions that such feedback generates. For example, Scale 6 descriptors that refer to sensitivity to criticism and attentiveness to other people's reactions to them are better ways to open a discussion of this result and the descriptors that refer to suspiciousness. Extremely threatening results may need to be postponed until the therapeutic alliance and client ego are strong enough to endure this level of threat.

Using Finn's (1996) approach implies that clinicians should avoid a front-to-back approach to test feedback that starts at Basic Scale 1 and ends with the Critical Items. Instead, clinicians should start with whatever information fits in Level 1 and proceed from there. This may mean beginning with the Content Scales, moving next to the Basic Scales, and then to the Supplemental Scales. Although the lack of a one-size-fits-all approach to discussing MMPI-2 results makes the clinician's task more complicated in the short run, varying the order of presentation of findings according to client receptiveness pays better dividends in the long run. Most of all, it helps the client absorb information that is uncomfortable and allows the client and clinician to come to a gradual and comfortable understanding of the implications of the findings for treatment.

During the discussion of the clinical findings, mental health professionals need to be vigilant about several counseling process factors. The breadth of information obtained from the MMPI-2 or MMPI-A can inadvertently lead a clinician to dominate the conversation by presenting such a long list of descriptors that the client cannot absorb all the information or respond fully. When this happens, the client often offers monosyllabic responses, and the opportunity to translate the feedback session into a truly therapeutic activity is lost. To avoid this pitfall, clinicians should present only a few descriptors at a time and follow up with questions such as, "Does that ring true for you?" or "How does that fit with your experience?" Second, because the test feedback session is an intellectually interesting experience for both clients and clinicians, both parties can overlook the emotional power of the feedback during the session. If clients leave a session with many feelings about the feedback that they cannot process effectively, they may be reluctant to return to any further review of findings or may lose motivation to apply findings to the treatment goals. Thus, clinicians ought to periodically stop the process of discussing descriptors to explore the client's emotional reactions to the feedback even if the client presents no obvious nonverbal signs of distress. Simple questions such as, "How are you doing hearing all this feedback right now?" or "Sometimes the feedback process stirs up some strong feelings; are you aware of any strong emotions in yourself right now?" Finally, because of the wealth of information presented, therapists are wise to ask the client to summarize findings so that they can be sure that clients have an accurate perception of the communication. This request can be made without transforming the session into a test of the client's memory by using a question such as, "Since we have covered a lot of territory so far today, I'd like to get a sense of what you are taking away from our discussion. If you were to tell a loved one about your MMPI results so far, what would you say?" A clinician should also offer periodic summaries of findings and, at that point, offer the client another opportunity to ask questions about the test.

If these counseling process factors have been adequately attended to, the clinician has prepared the client for the transition to the next step in the process, a discussion of the implications of the findings for the client's overall self-understanding and for treatment planning. An ideal method for beginning this task is to return to the goals that the client identified for testing prior to administration. Clinicians can introduce the topic with the following comment: "I remember that when we first discussed the MMPI, you said you were interested because you were pretty baffled by the reasons you and your spouse argue so much. I'd like to turn our focus to what, if anything, the test results may have revealed to you about that issue. What comes to mind first?" After the client has disclosed the insights gained, the clinician can add additional material to this discussion to further extend the client's insights. For instance, a client might describe a new understanding of how irritable his depression has made him and how clear it is now that his own irritability has played a role in his arguments with his wife. The clinician may extend this discussion by including the possible influence of his high score on obsessiveness on marital conflict, an issue that the client did not volunteer. Should the client reject that material, the clinician is wise to move on to other less sensitive client insights about the implications of the results. Once the important insights have been sufficiently explored, the next part of the process involves the development of a revised treatment plan that integrates the test findings with the other data the clinician and client possess. Because this is likely to be a lengthy process that cannot be squeezed into the end of a feedback session, the clinician's aim here should be to set the stage for a fuller discussion of this issue at the next session. Suggesting that the client use the time between sessions to think about the implications of the results for future treatment is a good strategy.

At the close of a feedback session, the client should be reassured that he or she will receive a written summary of results once it has been completed and may contact the clinician between sessions if questions arise for which the client feels he or she need immediate answers. Time for one last question should be included along with a processing of emotions provoked by the process. Finally, the clinician should again thank the client for his or her commitment to the testing process and highlight the value the clinician believes has been derived from the test data.

Adapting the Feedback Session When the Test Taker Is Not an Ongoing Client

Frequently, clinicians with competence in testing give the MMPI-2 or MMPI-A to other people's clients. Under these circumstances, clinicians can derive maximum value from the testing if they involve the ongoing therapist in the assessment process and conduct both an orientation and a feedback session with the regular therapist and the client. In the orientation meeting, the clinician needs to assess the client's appropriateness for testing, help the client to develop an invest- ment in the potential value of test results, and explain to both therapist and client the strengths and limitations of the MMPI-2. Including the ongoing therapist not only ensures that he or she has a clear picture of the process and outcomes of testing but also encourages the client to trust the new and unknown clinician—some of the rapport with the ongoing therapist may transfer to the test administrator. That trust is important if the clinician is to obtain accurate client information. Clients feel freer to discuss sensitive personal information if their regu- lar therapist is supporting them and the therapist can, in turn, offer additional details or encourage the client to comment on other aspects of their functioning that did not first come to mind.

Including the ongoing therapist in the feedback session is even more crucial, perhaps, because the ultimate value of the MMPI-2 and MMPI-A is in their capacity to make treatment more effective and efficient for the client. Therefore, no meaningful discussion of treatment implications can really occur without the ongoing thera- pist present at the same time as the client. If a meeting with the client alone is unavoidable, the clinician should schedule a separate consul- tation meeting with the therapist in which the test results and the client's reactions to the results are reviewed.

Writing the Final MMPI-2/MMPI-A Report

The final report includes the same sections used in the preliminary notes and is best written with the expectation that the client will have access to a copy of the report. Clients have an ethical and legal right to copies of all information kept in their record, and clients or their representatives often ask for copies of test reports (see Welfel, 2002, for additional discussion of this issue). As described in Chapter 4, the organization for the MMPI-2 or MMPI-A report that we prefer is the model recommended by Butcher and Williams (2000):

- Validity of the Test and Client Attitude Toward Testing
- Symptomatic Behavior
- Interpersonal Behavior
- Stability of the Profile
- Diagnostic Considerations
- Treatment Implications

The content of the final report should begin, of course, with a brief description of the client and the reason for entering therapy. If client ethnicity, language, or other characteristics are substantially different from the norm group, that information should also be presented. If, for example, a client took the test in a second language or represented an ethnic group either not included in the norm group or for which research shows some variation in the meaning of test results, those are the characteristics to note in this section.

The language in the report is crucially important to accurate interpretation. Each section of the model should be phrased so that the reader understands that the test results represent plausible explanations of client problems and behaviors rather than absolute truths. The following chart includes both desirable and inappropriate language:

Acceptable Wording	Unacceptable Wording
The test supports the interpretation that Maria was honest and nondefensive in her responses to items.	Maria is honest and nondefensive.
People with these elevations tend to be at high risk for suicide, and Maria's results strongly suggest that she be evaluated for suicidality.	Maria is highly suicidal.
Maria endorsed items that acknowledged problem usage of drugs and alcohol.	Maria is either an alcoholic or a drug abuser or both.
Paul's responses are consistent with those of an adolescent who gets disciplined often at school and is at risk for suspension or expulsion.	Paul will probably be suspended or expelled from school.

In addition, if the test is inconclusive about any aspect of client functioning or is inconsistent with other client data, that contradiction should be disclosed in the test report. Along with the description of that inconsistency, clinicians should discuss any recommendations for future treatment or additional testing such findings suggest. For example, a report on a college student might read, "No problematic pattern of substance use was identified in the client's pattern of MMPI-2 scores, but the client reports bingeing on alcohol at college parties numerous times during a semester. Therefore, the client's pattern of substance use should probably continue to be monitored even though the MMPI-2 results were not elevated."

Novice MMPI users often inquire about the degree of detail about individual scale results that needs to be included in the test report. No single standard for detail exists in the profession. Some reports refer directly to particular scales and T scores, whereas others focus only on the descriptors and let the reader refer to the graphs for the particular T scores. Generally, we recommend that a minimum of detail be presented in a final report and that if a report is to be forwarded to another professional, a copy of the profile accompanies the report. This strategy also makes the report more accessible to the client. If a report is being prepared for a court and its accuracy is likely to be challenged, additional reference to particular scale scores may be wise.

All reports should be signed by the professionals who prepared them, with their licenses to practice noted along with contact information in the event that the reader has questions about the report. A copy should be placed in the client's file, and other copies should be sent to those designated by the client to receive them, provided the client has signed the proper releases and the recipients are competent to use the report responsibly.

The following is a sample final report for Margot, the client whose MMPI-2 scores are presented in Chapter 4.

Report of MMPI-2 Findings on Margot

Client Background Data

Margot is a 23-year-old graduate student in biochemistry who is feeling depressed and anxious and is experiencing increasing levels of conflict with her spouse of 18 months. Margot is of European American background, speaks English as her first language, and denies any disabilities that might affect her scores on the MMPI. She has never before taken the MMPI or MMPI-2, nor has she ever been in psychological treatment aside from counseling with the school counselor during high school because of boredom with her classes. Margot came to therapy 2 months ago on the advice of her graduate adviser because her symptoms were interfering with her progress on her degree and her pleasure from her marriage. The MMPI-2 was administered under secure conditions on June 1, 2001. The client completed testing in 1.5 hours without interruption.

Validity Findings

Margot cooperated with the testing by answering nearly all the questions in a way that suggested that she understood and consistently paid attention to the content of the items. The validity scales also show no indication that she responded defensively or attempted to present herself as being exceptionally virtuous. Nor did she seem to significantly exaggerate her problems, although her scores are in the range that show that she is experiencing symptoms and is willing to acknowledge a variety of problems.

Symptomatic Behavior

The pattern of MMPI-2 results suggests that Margot's primary symptoms center on anxiety and depression. The items she endorsed indicate that she is likely to be feeling sad, overwhelmed, hopeless, guilty, tense, worried, vulnerable, and inadequate. Margot's elevated scores are consistent experiences of brooding, rumination, difficulty concentrating and making decisions, perfectionistic thinking, pessimism, loss of interest in formerly pleasurable activities, and a tendency to be highly self-critical. She also endorsed items suggesting fatigue, sleep disturbance, appetite problems, social withdrawal, and difficulty carrying out her work and life tasks. All of these findings are consistent with Margot's self-report.

The findings also suggest some risk for suicide, particularly recent suicidal ideation, and perhaps a history of suicide attempts. During her interview, Margot reluctantly admitted some suicidal ideation but denied any history of suicidal attempts or any recent suicidal gestures. According to her self-report, Margot's suicidal ideation centers on feelings that she would rather be dead and not on any action plan for suicide. She also denies any access to guns or to any medication that might be easily used for self-destructive purposes.

Based on the MMPI-2 elevations, her secondary symptoms revolve around concerns about marital and family conflict, her current health, and her ability to be comfortable in social relationships at present. The test results are generally inconsistent with any concerns about substance abuse or dependency, psychotic processes, sociopathic behavior, or mania. The findings suggest potential strengths in forming close relationships with people, in making a commitment to psychotherapy, and in taking responsibility for self.

Interpersonal Behavior

Although the test does not suggest that Margot is typically an introvert, at this point she does not appear to be enjoying interpersonal contact, may tend to withdraw from others, and may act nonassertively and passively in relationships. She may feel particularly sensitive to criticism by others. The test results and Margot's self-report indicate that conflict and dissatisfaction mark her current relationship with her spouse. In the interview, Margot also confirmed that her other family relationships are generally unsatisfying to her, a pattern consistent with test results. However, both the test and the interview data suggest that Margot seems capable of establishing deep emotional ties with other people and is unlikely to act in narcissistic or self-interested ways in interpersonal relationships.

Behavioral Stability

The pattern of scores in this profile does not show high elevations and high definition, so they are likely to change with therapy or environmental changes in Margot's life. Her tendency to worry about herself and her own flaws rather than deflecting responsibility for her problems onto others is more likely to be stable, as is her score on social introversion.

Diagnostic Considerations

The diagnostic categories that merit further investigation based on these results are depressive disorders, anxiety disorders, and adjustment disorders. Margot may be experiencing an episode of major depression or generalized anxiety, or these symptoms may be secondary to her relationship problems. The profile shows no suggestion of substance abuse problems, sociopathic behavior, or thought disorder. These findings are consistent with the tentative diagnosis of adjustment disorder with mixed anxiety and depressed mood given to Margot at the intake interview. A diagnosis of substantial conflict with her marital partner should also be noted based on the client's self-report and her MMPI scores.

Treatment Implications

Individuals with the elevations shown in Margot's profile tend to be motivated for therapy, have hope that therapists can help them, and be capable of insight and behavior change. The depressive symptoms that appear on the profile suggest that, initially, it may be difficult for Margot to muster the energy she needs for behavior change and difficult for her to hear negative feedback, but in the long run, she is likely to be responsive to therapy. Unless behavioral data contradict the test findings, her therapist should probably be cautious about confrontation and about Margot's tendency to be passive, dependent, and nonassertive in relationships, behaviors that may also be exhibited in the therapeutic relationship.

This report was prepared on June 21, 2001. Questions about its findings can be directed to me at the address and telephone number indicated on the top of this letterhead.

Sincerely,

Janine Smithson
Licensed Psychologist, State of Ohio

Summary

Feedback sessions with clients are mandated by ethics codes of all the mental health professions and are also of substantial therapeutic and diagnostic value. They help clarify conflicting results, communicate respect for the investment the client has made in completing a long and difficult test, and, if done competently, advance the therapeutic goals of therapy. Feedback sessions can increase clients' insight into their problems and motivation for change.

If feedback sessions are to achieve these goals, clinicians must prepare carefully for them by being thoroughly familiar with the test scores, having a plan for presenting the findings that may be uncomfortable for clients to hear about, and having copies of the MMPI-2 or MMPI-A profile to bring to the session. During the session, clinicians should focus on involving the client in the feedback session, actively soliciting client reactions to the descriptors associated with elevations, and carefully attending to the emotional power of the feedback given. Clinicians should also pace the feedback so that the client understands and remembers what is being discussed and has time to formulate appropriate questions. Periodically, the clinician should ask the client questions aimed at confirming that he or she is comprehending the test findings. As time permits, the clinician should use the feedback session to discuss the implications of the test results for treatment plans, and this topic should be returned to in the next session. Before a feedback session terminates, the client should be informed that he or she can ask for additional clarification of test findings at a later point in therapy and is welcome to a copy of the report if he or she wishes one.

Discussion Questions

1. Clinicians are sometimes reluctant to provide clients with copies of their reports of testing. According to both legal precedent and ethics codes, clients have a right to such information, but is there any rational basis to that reluctance? If so, what might that be?

2. The chapter provides several examples of language that may be used in feedback sessions to explain test results. What other examples of helpful phrases for introducing and summarizing results come to mind?

3. Clinicians often have difficulty not dominating feedback sessions and giving clients enough encouragement to talk about their reactions to the test findings. What other strategies (in addition to those mentioned in the chapter) might be useful to clinicians in this circumstance?

4. What practical limitations come to mind in the model for feedback proposed in this chapter?

References

American Counseling Association. (1995). *Code of ethics and standards of practice.* Alexandria, VA: Author. Available at www.counseling.org/resources/codeofethics.htm

American Psychological Association. (1992). *Ethical principles of psychologists and code of conduct.* Washington, DC: Author. Available at www.apa.org/ethics/code.html

Butcher, J. N., & Williams, C. L. (2000). *Essentials of MMPI-2 and MMPI-A Interpretation* (2nd ed.). Minneapolis: University of Minnesota Press.

Finn, S. E. (1996). *Manual for using the MMPI-2 as a therapeutic intervention.* Minneapolis: University of Minnesota Press.

Pope, K. S. (1992). Responsibilities in providing psychological test feedback to clients. *Psychological Assessment, 4,* 268–271.

Welfel, E. R. (2002). *Ethics in counseling and psychotherapy: Standards, research, and emerging issues* (2nd ed.). Pacific Grove, CA: Brooks/Cole.

6

The Strong Interest Inventory*
and the Kuder Career Search

The topic of career assessment is a very wide brush stroke across the canvas of career development interventions. Career-concerned clients may need inventoried information about their career interests, values, skills, maturity, salience, decision making, beliefs, efficacy, barriers, personality, or job satisfaction. Career counselors typically recommend assessments to their clients to provide opportunities for learning more about themselves yet, secondarily, for counselors to gain more information about their clients. The canvas for this chapter is not large enough to address the multitude and variety of career assessment opportunities available for use with career clients, so the picture will focus merely on career interest assessment. Actually, only a snapshot of interest assessments will be viewed because information will be specific to the Strong Interest Inventory® (Consulting Psychologists Press, 1994) and the Kuder Career Search With Person Match (National Career Assessment Services, 1999). These two interest assessments were selected due their longevity and the quantity of research each has generated.

Career interests can be understood as those elements of work that attract our attention. A vocational interest, or interest in a career task, does not necessarily imply skill or ability in that area. As described in

---

*Strong Interest Inventory is a registered trademark of Stanford University Press.

Learning Experience 6.1 (presented at the end of this chapter), each of us can probably recall being drawn toward another's work yet know for a fact that we do not have the skills to do the job tasks ourselves. For example, one of the authors (S.T.) has an intense interest in the visual arts yet has no skill in applying paint to paper (or to walls, for that matter). Many career development theories provide rationales for including the measurement of interests in the process of helping career clients learn more about themselves. You may find the learning experiences in Chapters 6 and 7 to be useful for your own career development, as a classroom activity, or to copy to use with career clients.

Theoretical Guidelines for Use of Vocational Interest Assessment

One of the original career development theories, trait and factor theory (Parsons, 1909), provided early career practitioners with three counseling steps:

1. Gaining self-understanding

2. Gaining understanding of the work world

3. Fitting information about the self and the work world together

In the realm of Step 1, interest assessment offers one piece of self-understanding, and for Step 2, both the Strong Interest Inventory and the Kuder Career Search With Person Match generate job titles from the world of work for client research and exploration. A more sophisticated version of trait and factor theory, that of John Holland (1973), expanded the self-understanding and work world understanding steps to a hexagon model of explaining (a) workers' types and (b) work environment types as Realistic, Investigative, Artistic, Social, Enterprising, and Conventional. In 1974, these six types were included as the Basic Interest Scales of another edition of the Strong, and in 1999, a similar structure of six types was included in the Kuder Career Search as the Kuder Career Clusters.

Career interest assessment is also a component of the developmental theory of Donald Super. The authors of the career-development assessment and counseling model (C-DAC) (Super, Osborne, Walsh, Brown, & Niles, 1992) recommended combining measurement of career development, interests, and aptitude to create a more complete assessment package.

One of the most current career development theories, social cognitive career theory (SCCT) (Lent, Brown, & Hackett, 1996), also provides support for the assessment of career interests. In their model of interest development, self-efficacy (sense of competence) and outcome expectations (good performance produces positive outcomes) predict the establishment of an interest. This model explains how interests can change and develop over the life span, as new learning opportunities and reinforcers provide new cognitions and outcome experiences. Assessing interests can be useful in the SCCT model by providing learning opportunities that include accurate vocational information and by expanding career explorations to include those that can increase self-efficacy.

The choice of an interest assessment intervention for any particular career client or with a career exploration group can be easily justified and supported through the career development theories just mentioned. Beyond relying on theory for a rationale, though, the actual material brought to the session by the client may also justify the need for clarifying, structuring, or measuring career interests. Inventoried interests may generate more options for exploration, explain discrepancies between the client's interests and the interests of those who have influence in the client's world, or increase a client's confidence in his or her expressed career choices. In addition, Diamond (1990) described how inventoried interests are often more accurate than expressed interests: "People's occupational and educational choices are too often based on irrelevant influences and information rather than critical information about themselves and about the fields they are considering" (p. 215). In addition, in keeping with the scope of this book, interest assessment information may assist the client in identifying areas of strengths and support other assessments of cognitive abilities and/or personality. Learning Experience 6.2, presented on page 190, offers an opportunity for you to gain a sense of your Holland (1973) type and your own career interests.

Uses for Measured Interests

Other client-driven reasons for choosing to measure interests are noted by Anastasi (1982), who referred to considering the client's need for self-exploration, expansion of career titles to explore, and assistance with career decision making. In addition, Hansen (1990) claimed that interest measurement can be useful for choosing "leisure interests, preferences for various types of work, living and recreational environments, and an affinity for people with various interests" (p. 185). The process of explaining interest assessment results can also help clients build rapport, increase their sense of being heard or being known by their counselor, and provide an opportunity for them to tell the story of traveling their career path. Often interest assessments can verify clients' career choices or plans and empower them to pursue further training or complete any necessary additional credentialing.

Administration

The other assessments addressed in this book (most notably the Wechsler measurements of intelligence and the MMPI-2/MMPI-A) require extensive training and attention to standardized test administration. As mentioned in Chapter 1, use of vocational interest measures may not demand the same advanced level of training as intelligence and personality assessment but do require familiarity with test administration, knowledge of test construction and scores, and the delivery of inventoried information to clients. As with intelligence and personality assessment, it is important for clients to complete a career interest measure in a quiet environment with few distractions, but unlike intelligence testing, the only materials needed at the time of testing are the test questions, the answer sheet, and a Number 2 pencil. For those completing interest assessments online, even booklets, answer sheets, and pencils have become obsolete. The Strong Interest Inventory (SII®) (Harmon, Hansen, Borgen, & Hammer, 1994) and the Kuder Career Search (KCS) (Zytowski, 2002) manuals recommend specific wordings and instructions for a standardized administration process. Administration of either the SII or KCS can take place in individual or group (class) settings.

The Strong Interest Inventory

History

Chronologically, the Strong Interest Inventory® is the oldest of the *currently* used interest assessments but was not the first. Following

World War I, a seminar at the Carnegie Institute of Technology resulted in the generation of 1,000 interest assessment items that were eventually used in the Occupational Interest Inventory (Freyd, 1923), the General Interest Survey (Kornhauser, 1927), the Purdue Interest Report (Remmers, 1929), and Strong's (1927) Vocational Interest Blank (Hansen, 1990). Lowman (1991) stated that these early assessments "rank on par with early measures of intelligence for their impact on the practice of psychology and for their contribution to the scientific-professional model of psychological practice" (p. 16). The current edition of the 1927 Vocational Interest Blank, the Strong Interest Inventory (Consulting Psychologist Press, 1994), is the only interest assessment still remaining from this pioneering work of the 1920s.

Revisions of the original Strong interest assessment have included increasing the number of occupational scales, adding a form for women (Strong, 1933), developing the Basic Interest Scales (Campbell, Borgen, Eastes, Johansson, & Peterson, 1968), including Holland's (1973) vocational typology (Campbell, 1974), and increasing expansion of the criterion sample (Hansen & Campbell, 1985; Harmon et al., 1994). The most current edition of the Strong Interest Inventory, the fifth edition (Consulting Psychologists Press, 1994), includes extensive updating of the reference pool, new occupational titles, and a restructuring of the Special Scales. Product information is available on the publisher's Web page at www.cpp-db.com.

Administration

The latest editions of the SII ask test takers to indicate whether they "like," "dislike," or feel "indifference" for occupations, school subjects, work activities, leisure activities, types of people, and characteristics. It is advisable to administer the SII after interest patterns have begun to stabilize (typically after age 14) and with a reading level of at least the eighth grade (Walsh & Betz, 2001). To prepare clients for the assessment, the clinician and client should read together the following general instructions:

This inventory is used to help you understand your interests in a general way, and to show some kinds of activities and work in which you might be comfortable. The booklet lists many jobs, activities, school subjects, and so forth, and you are asked to show your liking or disliking for each. Your answers will be compared with the answers given by people already working in a wide range of jobs, and your scores will show how similar your interests are to the interests of these people. But this is not a test of your *abilities*; it is an inventory of your *interests*. (Hansen, 1985, p. 6)

Alternatively, the instructions on the SII item booklet and answer sheet (Consulting Psychologists Press, 1994) could be read with an individual client or group (class) participants:

The *Strong Interest Inventory* is used to help you understand your work interests and to show you some kinds of work in which you might be comfortable. The following pages list many jobs, activities, school subjects, and so forth, and you will be asked to show whether you like, are indifferent to, or dislike each of them. Your answers will be compared with the answers given by people already working in a wide range of jobs, and your scores will show how similar your interests are to the interests of these people. The *Strong* is not a test of your *abilities*; it is an inventory of your *interests*. Your report will be presented to you later on a *Strong Interest Inventory* report. The report will provide information to help you understand your results. (Consulting Psychologists Press, 1994, p. 3)

The 317 SII items are typically completed in 35 to 40 minutes. It can be useful to remind clients that there are no correct or incorrect answers and that the inventory is not a measurement of how well they believe they could do an activity or occupation but rather will assist them in organizing their interest patterns. Clinicians are encouraged to review *The Strong Interest Inventory: Applications and Technical Guide* (Harmon et al., 1994) for detailed chapters concerning validity and reliability data as well as interpretation recommendations (see Figure 6.1 to view the four scales of a Strong Interest Inventory report).

The General Occupational Themes

The first page of the SII results protocol provides a snapshot (or summary) of results obtained by the client on each of the four scales

(Text continues on page 165)

STRONG INTEREST INVENTORY™

Profile report for **ANNA**
ID: **624**
Age: **35**
Gender: **Female**

Date tested: **3/1/01**
Date scored: **3/8/01**

Page 1 of 6

SNAPSHOT: A SUMMARY OF RESULTS FOR ANNA

GENERAL OCCUPATIONAL THEMES

The General Occupational Themes describe interests in six very broad areas, including interest in work and leisure activities, kinds of people, and work settings. Your interests in each area are shown at the right in rank order. Note that each Theme has a code, represented by the first letter of the Theme name.

You can use your Theme code, printed below your results, to identify school subjects, part-time jobs, college majors, leisure activities, or careers that you might find interesting. See the back of this Profile for suggestions on how to use your Theme code.

THEME CODE	THEME	VERY LITTLE INTEREST	LITTLE INTEREST	AVERAGE INTEREST	HIGH INTEREST	VERY HIGH INTEREST	TYPICAL INTERESTS
S	SOCIAL	☐	☐	☐	☑	☐	Helping, instructing
C	CONVENTIONAL	☐	☐	☐	☑	☐	Accounting, processing data
A	ARTISTIC	☐	☐	☑	☐	☐	Creating or enjoying art
E	ENTERPRISING	☐	☑	☐	☐	☐	Selling, managing
R	REALISTIC	☑	☐	☐	☐	☐	Building, repairing
I	INVESTIGATIVE	☑	☐	☐	☐	☐	Researching, analyzing

Your Theme code is SCA—(see explanation at left).
You might explore occupations with codes that contain any combination of these letters.

BASIC INTEREST SCALES

The Basic Interest Scales measure your interests in 25 specific areas or activities. Only those 5 areas in which you show the *most* interest are listed at the right in rank order. Your results on all 25 Basic Interest Scales are found on page 2.

To the left of each scale is a letter that shows which of the six General Occupational Themes this activity is most closely related to. These codes can help you to identify other activities that you may enjoy.

THEME CODE	BASIC INTEREST	VERY LITTLE INTEREST	LITTLE INTEREST	AVERAGE INTEREST	HIGH INTEREST	VERY HIGH INTEREST	TYPICAL ACTIVITIES
C	OFFICE SERVICES	☐	☐	☐	☐	☑	Performing clerical and office tasks
S	RELIGIOUS ACTIVITIES	☐	☐	☐	☑	☐	Participating in spiritual activities
A	CULINARY ARTS	☐	☐	☐	☑	☐	Cooking or entertaining
C	COMPUTER ACTIVITIES	☐	☐	☑	☐	☐	Working with computers
A	MUSIC/DRAMATICS	☐	☐	☑	☐	☐	Performing or enjoying music/drama

OCCUPATIONAL SCALES

The Occupational Scales measure how similar your interests are to the interests of people who are satisfied working in those occupations. Only the 10 occupations on which your interests are *most* similar to those of these people are listed at the right in rank order. Your results on all 211 of the Occupational Scales are found on pages 3, 4, and 5.

The letters to the left of each scale identify the Theme or Themes that most closely describe the interests of people working in that occupation. You can use these letters to find additional, related occupations that you might find interesting. After reviewing your results on all six pages of this Profile, see the back of page 5 for tips on finding other occupations in the Theme or Themes that interest you the most.

THEME CODE	OCCUPATION	VERY DISSIMILAR	DISSIMILAR	MID-RANGE	SIMILAR	VERY SIMILAR
S	ELEMENTARY SCHOOL TEACHER	☐	☐	☐	☐	☑
SE	SPECIAL EDUCATION TEACHER	☐	☐	☐	☐	☑
SA	SPEECH PATHOLOGIST	☐	☐	☐	☐	☑
S	CHILD CARE PROVIDER	☐	☐	☐	☐	☑
CE	BANKER	☐	☐	☐	☐	☑
RIS	RADIOLOGIC TECHNOLOGIST	☐	☐	☐	☐	☑
CE	PARALEGAL	☐	☐	☐	☐	☑
IS	AUDIOLOGIST	☐	☐	☐	☐	☑
CES	FOOD SERVICE MANAGER	☐	☐	☐	☐	☑
CE	CREDIT MANAGER	☐	☐	☐	☑	☐

PERSONAL STYLE SCALES measure your levels of comfort regarding Work Style, Learning Environment, Leadership Style, and Risk Taking/Adventure. This information may help you make decisions about particular work environments, educational settings, and types of activities you would find satisfying. Your results on these four scales are on page 6.

Figure 6.1a   Anna's Strong Interest Inventory®

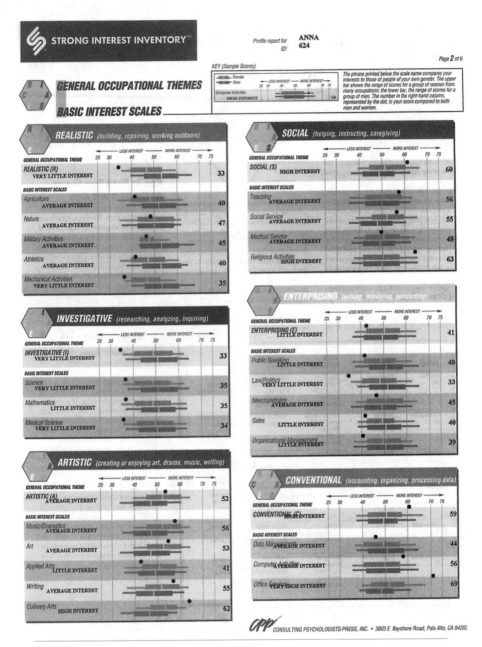

Figure 6.1b

OCCUPATIONAL SCALES

KEY (Sample Scores)

( ) You can find your score compared to this gender under the Theme represented by the first letter of this code. For example, your score compared to male dietitians is shown under the S or Social Theme.

- The position of the dot shows how similar your interests are to those of individuals of your gender who say they are satisfied in their occupation.
- Not enough people of this gender who work in this occupation could be found to make a good comparison.

NOTES

REALISTIC (building, repairing, working outdoors)

THEME CODES FEMALE	MALE		YOUR SCORES FEMALE	MALE	DISSIMILAR INTERESTS 15	20	30 —MID-RANGE— 40	SIMILAR INTERESTS 50	55
RIS	(SIR)	Athletic Trainer	2	(SIR)					
R	R	Auto Mechanic	14	20					
RIA	REA	Carpenter	3	13					
RIA	RIC	Electrician	10	-5					
RCI	RI	Emergency Medical Technician	23	17					
RI	RI	Engineer	11	8					
(CSE)	RC	Farmer	(CSE)	26					
RI	RI	Forester	22	22					
RC	RE	Gardener/Groundskeeper	26	32					
REI	REI	Horticultural Worker	14	11					
(CRE)	RCE	Military Enlisted Personnel	(CRE)	28					
REI	REC	Military Officer	16	8					
*	R	Plumber	.	24					
RE	R	Police Officer	25	24					
RIS	RI	Radiologic Technologist	55	41					
(CE)	RE	Small Business Owner	(CE)	23					
RSI	RSE	Vocational Agriculture Teacher	15	9					

INVESTIGATIVE (researching, analyzing, inquiring)

THEME CODES FEMALE	MALE		YOUR SCORES FEMALE	MALE	DISSIMILAR INTERESTS 15	20	30 —MID-RANGE— 40	SIMILAR INTERESTS 50	55
IS	IA	Audiologist	53	26					
IRA	IA	Biologist	10	23					
IR	IR	Chemist	10	7					
IR	IRA	Chiropractor	23	23					
IAR	IAS	College Professor	21	18					
IR	IAR	Computer Programmer/Systems Analyst	15	16					
IRA	IR	Dentist	5	9					
IES	(SEC)	Dietitian	17	(SEC)					
IRA	IA	Geographer	9	2					
IRA	IRA	Geologist	1	6					
IRC	ICA	Mathematician	-11	-2					
IRC	IRE	Medical Technician	28	12					
IRC	IRC	Medical Technologist	4	18					
IR	IR	Optometrist	17	-6					
ICR	ICE	Pharmacist	21	25					
IAR	IAR	Physician	6	5					
IRA	IRA	Physicist	-4	4					
IA	IA	Psychologist	-1	8					
IR	IRC	Research & Development Manager	-4	-8					
IRA	IRS	Respiratory Therapist	26	20					
IRS	IRS	Science Teacher	7	13					
IAR	(AI)	Sociologist	-3	(AI)					
IRA	IR	Veterinarian	14	14					

CPP CONSULTING PSYCHOLOGISTS PRESS, INC. • 3803 E. Bayshore Road, Palo Alto, CA 94303

Figure 6.1c

OCCUPATIONAL SCALES (continued)

ARTISTIC (creating or enjoying art, drama, music, writing)

THEME CODES FEMALE	MALE		YOUR SCORES FEMALE	YOUR SCORES MALE
AE	AE	Advertising Executive	29	44
ARI	ARI	Architect	-2	15
ARI	A	Artist, Commercial	2	19
AR	A	Artist, Fine	5	23
ASE	AS	Art Teacher	11	33
AE	AE	Broadcaster	26	29
AES	AES	Corporate Trainer	16	21
ASE	ASE	English Teacher	33	40
(EA)	AE	Interior Decorator	(EA)	43
A	A	Lawyer	20	29
A	A	Librarian	38	55
AIR	AIR	Medical Illustrator	-14	13
A	A	Musician	35	43
ARE	ARE	Photographer	23	24
AER	ASE	Public Administrator	11	14
AE	AE	Public Relations Director	14	32
A	A	Reporter	10	26
(IAR)	AI	Sociologist	(IAR)	12
AIR	AI	Technical Writer	25	39
A	AI	Translator	37	51

SOCIAL (helping, instructing, caregiving)

THEME CODES FEMALE	MALE		YOUR SCORES FEMALE	YOUR SCORES MALE
(RIS)	SIR	Athletic Trainer	(RIS)	8
S	*	Child Care Provider	61	*
SE	SE	Community Service Organization Director	44	33
(IES)	SEC	Dietitian	(IES)	45
S	S	Elementary School Teacher	68	68
SAE	SA	Foreign Language Teacher	44	54
SE	SE	High School Counselor	27	35
SE	*	Home Economics Teacher	41	*
SAR	SA	Minister	13	31
SCE	SCE	Nurse, LPN	45	48
SI	SAI	Nurse, RN	41	36
SAR	SA	Occupational Therapist	48	44
SE	SE	Parks and Recreation Coordinator	32	32
SRC	SR	Physical Education Teacher	16	17
SIR	SIR	Physical Therapist	34	25
SEA	SEC	School Administrator	15	22
SEA	SEA	Social Science Teacher	28	36
SA	SA	Social Worker	40	49
SE	SEA	Special Education Teacher	62	63
SA	SA	Speech Pathologist	62	56

NOTES

Figure 6.1d

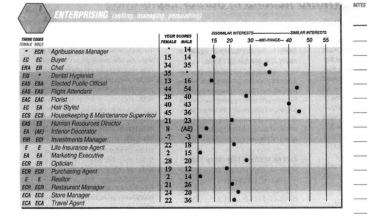

STRONG INTEREST INVENTORY

Profile report for **ANNA**
ID: **624**

KEY (Sample Scores)

OCCUPATIONAL SCALES (continued)

ENTERPRISING (selling, managing, persuading)

THEME CODES FEMALE	MALE		YOUR SCORES FEMALE	MALE
*	ECR	Agribusiness Manager	•	14
EC	EC	Buyer	15	14
ERA	ER	Chef	34	35
EIS	*	Dental Hygienist	35	*
EAS	ESA	Elected Public Official	13	16
EAS	EAS	Flight Attendant	44	54
EAC	EAC	Florist	28	40
EC	EA	Hair Stylist	40	43
ECS	ECS	Housekeeping & Maintenance Supervisor	45	36
EAS	ES	Human Resources Director	21	23
EA	(AE)	Interior Decorator	8	(AE)
EIR	ECI	Investments Manager	-7	-3
E	E	Life Insurance Agent	22	18
EA	EA	Marketing Executive	2	15
ECR	ER	Optician	28	20
ECR	ECR	Purchasing Agent	19	12
E	E	Realtor	2	14
ECR	ECR	Restaurant Manager	21	26
ECA	ECS	Store Manager	24	20
ECA	ECA	Travel Agent	22	36

CONVENTIONAL (accounting, organizing, processing data)

THEME CODES FEMALE	MALE		YOUR SCORES FEMALE	MALE
CE	CE	Accountant	30	16
CI	CI	Actuary	16	8
CE	CE	Banker	55	32
C	C	Bookkeeper	31	36
CES	CES	Business Education Teacher	39	47
CE	CE	Credit Manager	49	24
CSE	*	Dental Assistant	45	*
CSE	(RC)	Farmer	43	(RC)
CES	CES	Food Service Manager	50	38
CIR	CIS	Mathematics Teacher	14	10
C	C	Medical Records Technician	46	47
CRE	(RCE)	Military Enlisted Personnel	43	(RCE)
CES	CES	Nursing Home Administrator	39	44
CE	CA	Paralegal	54	47
CES	*	Secretary	42	*
CE	(RE)	Small Business Owner	39	(RE)

NOTES

Figure 6.1e

STRONG INTEREST INVENTORY™

Profile report for **ANNA**
ID: **624**

Page **6** of 6

PERSONAL STYLE SCALES

KEY (Sample Scores)

The upper bar shows the range of scores on this scale for a group of women from many occupations; the lower bar, the range of scores for a group of men. The number in the right-hand column, represented by the dot, shows your preference on this scale compared to both men and women.

NOTES

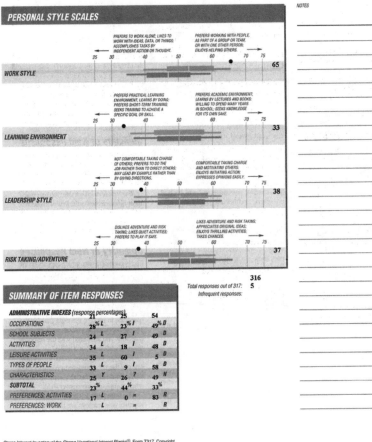

Total responses out of 317: **316**
Infrequent responses: **5**

Figure 6.1f

SOURCE: Modified and reproduced by special permission of the Publisher, Consulting Psychologists Press, Inc., Palo Alto, CA 94303 from the *Profile Report of the Strong Interest Inventory of the Strong Vocational Interest Blank®*, Form T317. Copyright © 1933, 1938, 1945, 1946, 1966, 1968, 1974, 1981, 1985, 1994 by the Board of Trustees of the Leland Stanford Junior University. All rights reserved. Printed under license from Stanford University Press, Stanford University, Stanford, CA 94305. Strong Vocational Interest Blanks is a registered trademark of Stanford University Press. Further reproduction is prohibited without the Publisher's written consent.

of the inventory. The first scale, General Occupational Themes, indicates the order of preferred Holland (1973) types. It is necessary for the clinician to begin the SII explanation session with a description of each of the six Holland types (Realistic, Investigative, Artistic, Social, Enterprising, and Conventional [RIASEC]) because the entire protocol is structured around the RIASEC titles. Detailed RIASEC explanations, reproducable transparencies, and handouts are available in *Using the Strong in Organizations* (Hirsh & McEvoy, 1986). In addition, the six Holland (1973) types are briefly described in this chapter's Learning Experience 6.2 (p. 190).

It is also important for the clinician to illustrate to his or her clients how the RIASEC types are positioned around the hexagon model. Three additional aspects of Holland's (1973) theory of types (consistency, congruence, and differentiation) may also be useful for clients:

1. The notion of *consistency* provides an explanation for similarities between the six types represented at each corner of the hexagon. For example, if the client's three highest types are Investigative, Artistic, and Conventional, there is similarity or consistency between Investigative and Artistic (for they are next to each other on the hexagon) but not much similarity between Artistic and Conventional (far apart on the hexagon). Higher consistency may indicate that the client will find more occupational matches (work environments and job tasks can also be categorized using the same RIASEC hexagon model) because one job may not reinforce both Artistic and Conventional interests.

2. The notion of *congruence* can also be important for understanding and interpreting SII results. Congruence is the degree of match between the client's three letter preferences and the three-letter type that characterizes the occupational setting or job tasks. If the client's preferred type is Investigative, Artistic, and Conventional and he or she works in an environment that supports Social, Artistic, and Enterprising interests, the congruence or similarity between individual and work preferences is minimal. Such a lack of congruence could explain a client's discomfort or lack of satisfaction with his or her work environment and tasks.

3. The notion of *differentiation* indicates a client's distinction between those things that catch his or her interest and those that do not. The General Occupational Themes scores on the SII assess interests from very high to very low. A client who has differentiated interests may demonstrate a career history that falls within the same three RIASEC types, in which an undifferentiated client may have selected, in the past, careers that appear to be from all over the hexagon. Undifferentiation can be a positive factor, in that it gives the client a theoretical explanation for his or her diversity of interests, experiences, and vast range of occupational choices, or undifferentiation can be experienced as a negative if the client is confused and stuck in the choice process by an overly wide array of possibilities.

Holland's (1973) theory is one of the most widely researched approaches in the career development literature. There is not only research support for his theory, but clinical experience with clients also validates the efficacy of using such a parsimonious model. However, some research (e.g., Shivy, Phillips, & Koehly, 1996; Shivy, Rounds, & Jones, 1999) suggests that other structural models may be preferable. With a little effort, the Strong Interest Inventory results can be adapted to match Prediger's (1982) things/people and data/ideas dimensions, Gati's (1979) three-group (RI, AS, EC) model, or Roe's (1956) hierarchical cone model. The reader is encouraged to further explore the use of other models, even though this text follows the SII's use of Holland's (1973) hexagonal model.

The General Occupational Themes section of the SII often requires an educative approach to inventory interpretation. Explanation of Holland's (1973) RIASEC typology and the concepts of consistency, congruence, and differentiation provide a fundamental groundwork for the scale results that follow. After completing Learning Experience 6.2, place the three types you associated with the most on the (RIASEC order) hexagon to evaluate your own comprehension of the RIASEC types, consistency, congruence, and differentiation.

Basic Interest Scales

The snapshot on the first page of the report does not contain scores for all of the 25 Basic Interest Scales but identifies only those with the highest scores. Later in the protocol, the complete set of Basic Interest Scales is organized in the same RIASEC structure as presented in the General Occupational Themes. It is important to remember the following:

1. Standardized scores for the General Occupational Themes and the Basic Interest Scales were developed by comparing the client's responses to the responses of both men and women in the General Reference Sample. The mean of the standard scores is 50, and standard deviation is 10.

2. The protocol also contains "interpretive comments" (Hansen, 1990). The six possible interpretive comments range from "very high" interest to "very low" interest and coincide with same-gender reference group percentile scores.

3. "Interpretive bars" (Hansen, 1990) visually depict a flattened bell curve or normal distribution for the women in general or the men in general in the reference group. The middle of the bar is 50% of the sample, but the middle of the distribution may fall between different actual scores for women and for men. Therefore, the client can compare his or her own Basic Interest Scale scores to reference group scores of both genders (see Figure 6.1b for a depiction of the interpretive bars found on this scale).

Clients often enjoy reviewing their lowest Basic Interest Scale scores, along with their highest scores. This is the section of the Strong Interest Inventory where clients usually express the most surprise concerning how well these Basic Interest scores capture their prior work histories and leisure interests. Conversation can continue with how well their current or future employment may support the expression of their basic interests.

Occupational Scales

Again, the snapshot of occupations (on the first page of the protocol) lists only the job titles to which the client scored most similarly to the reference group representatives of those occupations (individuals who have stated they are satisfied with their work for at least 3 years and are 25 years of age or older). To locate the complete scores, the reader can access all 211 occupational scales (comprising 109 occupational titles), which are arranged (as in all sections of the SII) in RIASEC order (see Figure 6.1c, d, e). Each occupational score is standardized with a mean of 50 and described with phrases from "very similar" to "very dissimilar." Along with each occupational title is the designated Holland (1973) code. Clients may wish to explore or research only a handful of their highest scored occupations, or they may use their results to expand their search. Even "dissimilar" scores can include occupations worth further exploration because with career maturity, study/training, and life experience, vocational interests can take on new patterns. The clinician should repeat to clients that their scores are based on their current interests and do not necessarily relate to their ability to do the job tasks. It is also important to emphasize that these occupational scales are recommendations for exploration and are not their only career or college major choices. The assessment results can be expanded by comparing the inventoried occupational preferences to the job descriptions contained in references such as the *Dictionary of Occupational Titles* (U.S. Department of Labor, 1991) or the *Occupational Outlook Handbook* (U.S. Department of Labor Statistics, 2000).

Personal Style Scales

This final section of the SII includes four scales that assess personal styles: Work, Learning, Leadership, and Risk Taking/Adventure. The client's scores are presented on four continuum scales, indicating the degree of preference from one side of the pole to the other. The polarity depicted on the Work Style scale ranges from (left) prefers to work alone to (right) prefers to work with people. These scores usually coincide with the data/things versus the people qualities of the six General Occupational Themes. The Learning Environment continuum goes from displaying a preference for learning by doing (left) to learning academically through reading and lecture (right). If clients are reminded that the SII does not assess abilities or skills, this scale can be very reassuring to college students whose scores fall on the left end of the continuum. Those students typically find they must force themselves to study for class, yet if they do study, they can obtain high grades and graduate. For Leadership Style, the continuum measures (left) doing the work oneself and not leading others to (right) managing and leading others in doing the work. This scale can elicit stories about previous work experiences with coworkers and managers. The final continuum, Risk Taking/ Adventure, depicts for clients their preference for playing it safe (left) to taking risks (right). The previous edition of the SII included this scale as one of the Basic Interest Scales under the Realistic theme. Now that the risk-taking/adventure continuum is depicted as a Personal Style scale, the score can be applied to many aspects of the client's career history, not merely in relation to the Realistic Holland (1973) type.

Summary of Item Responses

The Administrative Indexes provide summaries of all the response percentages (such as "like," "indifferent," or "dislike") completed by the test taker on the answer sheet. The percentages for each section of the SII answer sheet (Occupations, School Subjects, Activities, Leisure, Types of People, and Characteristics) are calculated, along with an overall subtotal percentage. Any pattern of answers across the sections can be indicative of a response set (a tendency to answer all the items in a particular style). If the percentages are predominately "dislike" (80% or more), the individual may be displaying such attributes as negativity toward work, toward the assessment, toward meeting with a counselor, or a general negativity. It is important to assist the client in determining the meaning of a response set because high percentages (of "likes" or "dislikes") can influence the scores on the other SII scales.

There are also two ways to check the validity of the results. A Total Responses statement (located adjacent to the Administrative Indexes) indicates how many items were completed by the test taker out of 317 possible responses. If the number of completed responses is below 300, the results may not be a valid indication of the test taker's vocational interests. Also, Infrequent Responses are noted on the profile under the Total Responses. This measure indicates differences in the test taker's responses as compared to typical test responses by others of his or her gender. The range of scores is 5 to −7 for women and 7 to −8 for men. Only negative scores need to be addressed with clients because negative scores may be reflective of nontraditional interests or an indication that the test taker merely filled in random bubbles on the answer sheet. It is important to discuss Total Responses and Infrequent Responses with clients to determine how validly the scores reflect their interests.

Strengths and Weaknesses of the SII

The Strong Interest Inventory has stood the test of time as one of the most important contributions to the field of vocational assessment over the past 70 years. The SII is useful with clients over a wide variety of career concerns—from generating a variety of occupations to explore, to fine-tuning a vocational choice, to confirming what one already knows about one's self. Prince and Heiser (2000) noted other strengths of the SII: large sample sizes for test construction and analysis; excellent reliability; an easy profile to read, interpret, and customize; the incorporation of Holland (1973) typology; and a manual that is useful for technical information, interpretation guidelines, and related occupational appendixes.

However, to explain the SII results, some clinicians may often need to change their style from one of vocational therapist to one of a teacher of vocational typology. Much time can be consumed in a session explaining Holland codes, consistency, differentiation, and congruence with vocational environments. It is also necessary to invest time in discussing normative scoring, norm groups, and score distributions. Prince and Heiser (2000) also mentioned how time-consuming it can be to interpret "discrepancies between scores on different types of scales" to explain "profiles with few or numerous elevations" and to teach the importance of "opposite-sex scales" (p. 58). Also, due to the collection of occupations listed on the SII, this particular interest assessment can be most useful with individuals who already have some experience in the world of work and who aspire to occupations requiring a college education, although this limitation can be remedied by using the various reports (high school, college, professional, business) available from Consulting Psychologists Press (www.cpp-db.com). As with most interest assessments, a primary limitation is the lack of integration with career abilities, values, beliefs, barriers, or readiness assessments.

The publishers of the Strong Interest Inventory offer a variety of administration options: paper-and-pencil mail-back inventory, onsite scanning, and Internet versions. Through its long history, the SII has been identified as a very cost-effective, paper-and-pencil interest assessment. We turn now to another vocational interest assessment first introduced nearly 70 years ago, the Kuder Career Search With Person Match (KCS). The KCS is currently available in several formats, including an online assessment that provides nearly instantaneous results.

The Kuder Career Search With Person Match

History

Frederic Kuder began his study of the relationship between interests and careers in the early 1930s as a graduate student at The Ohio State University (Diamond, 1990). The first Kuder interest assessment, the Kuder Preference Record, appeared in 1939 and was subsequently published in 1941 by Science Research Associates. The KPR was different from the other vocational assessments of that time, in that it included respondents' preferences of everyday activities, not just occupations. The assessment was completed by punching a hole through the answer pad with a pin and counting the holes in the answer key to determine scores on 10 interest scales. (We can all be grateful that today's users are completing their responses with the click of a mouse rather than by yielding holes in paper with pins!)

In 1943, a revised version of the Kuder Preference Record was used to assess the vocational interests of those in the armed services during World War II and later became a standard for postwar veterans continuing their education under the GI Bill. This version was further revised to extend the age range downward to the sixth grade and included capabilities for the first computer scoring.

The second generation of Kuder interest measurements appeared in 1966 as the Kuder Occupational Interest Survey (Kuder, 1966). This version included client assessment on 10 interest scales but also provided the test taker's similarity to workers in 100 occupational and 40 college major groups. In 1969, Donald Zytowski published his first of more than 25 publications on the Kuder assessments. Since 1980, he has been the primary Kuder inventory developer, continuing revisions and constructing additional occupational scales. The latest edition is the KCS (National Career Assessment Services, 1999).

The third generation of Kuder assessments includes the 10 traditional interest scales (now called the Activity Preference Profile), along with six Kuder Career Clusters and more than a hundred occupational titles linked for further reference to the *Occupational Outlook Handbook* (U.S. Department of Labor Statistics, 2000). The KCS does not rely on punching pins in a pad or even the necessity of filling bubbles with Number 2 pencil marks. The new options include a mail-back paper-and-pencil version of the KCS, a PC-based (CD compatible with Windows 95/98/NT) version, and, most notably, an online version (at www.kuder.com).

Also new to the KCS is the incorporation of a different philosophy of matching, which was introduced by Kuder in 1980 as person-to-people matching. Each individual user is matched to 25 similar individuals in the Person Match. Each of the 25 matches is identified with a job title but also comes with an autobiographical sketch. This KCS feature can open the counseling session to the discussion of career stories rather than merely assessment scores.

Administration

Kuder and Zytowski (1991) suggested that the assessment of vocational interests is most appropriate beginning in Grade 10. As with the Strong Interest Inventory, it is advisable for the clinician to read the directions for testing with the client, highlighting that there are no wrong answers. The KCS administration instructions noted in the preview manual (Zytowski, 1999) are as follows:

> Now open the survey to the inside left page. Read the directions to yourself. (After a pause) Notice that the survey wants you to mark each activity in the groups of three: 1 for most preferred, 2 for next most preferred, and 3 for least preferred. Be sure to mark each of the activities in a group with 1, 2 or 3. (p. 3)

The example provided on the KCS answer sheet is the following:

Have ice cream for dessert

Have cake for dessert

Have pie for dessert

Often, assessment completion errors are made when clients do not understand that they must indicate first, second, and third choices, not just their first choice. These rank-order responses are compared with responses from the reference group members, who also completed their first, second, and third choices to the same items. Test takers should be encouraged to not skip any items.

The online administration directions are similar, except that the most preferred, next most preferred, and least preferred choices are selected with mouse clicks. One advantage to online administration is that the computer will not begin the scoring process if all items are not marked as first, second, and third preferences. The 60 items can be completed by those with a sixth-grade reading level, and most people will finish the online version in 20 to 30 minutes. Also, a Spanish-language KCS assessment is available in the print or online versions.

Interpretation

The mail-back versions are scored by the publisher the same day they are received and are returned by postal service. Results can be printed from the PC-based version in minutes, whereas the online assessments are scored in less than 9 seconds! Supplemental materials, containing masters for transparencies, are available from the publisher for group interpretations of the KCS With Person Match. In addition, there is an online tutorial available (at www.kuder.com) to help clinicians become familiar with the various KCS scales. Whether interpreting the results to individuals or groups, from the mail-back version or the online version, information from each of the four sections or scales (Activity Preference Scales, Education levels, Career Clusters, and Person Matches) should be addressed with your clients in a collaborative style, with the emphasis on generating career options for further exploration and research (refer to Figure 6.2 for clarification of the four scales on the KCS results protocol).

(Text continues on page 183)

Dear *Anna Case;*

Your results to the Kuder Career Search™ are presented here in five parts: 1) your Activity Preference Profile, which shows your relative preference among ten different kinds of activities; 2) your preferred career clusters; 3) your career chart, showing the level of education needed for occupations within the career clusters; 4) your top 25 Person Matches™ to explore and 5) steps for continuing your career exploration.

I. Your Activity Preference Profile

Your personal activity preference profile is shown below. It should help you develop a clear picture of yourself, what activities you most and least prefer. Try to keep your top two or three in mind as you think about your future plans.

Scale	Score	Profile
HUMAN SERVICES	95%	
NATURE	87%	
OFFICE DETAIL	79%	
MUSIC	71%	
COMMUNICATIONS	66%	
ART	61%	
COMPUTATIONS	31%	
SALES/MANAGEMENT	29%	
MECHANICAL	15%	
SCIENCE/TECHNICAL	13%	

Definitions of each of the activity preference scales are given on the next page. Read them carefully before you continue.

Your scores are shown in percentiles, based on a combined norm group of males and females. If you scored 38 on the Nature scale, that means you scored higher than 38 percent of the norm group. Scores above 75 are considered high; scores below 25 are considered low. Scores above 90 are very high; scores of less than 10 are very low.

THE IMPORTANT INFORMATION IS THE RANK ORDER OF THE SCALES, NOT THE EXACT SCORES. You should think of your results in terms of, "I most prefer (highest ranked scale), next most on (second ranked scale)", and so on, to "I least prefer (lowest ranked scale) activities."

Occupations typically involve two or three kinds of activities. An engineer might score highest on Mechanical and Science/Technical activities; a writer of computer manuals might score highest on Science and Communications; a psychologist highest on Science, Communications, and Human Services.

As well, not everyone with a given occupational title has exactly the same activity preference profile. One engineer might be highest on Mechanical and Science/Technical and working in research and development; another highest on Science/Technical and Sales/Management and working in technical sales; and another on Art and Mechanical, working for an engineering firm and drawing cartoons for fun.

Figure 6.2a   Anna's Kuder Career Search With Person Match

SOURCE: Used by permission of the publisher, National Career Assessment Services, Inc.

Definitions of the Activity Preference Scales

As shown on page one, your preferences have been ranked according to 10 career-related categories. Following are the definitions of each. You may print this report and mark each definition below with a 1 through 10 as it corresponds to your preferences above.

Nature:

activities you do outdoors, such as growing or caring for plants or animals. Farmers, gardeners and people who raise animals score high on this scale. These preferences often lead to hobbies like growing flowers or vegetables, entering animals in shows or outdoor recreation like camping or hiking.

Mechanical:

activities that come from knowing how things work and using tools and machines to make or repair things. People who build houses, or repair cars or office machines usually score high on this scale. Enjoyment of these activities can lead to hobbies like woodworking, flying model airplanes and many kinds of handicrafts.

Science/Technical:

activities such as discovering or understanding the natural and physical world. People who score high on this scale are scientists, doctors, engineers, medical technicians, nurses and computer repairers, among others. People who like to try new cooking recipes, keep weather records or breed new flowers for fun may score high on this scale.

Art:

creative activities that make beauty. High scorers work with colors and designs in painting, photography and decorations. This includes clothing designers, architects, illustrators and florists. People with artistic hobbies do things like watercolor painting, cartooning and flower arranging.

Music:

activities that involve making or listening to music, singing or playing an instrument, or leading a musical group. Few people make their living as professional musicians, but many play music for fun, collect records or enjoy going to concerts.

Communications:

activities that use language, either writing or speaking it. People high on this preference may be English teachers, write books, or work for TV stations, newspapers and magazines. Hobbies include acting in community theater, reading for enjoyment or keeping a journal.

Human Services:

activities that help other people. Those who score high on this scale may be teachers, counselors or work for a church. Others are sales persons and child care workers. Many people do volunteer work besides their regular jobs - another way to use this preference.

Sales/Management:

activities that deal with people, like leading a team of workers or selling things or ideas. Auto, home and insurance salespeople, sales managers and people elected to government positions prefer these activities. Volunteering on a political campaign or asking for contributions for charity are other examples.

Figure 6.2b

Computations:

activities that use numbers. Accountants, tax preparers, bookkeepers, claims adjusters and inventory clerks generally score high on this activity. People who score high on this scale may enjoy hobbies such as card games or keeping statistics on their favorite sports team.

Office Detail:

activities that require keeping track of things, people or information, like those involved in word processing and database management. People who like these activities are likely to be office managers, ticket agents, hotel clerks, among others. Doll, baseball card or other collectors would score high on this scale.

II. YOUR PREFERRED CAREER CLUSTERS

Occupations have similarities and differences that enable them to be grouped together into career clusters. Each interest area has similarities in job duties and outcomes (such as pay level and satisfaction), and educational requirements, that make them different from the others. Ohio uses six career clusters.

Your activity preferences have been compared with the composite profiles of occupations in the six career clusters. They are shown here in order of your similarity. You may print this report and mark each definition below with the number that corresponds to your interest area ranking.

1 Human Resources/Services

2 Arts and Communication

3 Health Services

4 Business and Management

5 Environmental/Agricultural Systems

6 Industrial/Engineering Systems

DEFINITIONS OF THE CAREER CLUSTERS

Environmental & Agricultural Systems

This cluster includes the entry, technical, and professional level careers within environmental and agricultural industries. This cluster includes careers related to service, research, education and production. Numerous career opportunities exist in agricultural sales and services, animal and crop production, education, engineering and mechanical systems, food processing, horticulture, and natural resources.

Arts & Communications

This cluster includes the entry, technical, and professional level career options within the performing, visual, written, and media arts. This cluster includes but is not limited to the following industries: theater, film, mass media, journalism, literature, fine arts, TV/radio broadcasting, advertising, public relations, graphic design, printing/publishing, telecommunications, and technical writing.

Business & Management

This cluster encompasses the entry, technical, and professional level careers within the world of business, management, and marketing. Students may major in at least one of the following areas: banking and finance, accounting, administration and management, marketing, administrative support, computer information systems, information technology, travel and tourism, retail management, culinary and food service management, and distribution and warehousing.

Figure 6.2c

Health Services

This cluster includes the entry, technical, and professional level careers within the health services industry. This cluster includes service, research, education and manufacturing areas of the health industry. Many career opportunities exist within medicine, dentistry, nursing, radiology, optometry, nutrition, biotechnology, physical therapy, occupational therapy, rehabilitation, and prevention and wellness.

Human Resources/Services

This cluster includes the entry, technical and professional level career options within a variety of industries related to economic, political, and social systems. These industries encompass personal, protective, legal, educational, and children's and family services.

Industrial & Engineering Systems

This cluster includes the entry, technical and professional level careers within industrial and engineering related fields. This cluster is divided into three subclusters: manufacturing, construction, and transportation. Each of these industries offers many career options depending upon the level of education and training desired. The manufacturing subcluster involves all aspects of the manufacturing industry, from product design to production and delivery. The construction subcluster involves all aspects of the building trades (such as carpentry and technical work related to electrical, heating, ventilation and air conditioning systems) as well as engineering, architecture and surveying. The transportation subcluster includes all aspects of the industry, automotive, airline, maritime, rail and trucking.

Figure 6.2d

III. Exploring Careers By Education Level

ENVIRONMENTAL & AGRICULTURAL SYSTEMS

On-the-job Training and/or Specialized Training *	Community College	University
Animal Caretaker	Forester & Conservationist	Landscape Architect
Farm Worker	Forestry Technician	Cooperative Ext. Service Worker
Groundskeeper	Ornamental Horticulturist	Economist
Logging Worker	Chemical Technician	Biological Scientist
Veterinary Assistant	Fish and Game Warden	Botanist
Farm Supervisor	Tree Surgeon	Compliance/Enforcement
Horticultural Nursery Worker	Water Plant Operator	Geographer
Pest Controller	Weather Observer	Geologist
Food/Dairy Processing Operator		Geophysicist
Grain & Feed Miller		Agricultural Engineer
Cannery Worker		Teacher (Agriscience)
Chemical Applicator		Animal Scientist
Field Inspector		Food Scientist
Agricultural Equipment Sales		Agronomist
Dairy Herder		Entomologist
Turf Grass Manager		Hydrologist
Agriculture Crop Sales		Marine Biologist
Animal Health Products Sales		Zoologist
		Life Scientist

* includes high school/technical education

INDUSTRIAL & ENGINEERING SYSTEMS

On-the-job Training and/or Specialized Training *	Community College	University
Assembly Line Worker	Microcomputer Specialist	Chemical Engineer
Aircraft Mechanic	Biomedical Equipment Repairer	Chemist
Building Maintenance Worker	Chemical Technician	Electrical/Electronic Engineer
Carpenter	CAD Repairer	Industrial Engineer
Construction Laborer	Electronics Technician	Manufacturing Engineer
Small Engine Repairer	Mechanical Engineering Technician	Marine Architect
Electrician	Metallurgical Technician	Marine Engineer
Utilities Lineperson	Nuclear Technician	Mechanical Engineer
Household Appliance Installer	Printer	Mining Engineer
Auto Mechanic	Robotics Technician	Petroleum Engineer
Manufacturing Painter	Surveyor	Plant Manager
Institutional Housekeeper	Industrial Designer	Production Manager
Dry Wall Installer	Broadcast Technician	Quality Control Engineer
Sheet Metal Worker	Aircraft Pilot/Technician	Quality Control Manager
Drafter	Laser Technician	Robotics Engineer
Electronic Components Worker		Civil Engineer
Welder		Automotive Engineer
Furniture & Wood Finisher		Architect
		Ceramic Engineer

* includes high school/technical education

Figure 6.2e

ARTS & COMMUNICATIONS

On-the-job Training and/or Specialized Training *	Community College	University
Engraving Press Operator	Screen Printing Machine Operator	Musician
Offset Press Operator	Photoengraver	Interpreter/Translator
Phototypesetter Operator	Scanner Operator	Columnist
Paste-up Artist	Lithographic Photographer	TV Production Designer
Computer Typesetter	Compositor	Technical Writer
Disk Jockey	Announcer	Writer/Author
Dramatic Reader	Freelance Writer	Journalist
Impersonator	Advertising Agent	Art Director
Comedian/Comedienne	Sign Language Interpreter	Choreographer
Model	Graphic Designer	Film Maker
Cartoonist	Illustrator	Teacher
Dancer	Medical & Scientific Illustrator	Art Historian
Merchandise Displayer	Decorator	Cartographer
Photographic Process Worker	Commercial Artist	Archeologist
Airbrush Painter	Photojournalist	Landscape Architect
Instrumental Musician	Music Director	Newscaster/Correspondent
Composer/Musician	Photographer	Archivist & Museum Curator
Singer	Cartoonist	Copywriter
Painter	Advertising Copywriter	
	Stage Technician	

* includes high school/technical education

HEALTH SERVICES

On-the-job Training Specialized Training *	Community College	University
Physical Therapy Aide	Physical Therapy Assistant	Physical Therapist
Dental Assistant	Dental Hygienist	Dentist
Dietetic Aide	Surgical Technician	Surgeon
EEG/EKG Technician	Dental Lab Technician	Hospital Administrator
Nurse Aide/Orderly	Dialysis Technician	Medical Scientist
Occupational Therapy Aide	Occupational Therapy Assistant	Pharmacist
Home Health Aide	Pharmacy Assistant	Psychologist
Medical Assistant	Mortician	Psychiatrist
Nursing Technician	Licensed Practical Nurse	Nuclear Physicist
Optometric Assistant	Optometric Technician	Medical Records Administrator
Hospice Worker/Assistant	MRI Technologist	Pathologist
Laboratory Assistant	Medical Technologist	Toxicologist
Histologist	Veterinary Technician	Veterinarian
Medical Records Technician	Histologic Technician	Physician
Admitting Clerk	Medical Records Technician	Occupational Therapist
Animal Caretaker	Administrative Clerk	Speech Pathologist/Audiologist
	Emergency Medical Technician	Medical Physicist
	Respiratory Therapist and Technician	Nurse Practitioner
	Registered Nurse	Nutritionist
	Ultrasound Technologist	Respiratory Therapist

* includes high school/technical education

Figure 6.2f

HUMAN RESOURCES/SERVICES

On-the-job Training and/or Specialized Training *	Community College	University
Child Care Worker	Police Supervisor	Administrative Law Judge
Author	Psychiatric Aide & Technician	Anthropologist
Commercial Artist	Substance Abuse Counselor	Preschool Teacher
Court Administrator	Compliance/Enforcement	College Administrator
Halfway House Manager	Corrections Officer	College Instructor
Legal Assistant	Driving Instructor	Elementary School Teacher
Library Technician &	Interior Designer	Employment Counselor
Private Investigator	Interpreter & Translator	Historian
Refuse Collector	Hazardous Waste Technician	Human Resource Specialist
Flight Attendant	Recreation Leader	Judge
Religious Worker	Truck Driver	Lawyer
Sheriff & Bailiff	Bus Driver	Librarian
Social Service Aide	Journalist	Market Research Analyst
Teacher Aide	Police Officer & Detective	Placement Specialist
Exercise/Aerobic Worker	Food Service Worker	Psychiatrist
Chef/Cook		School Administrator
Food/Beverage Svc. Personnel		School Counselor
Postal Clerk		Social Worker
Geriatric Aide		Urban & Regional Planner
		Clergy

* includes high school/technical education

BUSINESS & MANAGEMENT

On-the-job Training Specialized Training *	Community College	University
Wholesale Sales	Automotive Parts Sales	Software Engineer
Payroll Clerk	Assistant Buyer	Programmer Analyst
Sales Clerk	Store Manager	Market Research Analyst
Ticket Agent	Billing Clerk	School Administrator
Meter Reader	General Bookkeeper	Health Service Administrator
Cashier	Electronic Funds Transfer Coord.	Job Analyst
Salesperson, General	Brokerage Clerk	Accountant
Collection Clerk	Court Clerk	Tax Accountant
Account Teller	Computer Support Specialist	Auditor
Hotel Clerk	Systems Programmer	Health Services Administrator
Automotive Rental Clerk	Legal Assistant/Secretary	User Support Analyst
Payroll Clerk	Restaurant/Food Service Manager	City Manager
Tax Preparer	Medical Secretary	Air Traffic Controller
Radio Dispatcher	Travel Agent	Employee Benefits Manager
File Clerk	Property Manager	College Administrator
Computer Technician	Office Manager	Economist
Mail Clerk	Insurance Agent/Manager	
Messenger	Caterer	
	Claims Representative	
	Real Estate	

Figure 6.2g

IV. Your Top 25 Person Matches™ To Explore

You are a person, not a job title. Yet, when it comes to choosing careers, people tend to only think in terms of job titles or job descriptions, not the individuals behind them. That's why the Kuder Career Search developed Person Match™. Person Match™ compares your interests with over 1500 real people in satisfying careers. Below are 25 persons whose activity preferences are most like yours. They have all been fortunate to get into occupations they like – that are satisfying to them in significant ways. You can learn more about them by reading their job sketches online at www.kuder.com. Simply double click on the title you would like to explore.

Credit Representative

Executive Secretary #1

Teacher, Jr. High Social Studies

State Legislator

Librarian, School #2

Market Communicate Specialist

Manager, Auto Tire Company

Bank Teller #1

Manager, Personnel Dept.

Elementary School Aide

Salesperson, Mortgage Firm

Office Manager #8

Nurse (RN) #5

Foreign Services Officer, State

U.S. Army, Soldier/Recruiter

Religious Leader #8

Manager, Parole Office

Teacher Elementary Level, Librarian

Religious Leader #14

Federal Clerical Employee

Biological Technician

School Administrator #2

Medical Assistant #2

Vice President of Manufacturing #1

Commercial Bank Jr. Loan Officer

Now continue to the next page for information on how to continue your exploration.

Figure 6.2h

V. Continuing Your Career Exploration

So now you know many people who have similar interests to your own. You know what careers they are in, what they do in a normal day, what they like and dislike, how they got started and what they might do next. But what are YOU going to do next? How about beginning to make some career plans? The steps below will help you get started.

1. From the information in this report, you may formulate a tentative career goal of your own.

Using your career activity preferences, write in a possible career goal here:

2. Explore the information sources available to assist you.

Find the Occupational Outlook Handbook in your school or community library or online at www.bls.gov/ocohome.htm. Look over the description of the work in the goal you wrote above. Write here the occupational outlook and/or salary levels you found:

Or, check out your state Career Information Delivery System. Your school guidance counselor or career education coordinator can assist you in accessing the system. Write here the outlook and salary or a summary of the knowledge, skills and abilities needed for success in your career goal:

Use the power of the Internet to locate schools, colleges or universities that have programs of study that will help you achieve your goals. Write the names of two or three in here: (Be sure to visit the Kuder Career Search™ web site at WWW.KUDER.COM for links to helpful sites!)

3. What other jobs and careers are similar to the goal you named above? Write them here.

4. Who can you find working in a career similar to your goal?

Ask them the same questions we asked your Person Matches™, like what they do in a normal day, how they got started, what they like and what they plan to do next.

5. Have you begun a portfolio of your school and work achievements that you could show a potential employer? Yes? No? Why not?

6. Do you have a resume?

Can you write a persuasive cover letter? Can you make a positive impression in a job interview? If you answered "no" to any of these questions, who can you find to help you?Write their names here:

7. Be sure to re-assess your career interests.

Interests change and develop as you get older. Students should complete the Kuder Career Search™ at approximately two year intervals; adults should re-assess every five years.

Figure 6.2i

Activity Preference Profile

The first section of the KCS, the Activity Preference Profile, systematically samples the test takers' preferences on 10 career-related scales: Art, Communications, Computations, Human Services, Mechanical, Music, Nature, Office Detail, Sales/Management, and Science/Technical. Brief descriptions of each of the 10 scales are included on the test results report. The 10 preference scales are listed in rank order, with scores shown in percentiles based on combining the results from males and females in the reference pool. For example, if the client's protocol lists the Sales/Management preference first, with a score of 98, that indicates that the client's primary interest preference is in business and that she or he scored higher than 98% of the reference pool.

The norm group consists of workers who have been in their jobs for 3 or more years and describe themselves as satisfied and happy. They completed the identical KCS items that the clients completed. It is important to remind clients that their own list of activity preferences ranks the activities they most prefer to those they least prefer, and the scales may or may not have a relationship to their skills and abilities in those areas. Occupations typically include more than one or two of the career-related activities measured in the Activity Preference Profile section of the KCS. One artist may have his or her top three activity preference rankings as 1) Art, 2) Human Services, and 3) Sales/Management, whereas another artist may rank 1) Communications, 2) Sales/Management, and 3) Art, as the top three preferences. Not every employee in the same occupation has identical Activity Preference Profile rankings. It is important to introduce early in the interpretation process that the client's pattern of responses on the KCS will be compared with those of other people. Complete Learning Experience 6.3 (presented later in this chapter) to learn more about the 10 Activity Preferences.

Kuder Career Clusters

The second section of the KCS protocol, the Kuder clusters, depicts groupings of occupational similarities and differences. Each cluster contains similarities in interests, distinguishing each cluster from the other clusters. The standard clusters on the KCS resemble the six types of Holland (1973), as described earlier under General Occupational Themes of the Strong Interest Inventory. Each Kuder cluster (Arts/Communication, Business/Management, Environmental/ Agriculture, Health Services, Human Resources, Industrial/ Engineering) is defined on the KCS protocol. Cluster scores are the test taker's mean scores "on an aggregate of all criterion persons in occupations subsumed in each cluster" (Zytowski, 1999); that is, a person who scores high on the Human Resources cluster can be said to have the interests of those persons.

One of the innovative changes with the 1999 KCS is the capability of customizing the number and description of the clusters for each customer. This customization process is particularly useful for assisting schools with the implementation of their school-to-work pathways or clusters. In 1994, the School-to-Work Opportunities Act was signed into law, making it advisable for schools to have career assessments available to assist students with their career exploration and decision making. The KCS can be customized to coincide with the same clusters or pathways used by individual schools, school systems, or states. For example, the state of Michigan uses six clusters or pathways (Arts and Communication; Business, Management, Marketing, and Technology; Engineering/Manufacturing and Industrial Technology; Health Sciences; Human Services; and Natural Resources and Agriscience), whereas the state of Indiana uses 14 clusters or pathways (Agriculture and Natural Resources; Art, Media, and Communications; Engineering, Science, and Technologies; Manufacturing and Processing; Mechanical Repair and Precision Crafts; Business, Management, and Finance; Building and Construction; Educational Services; Health Services; Personal and Commercial Services; Legal, Social, and Recreational Services; Protective Services; Marketing, Sales, and Promotion; and Transportation). The results on the Career Clusters section of the KCS report can be depicted to coincide with the clusters or pathways of individual states' or school systems' pathways or can be scored with the traditional six Kuder clusters.

Exploring Careers by Educational Level

The third section on the Kuder Career Search protocol is depicted in the same clusters assigned in the second section, except that in this third section, occupational titles are listed alphabetically under each cluster heading. The occupational listings are separated into three categories: those requiring (a) on-the-job or specialized training, (b) community college education, and (c) a university education. These occupational titles are presented to encourage further career exploration within the client's preferred clusters. Further descriptions of all the occupational titles can be found in the *Occupational Outlook Handbook* (U.S. Department of Labor Statistics, 2000).

Person Match

The Person Match section of the KCS is not only the newest addition to the Kuder assessments but also a new conceptualization of the notion of vocational matching. This KCS section uses Spearman's rank-order correlation to compare the client's activity preference profile with each of the profiles of more than 2,500 men and women in the reference pool. To construct the Person Match section, each individual completes a seven-item Occupational Survey inquiring about his or her education, job description, entrance into current occupation, future plans, and satisfaction. These mini-autobiographies comprise the Person Match scale of the KCS.

In 1980, Kuder wrote that "instead of matching people to jobs, why not match people to people in jobs?" (p. 1). This style of gathering vocational information and presenting information to clients requires a different approach to interpreting inventory results. The interpretation becomes based on stories and narratives instead of on the interpretation of numbers and scores. Zytowski (1999) recommended using the following phrase: "These people have preferences that are very similar to yours. They are in different kinds of jobs or occupations that might be satisfactory to you—possibilities you might consider" (p. 5).

The idea of "possible selves" is derived from the work of Markus and Nurius (1986), and its application to the counseling field was introduced by Meara, Day, Chalk, and Phelps (1995) and Krieshok, Hastings, Ebberwein, Wettersten, and Owen (1999). The career client completing a KCS will get a sense of the multiple vocational possibilities through the pattern of Activity Preferences and Kuder clusters, combined with the Person Match sketches (see Figure 6.2h for examples of Person Match sketches).

Each of the autobiographical job sketches was provided by a "real" worker who was asked to supply details about his or her career. The first collected sketches appeared in the *Kuder Book of People Who Like Their Work* (Hornaday & Gibson, 1995). The KCS mail-back protocols include the autobiographical sketches of the test taker's top 5 person matches. The online KCS provides links to examine the sketches of the top 25 persons (from more than 2,500) matched to the test taker.

The Person Match section relies on the notion of possible selves. The identified job sketches may represent a wide variety of occupations, which at first glance may not appear to be similar to the test taker. The similarities lie in the autobiographies, not in the job titles. Some sketches may offer similarities in themes (such as gaining satisfaction through assisting others, having organization and predictability in the course of the day) or similarities in values (such as independence through self-employment, high-prestige jobs, salary, or way of life). The autobiographical sketches provided on the test taker's protocol offer examples of how an individual person took his or her pattern of activity preferences and interests and expressed them in a career. The test takers may then realize that they, too, could express themselves and find satisfaction and success in a variety of careers.

As described in the next chapter, the practitioner can enhance the test takers' understanding of their results by assisting them in generating their own vocational autobiography and in identifying the themes and similarities between their story and the identified job sketches. This conversation may lead to exploration of the occupations in the job sketches, perhaps careers not previously considered, or even the generation of occupational titles closely related to those in the sketches. Savickas (1993) stated that career counseling in the 21st century will be about stories and not about scores. The Kuder Career Search With Person Match may be the first career assessment that addresses this philosophical shift and assists clients in designing their own career stories. Discover more about your own career story by completing Learning Experience 6.4, presented at the end of this chapter.

Strengths and Weaknesses

As is true of the Strong Interest Inventory, the Kuder vocational interest assessments have been in existence since the first third of the 20th century, a strength unmatched in any other area of vocational assessment. The Kuder assessments have developed along with vocational advancements (adding new job titles and providing information on training requirements) and technological advancements (updating scoring procedures and offering online assessment). Being a forerunner in online assessment speaks to the test developer's and publisher's commitment to accessibility. A variety of tutorial exercises, case study materials, and client worksheets are also available on the Kuder Web page. Another strength of the KCS is the capability to customize the reports to match an individual state's career pathways or clusters. To provide an even more complete vocational assessment package, the publishers are also developing work values and vocational skills assessments, which will combine with results from the KCS to form the base of the Kuder Online Portfolio.

Weaknesses of the KCS include the newness of the administration format and the Person Match concept. Although both are valuable tools from a clinical viewpoint, neither has been adequately researched to offer validity and reliability data of equal magnitude to previous versions of the Kuder assessments (such as the Kuder Occupational Interest Survey) (Kuder & Zytowski, 1991) or of other current vocational interest inventories. The person matches are based on a new way of conceptualizing vocational matching (Kuder, 1980), of scoring (Zytowski, 1999), and of interpretation. More materials need to be published that support the psychometrics, online administration, and interpretative procedures.

SII and KCS Strengths and Limitations With Various Populations

Not all career clients aspire to higher education. When choosing an interest inventory for non-college-bound clients, the clinician should not only preview the occupational titles included on the assessment protocol but also consider the appropriateness of the reading level when making an assessment selection. Interest inventory results should assist clients in further exploration, and occupational titles and/or reading levels that are beyond the understanding of the client could negate potential benefits.

Researchers have been examining cross-cultural vocational interest differences for decades, and the results have been conflicting. Many of the more recent studies have looked for patterns of interests across cultures, mostly assessed with Holland typology (Day & Bedeian, 1995; Fouad & Dancer, 1992; Leung, Ivey, & Suzuki, 1994; Swanson, 1992). Yet several debates still remain: (a) Do interest inventories accurately access interests across cultures? (b) Does interest assessment merely reflect the held stereotypes of our culture? or (c) Does interest assessment perpetuate stereotypes? Because research could be cited to support all sides of those debates, it is beyond the scope of this book to offer definitive answers and conclusions. However, in this chapter, recommendations for the selection and administration of interest inventories have been considered.

When selecting an interest assessment for any client, it is important to consider the client's access to vocational information. Clients with limited experience with the world of work, due to such things as socioeconomic level, lack of role models, isolated environment, or inadequate public education, may not have the resources necessary to complete an interest inventory. This may be more true of the Strong Interest Inventory because it queries test takers about their interests in specific occupational titles, whereas the Kuder Career Search asks clients to react to everyday activities rather than occupations. All clients do not have equal access to information about occupations. Clinicians also need to consider access to information when interpreting results to clients because both the SII and KCS include occupational titles in their scales, and both are used to promote exploration.

Another selection consideration is the representation of diversity in the norm pools. Demographics are generally reported in technical manuals (SII) (Harmon et al., 1994). We recommend that clinicians review the manuals prior to administration to confirm that the inventory is appropriate for their clients. Because the KCS has been available only since 1999, the test developers and publishers are in the process of preparing such information about the KCS scales, specifically about the use of Person Match with diverse populations. Because the Person Match autobiographies do not contain information about race or gender, intuitively it would seem that eliciting individual vocational stories in relationship to the Person Match sketches reduces the likelihood of promoting stereotypes and discrimination. Further study and research are necessary to confirm this notion.

A third recommendation is to maintain standardization of inventory administration, as outlined in the SII and KCS materials. Deleting or adding administration instructions only provides the opportunity for offering a different assessment experience across cultures. Besides client understanding of administration instructions, there are additional factors to consider for administering English-language versions to international students. For example, it is not clear that all interest inventory scales (such as occupational titles or career clusters) are applicable to international vocational structures. It is also not clear that vocational titles and concepts easily translate to other languages.

Deciding to administer a vocational interest assessment to any client should include consideration of individual differences and the appropriateness of the information to the individual's career concerns. We suggest there may be more factors to consider in regards to test construction and individual needs when selecting and administering interest inventories across all cultures.

Summary

The use of vocational assessments can brighten the palette of vocational interventions for the benefit of the client and can highlight the clinician's understanding of the client's concerns. This chapter introduced interest inventory assessment, specifically in regard to the administration and use of the Strong Interest Inventory and the Kuder Career Search With Person Match. The content of each scale on both inventories was described and illustrated in Figure 6.1 (SII) and Figure 6.2 (KCS). The strengths and limitations of both were outlined, along with considerations for cross-cultural administration. We encourage the reader to complete the learning exercises found at the end of the chapter to increase familiarity with the experience of "being interest inventoried." We also encourage you to consider completing the assessments yourself. The Strong Interest Inventory can be obtained through Consulting Psychologists Press, 3803 East Bay Shore Drive, Palo Alto, CA 94303, and the Kuder Career Search With Person Match can be purchased online at www. kuder.com.

Learning Experiences

Learning Experience 6.1

The film *Rudy* depicts the outcome of a young man's interest in football, specifically the football played at Notre Dame University. Another film, *October Sky*, documents another young man's pursuance of an interest in rockets. After viewing both films, reflect for yourself (either on paper or with a peer) times in your life when having interests in things you never believed were possible led to varied outcomes.

Learning Experience 6.2

First you need to have access to the classified section of your local newspaper. Perusing every alphabetical listing, generate a list of job openings that attract your attention as interesting positions. Next, sort those job titles into your best estimate of their primary Holland (1973) type, as described in the following paragraphs:

Realistic—work done typically alone outdoors, with a preference for machines, animals, plants, and nature

Investigative—work done typically alone in discovering how things work; includes investigation, analyzing, and finding answers and solutions

Artistic—work done alone or in groups involving creative self-expression through art, music, dance, writing, and so on

Social—Work done with others; nurturing and looking out for others' interests and welfare

Enterprising—work typically done with others in business; influencing, buying and selling, managing, profit and loss

Conventional—work done with others or alone, but work with structure and organization, right and wrong answers, clarity, and distinct outcomes

You may begin to see a pattern of responses in which some of the RIASEC types have more job title listings than others. Those with the most job titles could be an indication of your Holland type because those are the fields that caught your interest.

Learning Experience 6.3

Estimate your own rank ordering of the KCS Activity Preference Profile scales, placing them in order from most prefer to least prefer. Next, list those individuals in your own life who you believe best represent each of the 10 preferences. Note any patterns you observe regarding family influence, friends and peers with whom you generally associate, and scales where you personally know the most individuals.

Art: creative activities that make beauty. High scorers work with colors and designs in painting, photography, and decorations. This includes clothing designers, architects, illustrators, and florists. People with artistic hobbies do things such as watercolor painting, cartooning, and flower arranging.

Communications: activities that use language, either writing or speaking it. People high on this preference may be English teachers, write books, or work for TV stations, newspapers, and magazines. Hobbies include acting in community theater, reading for enjoyment, or keeping a journal.

Computations: activities that use numbers. Accountants, tax preparers, bookkeepers, claims adjusters, and inventory clerks generally score high on this activity. People who score high on this scale may enjoy hobbies such as card games or keeping statistics on their favorite sports team.

Human Services: activities that help other people. Those who score high on this scale may be teachers, counselors, or church workers. Others are salespersons and child care workers. Many people do volunteer work besides their regular jobs—another way to use this preference.

Mechanical: activities that come from knowing how things work and using tools and machines to make or repair things. People who build houses or repair cars or office machines usually score high on this scale. Enjoyment of these activities can lead to hobbies such as woodworking, flying model airplanes, and many kinds of handicrafts.

Music: activities that involve making or listening to music, singing or playing an instrument, or leading a musical group. Few people make their living as professional musicians, but many play music for fun, collect records, or enjoy going to concerts.

Nature: activities you do outdoors, such as growing or caring for plants or animals. Farmers, gardeners, and people who raise animals score high on this scale. These preferences often lead to hobbies such as growing flowers or vegetables, entering animals in shows, or outdoor recreation such as camping or hiking.

Office Detail: activities that require keeping track of things, people, or information, such as those involved in word processing and database management. People who like these activities are likely to be office managers, ticket agents, or hotel clerks, among others. Doll, baseball card, or other collectors would score high on this scale.

Sales/Management: activities that deal with people, such as leading a team of workers or selling things or ideas. Auto, home, and insurance salespeople; sales managers; and people elected to government positions prefer these activities. Volunteering on a political campaign and asking for contributions for charity are other examples.

Science/Technology: activities such as discovering or understanding the natural and physical world. People who score high on this scale are scientists, doctors, engineers, medical technicians, nurses, and computer repairers, among others. People who like to try new cooking recipes, keep weather records, or breed new flowers for fun may score high on this scale.*

Learning Experience 6.4

Write your own vocational mini-autobiography by addressing the following items:

---

*Used by permission of the publisher, NCASI.

(a) Describe your educational background.
(b) Describe your current or most favorite job description.
(c) How did you enter your current occupation?
(d) What are your future vocational plans?
(e) What provides you the most satisfaction in your career?

If you have recently completed a Kuder Career Search With Person Match, compare your story with those of your top 25 Person Matches.

Discussion Questions

1. What theoretical explanations have been offered to explain the usefulness of learning about vocational interests? How could knowing the results of your own SII or KCS be useful to you?

2. What are the strengths and weaknesses of online vocational interest assessment?

3. Are interest inventories appropriate for all clients?

References

Anastasi, A. (1982). *Psychological testing* (5th ed.). New York: Macmillan.

Campbell, D. P. (1974). *Manual for the SVIB-SCII*. Stanford, CA: Stanford University Press.

Campbell, D. P., Borgen, F. H., Eastes, S., Johansson, C. B., & Peterson, R. A. (1968). A set of Basic Interest Scales for the Strong Vocational Interest Blank for men. *Journal of Applied Psychological Monographs, 52*(6), 1-54.

Consulting Psychologists Press. (1994). *The Strong Interest Inventory: Item booklet and answer sheet*. Palo Alto, CA: Author.

Day, D. V., & Bedeian, A. G. (1995). Personality similarity and work-related outcomes among African-American nursing personnel: A test of the supplementary model of person-environment congruence. *Journal of Vocational Behavior, 46*, 55-70.

Diamond, E. E. (1990). The Kuder Occupational Interest Survey. In C. E. Watkins, Jr. & V. L. Campbell (Eds.), *Testing in counseling practice* (pp. 211-239). Hillsdale, NJ: Lawrence Erlbaum.

Fouad, N. A., & Dancer, L. S. (1992). Cross-cultural structure of interests: Mexico and the United States. *Journal of Vocational Behavior, 40*, 129-143.

Freyd, M. (1923). *Occupational interests*. Chicago: C. H. Stoelting.

Gati, I. (1979). A hierarchical model for the structure of vocational interests. *Journal of Vocational Behavior, 15*, 90-106.

Hansen, J. C. (1985). *User's guide for the SVIB-SII*. Palo Alto, CA: Consulting Psychologists Press.

Hansen, J. C. (1990). Interpretation of the Strong Interest Inventory. In C. E. Watkins, Jr. & V. L. Campbell (Eds.), *Testing in counseling practice* (pp. 177-209). Hillsdale, NJ: Lawrence Erlbaum.

Hansen, J. C., & Campbell, D. P. (1985). *Manual for the SVIB-SCII* (4th ed.). Stanford, CA: Stanford University Press.

Harmon, L. W., Hansen, J. C., Borgen, F. H., & Hammer, A. L. (1994). *The Strong Interest Inventory: Applications and technical guide*. Palo Alto, CA: Consulting Psychologists Press.

Hirsh, S. K., & McEvoy, E. (1986). *Using the Strong in organizations*. Palo Alto, CA: Consulting Psychologists Press.

Holland, J. L. (1973). *Making vocational choices: A theory of careers*. Englewood Cliffs, NJ: Prentice Hall.

Hornaday, J. A., & Gibson, L. A. (1995). *The Kuder book of people who like their work*. Amherst, NH: Motivation Press.

Kornhauser, A. W. (1927). Results from a quantitative questionnaire of likes and dislikes used with a group of college freshmen. *Journal of Applied Psychology, 11*, 146-151.

Krieshok, T., Hastings, S., Ebberwein, C., Wettersten, K., & Owen, A. (1999). Telling a good story: Using narratives in vocational rehabilitation with veterans. *Career Development Quarterly, 47*, 204-214.

Kuder, F. (1966). *General manual: Kuder DD Occupational Interest Survey*. Chicago: Science Research Associates.

Kuder, F. (1980). Person matching. *Educational and Psychological Measurement, 40*, 1-8.

Kuder, F., & Zytowski, D. (1991). *Kuder Occupational Interest Survey Form DD, general manual*. Monterey, CA: California Testing Bureau.

Lent, R. W., Brown, S. D., & Hackett, G. (1996). Career development from a social cognitive perspective. In D. Brown & L. Brooks (Eds.), *Career choice and development* (3rd ed.). San Francisco: Jossey-Bass.

Leung, S. A., Ivey, D., & Suzuki, L. (1994). Factors affecting the career aspirations of Asian Americans. *Journal of Counseling and Development, 72*, 404-410.

Lowman, R. L. (1991). *The clinical practice of career assessment.* Washington, DC: American Psychological Association.

Markus, H., & Nurius, P. (1986). Possible selves. *American Psychologist, 41,* 954-969.

Meara, N. M., Day, J. D., Chalk, L. M., & Phelps, R. E. (1995). Possible selves: Applications for career counseling. *Journal of Career Assessment, 3,* 259-277.

National Career Assessment Services. (1999). *The Kuder Career Search With Person Match.* Adel, IA: Author.

Parsons, F. (1909). *Choosing a vocation.* New York: Agathon.

Prediger, D. J. (1982). Dimensions underlying Holland's hexagon: Missing link between interests and occupations. *Journal of Vocational Behavior, 21,* 259-287.

Prince, J. P., & Heiser, L. J. (2000). *Essentials of career assessment.* New York: John Wiley.

Remmers, H. H. (1929). The measurement of interest differences between students of engineering and agriculture. *Journal of Applied Psychology, 13,* 105-119.

Roe, A. (1956). *The psychology of occupations.* New York: John Wiley.

Savickas, M. L. (1993). Career counseling in the postmodern era. *Journal of Cognitive Psychotherapy, 7,* 205-215.

Shivy, V. A., Phillips, S. D., & Koehly, L. M. (1996). Knowledge organization as a factor in career intervention outcome: A multi- dimensional scaling analysis. *Journal of Counseling Psychology, 43,* 178-186.

Shivy, V. A., Rounds, J., & Jones, L. E. (1999). Applying vocational interest models to naturally occurring occupational perceptions. *Journal of Counseling Psychology, 46*(2), 207-217.

Strong, E. K., Jr. (1927). *Vocational Interest Blank.* Stanford, CA: Stanford University Press.

Strong, E. K., Jr. (1933). *Vocational Interest Blank for Women.* Stanford, CA: Stanford University Press.

Super, D. E., Osborne, W. L., Walsh, D. J., Brown, S. D., & Niles, S. G. (1992). Developmental assessment and counseling: The C-DAC model. *Journal of Counseling and Development, 71,* 74-80.

Swanson, J. L. (1992). The structure of vocational interests for African-American college students. *Journal of Vocational Behavior, 40,* 144-157.

U.S. Department of Labor. (1991). *Dictionary of occupational titles.* Washington, DC: Government Printing Office.

U.S. Department of Labor Statistics. (2000). *Occupational outlook handbook.* Washington, DC: Bureau of Labor Statistics.

Walsh, W. B., & Betz, N. E. (2001). *Tests and assessments* (4th ed.). Upper Saddle River, NJ: Prentice Hall.

Zytowski, D. (1999). *Kuder Career Search: Preview manual.* Adel, IA: National Career Development Services.

Zytowski, D. (2002). *Kuder Career Search: Users' manual.* Adel, IA: National Career Development Services.

7

Interpretation of Career Interest Inventories

There can be an artistic quality to the process of explaining interest inventory results to individual clients or to groups (or classes). The goal for this chapter is not only to present guidelines and procedural recommendations for interpretation methods but also to encourage you to be thoughtful of the process from the client's perspective and to inspire you to use your creativity in presenting results that correspond to the career dilemma of each and every client.

First, let's turn to the literature to learn what has already been discovered about offering vocational assessment results to career clients. The early recommendations for providing interest inventory interpretations coincided with the introduction of the Strong Vocational Interest Blank (Bixler & Bixler, 1946; Darley, 1941; Strong, 1943). One of the first empirical studies (Dressel & Matteson, 1950) included support for the use of a client-centered interpretation approach, stating that clients who participated in the interpretation process gained more self-understanding, more career choice certainty, and more satisfaction with the testing experience. Gustad and Tuma (1957) investigated four different interpretation methods but discovered the method itself had no significant impact on client self-learning. Wright (1963) assessed differences in individual and group interpretation methods of the Kuder Preference Record and learned that individually counseled students displayed more accurate recall and were more satisfied with the interpretation process. Oliver (1977) also endorsed individual inventory interpretations for enhancing career choice certainty after investigating the effectiveness of individual, group, and programmed materials. However, she found no significant differences between the three interpretation methods in regard to their influence on increasing the frequency of career information-seeking behavior. A study by Barak and Friedkes (1982) concluded that the content of the interpretation sessions affected client outcome, not the process or method. From this sample of research covering four decades, there appears to be more support for individualized interpretation procedures, yet no interpretation style was identified as the most efficacious.

The change in focus of the interest inventory interpretation research of the 1980s and early 1990s reflected the decades' fascination with the computer (Gati, 1987; Gati & Blumberg, 1991; Matarazzo, 1986; Murphy, 1987; Reardon, 1987; Sinnett & Albott, 1987). Gati and Blumberg (1991) concluded that reliance on computers may be useful in offering clients a more complete interest inventory interpretation. Another set of studies (Hoffman, Spokane, & Magoon, 1981; Randahl, Hansen, & Haverkamp, 1993; Toman & Savickas, 1997) considered the influence of interest inventory interpretations on increasing clients' career exploration behaviors. Randahl et al. (1993) identified this interpretation outcome as "exploration validity," which they defined as "the power of interest inventories to facilitate career exploration activities such as talking to professionals, seeking vocational counseling, and so on" (p. 423). Drawing from the conclusions identified in the career development and assessment literature, this chapter includes interpretation models that promote vocational exploration, as well as models that consider the efficacy of delivering individualized and computer-assisted interest inventory interpretations.

In the remaining sections of this chapter, two interpretation models will be presented along with client worksheets, handouts, and case examples. One interpretation model applicable for use with the Strong Interest Inventory® (SII) comes from a recent text by Jeffrey Prince and Lisa Heiser (2000), *Essentials of Career Interest Assessment*, and five interpretation principles authored by Donald Zytowski (1999) appear in *Vocational Interests: Meaning, Measuring, and Counseling Use.* The accompanying worksheets and exercises, however, were designed specifically for this text, and you are encouraged to consider them as catalysts for designing your own supplemental materials to fit your unique clientele and setting. Familiarity with the content of the Strong Interest Inventory and the Kuder Career Search With Person Match (KCS) is recommended prior to applying the materials in this chapter. That familiarity can be gained by first reviewing Chapter 6 or by reading the more complete materials found in the assessment manuals (SII [Harmon, Hansen, Borgen, & Hammer, 1994]; KCS [Zytowski, 1999]).

Chapter 6 presented two figures: Figure 6.1 contains the Strong Interest Inventory results of a fictitious client named Anna, whereas Figure 6.2 contains her Kuder Career Search With Person Match results. One of the authors (S.T.) completed the paper-and-pencil version of the SII and the online version of the KCS "as if" she were Anna, yet taking into consideration each element of her case study unique to her. Anna's complete case study is included in Chapter 8, but the results of her vocational interest assessments are included here to illustrate interest inventory interpretation procedures.

Interpreting the Strong Interest Inventory

Clinician Preparation

Prior to the interpretation session, clinicians should take the time to review the assessment report. Prince and Heiser (2000) stated that first it is important to "assess the validity of the profile" (p. 28) by referring to two numbers that appear on the final page of the SII report. Validity is indicated if at least 300 (out of 317 questions) are completed by the test taker, as indicated on the SII as "Total Responses" (Harmon et al., 1994). Refer to the end of Figure 6.1 to see that Anna has completed 316 of 317 possible Total Responses, indicating that her profile meets this first indication of validity.

The second score to consider is "Infrequent Responses," also located on the last page of the report. This score reflects the number of answers that are infrequently endorsed (as compared to the typical responses from those of the same gender), including 14 items for men and 11 for women with scores ranging from 7 to −8 for men and from 5 to −7 for women. Because infrequently endorsed items are subtracted from a given constant, only the negative scores need consideration for the purpose of assessing validity. A negative score on the Infrequent Response scale may indicate that the client completed answers at random or merely has comparatively unusual interest patterns. Unusual interests can be identified by considering patterns or combinations of scores on the Basic Interests Scales and Occupational Scales (Harmon et al., 1994). Anna's Infrequent Response score of 5 indicates no unusual response patterns.

Following confirmation of validity, it may be most efficient to proceed through the six pages of the SII report in consecutive order. Because the "Snapshot" on the first page of the report provides a summary of the following pages, the clinician could begin by comparing the snapshots of each scale (General Occupational Themes, Basic Interest Scales, and the Occupational Scales) to the larger pattern of all the high and low scores. Familiarity with Holland (1973) types is essential for proceeding with an SII interpretation session. The client's inventoried interests and Holland type could then be compared with interview and case note impressions of Holland type and expressed interests.

In reviewing Anna's SII results, the clinician would note that her three highest General Occupational Themes are Social, Conventional, and Artistic and that these coincide with her highest "Basic Interests" (office services, religious activities, culinary arts) and appear in her highest Occupational Scales (credit manager, elementary school teacher, speech pathologist, food service manager). For Anna, her inventoried interests coincide with her expressed interests in education and religion, as noted in the case study, and her previous employment as a nursing home aide and grocery store checkout clerk.

Before proceeding, the clinician should also review the Personal Style Scales and the Summary of Item Responses on the final page of the SII report. Each score on the four "Personal Style Scale" continuum could also be compared to the General Occupation Themes, Basic Interests, and previously acquired information about the client. The Summary of Item Responses could provide an indication of inflated or deflated scores throughout the SII, if the client answered consistently at an extreme (such as 80% dislike or 80% like) when

Step 1: Introduce the results

Step 2: Explain Holland's (1973) theory and General Occupational Themes

Step 3: Discuss the Basic Interest Scales

Step 4: Interpret the Occupational Scales

Step 5: Review the Personal Style Scales

Step 6: Summarize results

Step 7: Encourage exploration beyond the profile

The following paragraphs will contain recommendations for using Prince and Heiser's (2000) seven-step model, several client worksheets designed specifically for this text, and applications of the steps to the case of Anna.

Step 1: Introduce the Results

During an interpretation session, you may discover a tendency to sound more like a teacher than a clinician. To counteract this tendency, you could begin the interpretation session by asking the client for his or her thoughts, feelings, and reactions to the assessment experience. You could also ask the client to review with you the initial reasons for including an interest inventory in his or her career counseling process and to describe what he or she hopes to gain from the results. It is important to repeat several times throughout the course of the SII explanation that interest inventories assess interests and not vocational skills or work values. Also, remind clients that there is no vocational assessment that will tell them the "perfect" career for them but that the SII will give them a structure for further vocational exploration.

It may be important for some clients to know what happens to their results after the interpretation session. Confidentiality can be crucial for some clients pursuing a career change or for college counseling center clients who need reassurance that their assessment results are not in their permanent academic records, accessible by faculty members and academic advisers. Your introduction should include an explanation of your site's policies for storing assessment results.

completing the SII items. If extreme response sets are noted, the answer sheet could be reviewed by the clinician, item by item, to compare the style of responses with prior clinical information or psychological test results from the case file. Again, refer to Figure 6.1 to locate the Personal Style Scales and Summary of Item Responses on Anna's SII test report, noting that she indicated "disliked" (more than "liked") at a higher response percentage. Her percentage of "dislike" responses could indicate that she is already somewhat selective and can distinguish between what interests her and what does not. As well, a high percentage of "dislike" responses could indicate the need for further assessment of an overall negativity to life or possible depression. Refer to Chapter 8 for further assessment reports of Anna's personality and depression levels.

One purpose for reviewing each page of the SII report is for the clinician to gain familiarity with the results prior to explaining them to the client and to not go blindly into an interpretation session. Another reason for review is to begin the process of integrating the scales (comparing and contrasting results), a process that will continue during the interpretation session with the client. A third reason is to look for scores that may appear contradictory or problematic for the client and to anticipate the need for further details or discussion. A final reason for previewing the SII results prior to the session is to consider how the inventoried responses coincide with the client's story in preparation for merging the assessment results with expressed interests and vocational history. Learning Experience 7.1 (presented on page 217) can help you, as a student or as a clinician, practice the skill and artistry of merging SII scale results.

Explaining SII Results to the Client

It is important to enter an interpretation session with a game plan, but one that is flexible enough to address the unique situations each client brings to counseling. It is possible to adequately interpret SII results in one 50-minute session, but on many occasions it is necessary to extend the SII explanation into a second session. Prince and Heiser (2000, p. 35) have provided a seven-step interpretation model that is both a clear game plan and contains flexibility:

Your introduction could conclude with an agenda for the session, using the Snapshot on page 1 of the profile to illustrate the scales to be discussed. Clients are frequently tempted to turn immediately to the Occupational Scales, yet providing the Snapshot as an outline for proceeding through the results may help postpone their temptation to consider only occupational titles. Because the Snapshot contains a great deal of data, you could indicate that each section (General Occupational Themes, Basic Interest Scales, and Occupational Scales) will be explained in more depth as you and the client proceed through the explanation together.

Step 2: Explain Holland's Theory and General Occupational Themes

Using, again, the Snapshot on the first page of the SII, highlight the first block containing the six Holland (1973) types of Realistic, Investigative, Artistic, Social, Enterprising, and Conventional. Because the next two sections of the profile are structured around the six types, it is important to take the time during this step in the process to adequately explain the nature of each type, including Holland's theoretical concepts of consistency, congruence, and differentiation. It can be useful to draw the hexagon model for the client or to have prepared handouts containing graphics that illustrate consistency (closeness on the hexagon or similarities between adjacent types), congruence (degree of similarity between individual interests and interests supported in the work environment), and differentiation (differences between high scores and low scores, reflecting distinction between likes and dislikes). You can review Holland typology in Chapter 6 of this text. Outlines for client handouts are available in several sources, including Hirsh and McEvoy (1986) or Prince (1995).

The following worksheet could help you and your client extend your understanding of Holland (1973) typology, by identifying general work tasks for each of the six types or by considering the work tasks involved in the client's current or future work environments. Please feel free to use this worksheet for your clients, your students, or yourself and to modify it in any way that would be more fitting to the unique demands of your counseling setting.

Holland Typology Worksheet

Your SII results are structured using John Holland's (1973) model of typing individuals and work environments. Before reviewing your SII results, let's practice matching activities to the six Holland types. There are several ways to complete this worksheet: (a) match the work tasks on the next page with the RIASEC definitions, (b) fill in the work tasks of your current position and note which Holland type contains more

Holland Types	Work Tasks
Realistic people like to work outdoors, with machines, equipment, plants, animals. They are typically good at understanding mechanical things and not as comfortable working with ideas and people.	_____
Investigative people like to work with data and with information, analyzing how things work and solving problems through research or through investigation.	_____
Artistic people like to use their creativity through participating in or attending musical, art, dance, or writing activities. They highly value independence and creativity.	_____
Social people like to work with and help other people, nurturing and looking out for others' interests and welfare. They highly value friends and spending time with others.	_____
Enterprising people like to work in business management and tasks involving money and influence. They are often in the public eye or are climbing the corporate ladder.	_____
Conventional people like work that has structure, order, and organization. They appreciate tasks that have a right or wrong answer and prefer working with data and things.	_____

responses, or (c) fill in the work tasks that you hope to do in your future career and note which Holland type contains more responses.

Work Tasks	
Designing a brochure	Purchasing store merchandise
Repairing a tractor	Filing paperwork
Keeping bank records	Teaching in an elementary school
Determining a medical diagnosis	Fighting a forest fire
Singing in a Broadway show	Holding political office
Visiting ill church members	Writing greeting card texts
Working in a research lab	Owning a small business
Installing a new roof	Preparing billings
Counseling a career client	Analyzing statistics

After you are convinced that the client has a firm understanding of Holland theory and typology and of the interpretive comments accompanying his or her top two or three types (as depicted in the Snapshot), proceed to the second page of the SII report where the General Occupational Themes are depicted in RIASEC order with standard scores. The scores and score graphs may require some explanation if the client is not familiar with standard scores, score distributions, and reference groups.

The clinician typically can begin by explaining that the results can be viewed as standard scores (the numbers on the right side of each graph) or as comparisons to the reference group (the light and dark gray bar graphs in the center of each block). The standard scores may be of interest if the client wants to compare scores across the six Holland types or General Occupational Themes, whereas the bar graphs may be useful when considering the scores in relation to other people in the workforce. It can be useful to draw a bell curve over one of the bar graphs to illustrate how the center of the bar coincides with the mean, with 50% of the reference sample falling in the largest width of the bar, whereas the tails of the bar include 80% of the reference sample, and the remaining 10% fall at each end of the graph. The light gray bars (scores of females) and the dark gray bars (males) allow the clients to compare their own score (indicated as a dot) across genders, which could be useful if the client is entering a position where his or her coworkers would be mostly of the opposite gender.

By reviewing Figure 6.1b, you can see that Anna's three highest General Occupational Themes are Social, Conventional, and Artistic. The bar graphs indicate that her degree of similarity is highest with the Social types in the reference pool, with a standard score of 60, which falls near the 80% range for women. This score coincides with her expressed interests in education and helping professions.

Each General Occupational Theme (RIASEC type) should be addressed separately with your client, even those that contain the lowest scores. After so much time has been spent on instruction, it is advisable to draw the client back into the discussion by asking for his or her reaction to each score and graph and by asking for examples of how the General Occupational Themes match his or her history and self-understanding. The next section of the SII (Basic Interest Scales) depicts the scores in the same RIASEC format.

Step 3: Discuss the Basic Interest Scales

Under each (RIASEC) General Occupational Theme are 25 (more specified) interests typical of that theme type. Because the standard score and bar graph depictions should now be familiar to the client, the discussion can focus immediately on how each of the Basic Interest scores fits with the client's self-perception and vocational history. One way to approach the scales is to proceed in the order of the client's preferred Holland types; in the case of Anna, that would be in Social-Conventional-Artistic-Enterprising-Realistic-Investigative order. The assessment is sensitive enough to pick up interests the client may have expressed in hobbies, volunteer activities, or previous work environments. Some of the client's Basic Interests may be underdeveloped due to lack of training or exposure. Therefore, it is important to discuss the meaning of each in the client's life and to generate life and work history examples that reinforce (or contradict) the scores. To summarize the Basic Interest Scales, refer back to the Snapshot on the opening page of the profile. Anna's highest Basic Interests of office services, religious activities, culinary arts, computer activities, and music/dramatics coincide with her expressed interests, previous employment, and leisure activities.

Step 4: Interpret the Occupational Scales

Again, the organization of these scales coincides with the RIASEC types of the General Occupational Themes. One difference in this section, though, is that your client's scores are compared to those of individuals in those occupations rather than to the total reference group. Clients should be reminded, again, that these occupations drew their *interest* and are not indications of their skills or abilities. Also, it is advisable to repeat to clients that the occupational titles are intended to structure their continued career exploration and are not indications of their "perfect" jobs. You may get a laugh by suggesting to clients that they should refer to a psychic or tarot card reader for information about their "perfect" job, but that usually gets the point across. Discussion of each Occupational Scale can proceed in RIASEC order (as depicted on the report) or in the client's inventoried order (for Anna, that would be in SCAERI order).

For each theme, one column of information lists the Holland (1973) type code for that work environment using the same RIASEC types. Another column contains the individual's standardized score, with the final column depicting that score on a scale from "dissimilar interests" to "similar interests," in comparison to the interests of others in those occupations. Clients should be encouraged to research and explore those careers that scored highest for them. However, if an individual has been considering a career that received a low, midrange, or dissimilar score, clients should be reminded that interests can change as our life experiences and educational experiences change. The Occupational Scales that received the highest scores are listed in the Snapshot on the first page of the SII report. In addition, clients can go through each section of the Occupational Scales to identify other occupations they choose to include in their exploration process. The following worksheet may assist clients in identifying occupations to explore.

Vocational History Worksheet

To complete this worksheet, refer to the Occupational Scale scores reported on your *Strong Interest Inventory*. It may also be helpful to have a copy of your résumé handy to assist you in completing the left-hand column of the worksheet. The purpose of this exercise is to compare your past work history, volunteer activities, or hobbies with the Occupational Scales on which you received your highest scores. Begin by listing your past positions chronologically, with the most recent appearing on the top line.

Your Work, Volunteer Positions, or Hobbies	SII Occupational Scales
(List in chronological order with your most recent activities first)	(List the occupational scale that most closely resembles your work position or activity)
_____	
_____	
_____	
_____	
_____	
_____	
_____	
_____	

List here those occupations you plan to explore further—your exploration method—and the dates by which you would like to complete the method:

Occupation	Method of Exploration	Completion Date

Anna's Occupational Scale scores reveal that her further exploration activities could include gaining more information about elementary school teacher, special education teacher, speech pathologist, child care provider, banker, radiologic technologist, paralegal, audiologist, food service manager, and credit manager.

Step 5: Discuss the Personal Style Scales

The four scales assessing personal styles in work, learning, leadership, and risk/adventure are each measured along a continuum. The meanings of the right and left ends of each pole are clearly defined on the report. Midrange scores (46 to 54) indicate no strong preference. The Work Style continuum ranges from "prefers to work alone with data, things, and ideas" to "prefers to work with people as part of a team." Learning Environment styles are scored from "prefers practical learning; learning by doing" to "prefers academic environments." The Leadership Style scale goes from "not comfortable taking charge of others" to "comfortable taking charge and motivating others." The final scale, Risk Taking/Adventure, ranges from "dislikes adventure and risk taking" to "likes adventure and risk taking." Referring to Figure 6.1, you can see that Anna's styles include preferences for working with others (score of 65), learning by doing (score of 33), not leading or taking charge of others (score of 38), and a dislike of risk taking (score of 37).

Step 6: Summarize Results

During this portion of the SII explanation, your preparation and creativity will be valuable. After your client clearly understands the scores on each scale (General Occupational Themes, Basic Interest Scales, Occupational Scales, and Personal Style Scales) and has had the opportunity to respond to each score with examples from his or her own vocational history, you can begin to help the client merge and converge any similarities between scales. To begin, consider the context of the client's presenting career dilemma and his or her expressed interests, goals for counseling, and expectations of completing an interest inventory. Each client dilemma will require a unique merging of scale scores. Engage the client in uncovering the significance of the information for his or her unique vocational concerns. Some clients may be changing careers and need confirmation that their new direction fits their interests, other clients may find value in gaining understanding about why their current occupation is so unsatisfactory, some clients may be new entrants into the world of work and need a basic occupational structure, and others may need assistance choosing a college major. The Snapshot on the first page of the profile can be a good point of reference for a summary conversation.

Step 7: Encourage Exploration Beyond the Profile

Career exploration does not end with the administration of an interest inventory; rather, the assessment process is just the beginning.

Clinicians should have a variety of resources available for vocational clients, including reference books, worksheets, Web sites, and access to individual workers who would be willing to participate in job shadows or informational interviews. The workbook *Where Do I Go Next?* (Borgen & Grutter, 1995) may also assist clients in proceeding with their career exploration. Clients at different developmental stages may use their interest inventory results in different ways (Toman & Savickas, 1997), so it is important to design exploration activities that best match the developmental needs of each individual client. Scheduling follow-up sessions with clients often helps motivate them to complete and report exploration activities. In addition, further clarification may be necessary through additional assessments (such as skills, work values, career beliefs, career barriers), continued interviews, or even another interest inventory (such as the Kuder Career Search With Person Match).

For more detailed information about the construction and statistical properties of the Strong Interest Inventory, refer to the *Strong Interest Inventory Applications and Technical Guide* (Harmon et al., 1994). In this chapter, we will now turn to another interest assessment, the Kuder Career Search With Person Match.

Interpreting the Kuder Career Search With Person Match

Clinician Preparation

The KCS is the latest version of the Kuder interest assessments. One new feature is the online administration and scoring option. Clinician preparation, therefore, needs to include familiarity with the procedures for completing the assessment online, anticipating client questions about online confidentiality, and completing the standard preparation of reviewing clients' assessment results. One way to gain familiarity with the online version of the KCS is to go to www.kuder.com and complete a KCS. Also at that Web site, clinicians have access to the Kuder Tutorial, an online instructional page to assist with the interpretation process.

Zytowski (1999, pp. 280-283) identified five principles, addressed in the career assessment literature, that can assist the clinician in delivering an interest inventory interpretation:

1. Prepare for the discussion of the results

2. Involve clients in the communication process

3. Use simple, emphatic communication

4. Ask clients to recapitulate their results in their own words

5. Stimulate continuing career development

Zytowski (1999) considered the clinician as a mediator between the assessment results and the client. He stated that counselors are a "crucial variable" in the interpretation process and therefore "must know what is being measured and be prepared with vocabulary with which to report it sensibly to a person who is hearing about it for the first time" (p. 279). Considering Principle 1, preparation for a KCS interpretation should include familiarity with its four scales (Activity Preference Profile, Career Clusters, Educational Levels, and Person Match). Information about the KCS scales can be acquired by reviewing Chapter 6 or by referring to the *Kuder Career Search: User Manual* (Zytowski, 2002). Also, descriptions of each Activity Preference scale and each Career Cluster are printed directly on the report form to aid both the client and clinician.

As with the interpretation of the SII, clinicians providing KCS results should also inform clients about the confidential maintenance of their report forms. In the case of online administration, clinicians will have access to their clients' KCS results through assigned passwords and access codes. The KCS Administrative Data System (available from the publisher, National Career Assessment Services) allows clinicians to store, sort, or retrieve all assessments completed by their clients. One advantage of online storage is that clients can never lose their KCS reports as long as you, their clinician, catalog their passwords and access codes. However, following the ethical guidelines of your mental health field, assurance of confidential online assessment results is comparable to the standards of confidentiality applied to any case files and information.

Explaining KCS Results to the Client

The Kuder Career Search With Person Match presents results in two formats: in scores and in stories (autobiographies). The report form presents the scores, first, on the Activity Preference Profile and Career Cluster scales, followed by the autobiographical reports of the Person Matches. For this chapter, the interpretation procedure will follow the same structure as the report form, beginning with the Activity Preference Profile, followed by the Career Clusters and Careers by Education Level, and then concluding with the Person Matches.

In Principle 2, Zytowski (1999) reminded clinicians to involve clients in the interpretation process and cited Healy's (1990) and Garfield and Prediger's (1994) recommendations that the assessment be approached as something that can offer hypotheses to be verified by other data (e.g., self-knowledge, past experience, information from others). Another way to involve clients in the process is to begin the interpretation session by providing the unscored pages of the KCS report that contain only the definitions of the Activity Preferences and/or the Career Clusters. Clients are then asked to estimate a rank ordering of the activities and careers, forming their own hypotheses. (Definitions of the KCS Activity Preferences can be found in Chapter 6 in Learning Experience 6.4.)

Anna might have selected her first few preferences as (1) office detail, (2) human services, (3) communications, and (4) art, where the ranking depicted on her KCS report form was (1) human services, (2) nature, (3) office detail, (4) music, (5) communication, (6) art, (7) computations, (8) sales/management, (9) mechanical, and (10) science/technical. Discussing the ranking differences of the expressed and inventoried preferences is one example of involving the clients in forming hypotheses about their own career interests, as found in both work and leisure settings.

The same ranking exercise can be used with the second KCS scale, the Career Clusters. Clients from some high school settings may be familiar with school-to-work pathways or clusters. The KCS report can be customized to score Career Clusters in the same number and definition used by each state's school-to-work program. The cluster definitions would, therefore, be familiar to such students, but all other clients need to read, discuss, and rank order the standard six Career Clusters.

Clients should be encouraged to describe how each Activity Preference and each Career Cluster fits with their information about themselves, their work history, careers to which they aspire, and information from other sources, such as parents, coworkers, peers, relatives, teachers, bosses, spouses, and so on. Discussing the lowest ranked Activity Preferences and Career Clusters could also be useful because rankings can prompt clients to differentiate between likes and dislikes, which is useful when eliminating job titles for further research or exploration.

Anna's ranked Career Clusters of (1) human resources/services, (2) arts and communication, (3) health services, (4) business management, (5) environmental/agricultural systems, and (6) industrial/engineering systems coincide with her inventoried and self-ranked Activity Preferences. As with the interpretation of any vocational interest inventory, clients should be reminded that these are assessments of their interests and not of their skills, abilities, or values. This should be clearly stated, as specified in Principle 3: Use simple, emphatic communication (Zytowski, 1999). At this point in the interpretation, Zytowski (1999) might also recommend that the client and counselor together "develop custom-made summary reports on the order of the SII snapshot (Harmon et al., 1994) if a report form is too extensive or complex for the developmental level of our clients" (p. 282). For example, a summary worksheet of Anna's results could include the KCS scales and her work experiences, with lines drawn to indicate similarities between the columns.

Anna's KCS Summary Worksheet		
Activity Preference Rankings	*Career Cluster Rankings*	*Work Experiences*
Human services	Human resources/services	Factory
Nature	Arts and communication	Housekeeping
Office detail	Health services	Cashier
Music	Business and management	
Communications	Environmental/agricultural systems	
Art	Industrial/engineering systems	
Computations		
Sales/management		
Mechanical		
Science/technical		

The Activity Preference and Career Cluster definitions contain broad activity and career fields, whereas the next KCS scale, Exploring Careers by Education Level, provides further specification.

The third KCS scale is organized around the same career clusters used for Scale 2 (the "traditional" six Career Clusters or the number of school-to-work pathways specific to that state). Each cluster heading is followed by three levels of occupational titles, those that require (a) on-the-job and/or specialized training, (b) community college education, or (c) university education. Some clients may already know they prefer to pursue specialized training rather than a university degree, and the specified lists can assist them in refining their career research and exploration. After explaining the Careers by Education Level lists to clients, they should leave the session with a clear understanding that the lists serve as catalysts for further exploration and are not intended to indicate the "perfect" job for them.

Principle 4 (ask clients to recapitulate their results in their own words) could be initially introduced at this point in the interpretation session to highlight the distinction between the process of explaining scales (Activity Preferences, Career Clusters, Educational Levels) and explaining stories (as in Scale 4: Person Match). If the client is a high school student, the client and the clinician should review the most salient parts of the KCS in preparation for explaining the results to the client's parents. For others, a summary of what they have learned from the KCS so far or how their results address their initial presenting career concern can lead toward affirming or correcting perceptions of their assessment outcomes. Clients of all ages can be reminded that their results are stored online and that they (or their future counselors, parents, employers) can always print additional copies by going to www.kuder.com and entering their password and access code.

The final scale of the KCS, Person Match, involves a different style of interpretation or explanation. Most clients are familiar with the notion that their assessment responses are compared to a large norm group to form comparisons or similarities with those in various activities or careers. However, once familiarity with norm group scoring is reached, it often can be difficult for clients to think in a different way, to understand that for the Person Match scale, their responses are compared with other *individuals* who have also completed the KCS. Person matching was first introduced by Frederick Kuder (1980) when he wrote, "Instead of matching people to jobs, why not match people to people in jobs?" (p. 1). Each individual in the Person Match pool has written a mini-autobiographical career history. Assisting your client in "analyzing" the autobiographies instead of test scores is comparable to the difference between doing qualitative and quantitative research. For this portion of the KCS, you will be assisting your client in unearthing themes and patterns, rather than understanding high and low rankings.

The KCS report form identifies a client's top 25 Person Matches by their occupational title. For example, Anna's first Person Match (the individual with which her KCS responses matched the best) was a credit representative, and her second was an executive secretary. Even though those occupational titles only partially match with several of her Activity Preferences and Career Clusters (office detail, human resources, business and management), the similarity may be not in the actual careers but rather in the individual career stories. Some clients may receive Person Matches that seem unrelated to their expressed career interests. Clinicians and clients need to look into the details of each of the 25 Person Match stories to discover the themes and patterns. Those stories or mini-autobiographical career histories can be obtained by double-clicking on the occupational title. Below are the stories that accompanied Anna's first two person matches:

Credit Representative

I have now found a career which I like as a credit representative. Prior to this occupation, I was dissatisfied with my work in telephone sales and as a factory worker. As a credit rep., I make collection calls, analyze business reports, and work with financial statements. As orders are received, I obtain financial statements on the companies placing the orders and analyze their credit records. Based on this analysis, I release the order, set up a new account, and/or reject the order. In order to handle these kinds of responsibilities, it is important to have good communication skills and to have good judgment. This job appeals to me because I find satisfaction in making a successful judgment call and in seeing a problem through. I like the people I work for and find there is opportunity for advancement for me.

Executive Secretary

My job changes from day to day as a executive secretary. That is probably why I have liked this as my career for so many years. On a regular basis, I handle correspondence, appointments, the telephone, travel arrangements, act as an administrative assistant, plus an unknown quantity of things as they occur. At times, I say that I would like there to be more stability as to how daily things progress so as to avoid things like the "last minute" response to get "things" out of the way. However, I have to admit that I get enjoyment from this hectic, stressful, ever-changing job as an executive secretary. To perform well at this job, it is important to stay cool and calm, have quick responses, and be alert, conscientious, dedicated, and loyal. I chose this as a career while I was in high school and took the high school business courses that would prepare me for secretarial work. The rest of my training has been mostly on-the-job.

Anna may notice that the first person, a credit representative, began his or her work history in a factory, as did Anna. She might not identify, though, with the financial record-keeping tasks performed by this credit representative because Anna reports little confidence with her math abilities. Anna might appreciate having the credit representative's experience of liking his or her coworkers. The executive secretary reports day-to-day job changes, which might also appeal to Anna, yet not the "hectic, stressful, ever-changing" environment. She might agree that she, too, is "alert, conscientious, dedicated, and loyal." Anna might feel encouraged to learn that most of the executive secretary's training was acquired on the job. After reviewing all or most of the 25 Person Matches in this fashion, themes and patterns begin to emerge that can then be considered during the exploration process. The KCS Person Match scale may help clients broaden their search and exploration, demonstrating how individuals with similar interests can find satisfaction in a large variety of careers. The Person Match scale also elicits clients' career stories, providing additional sources of information and an alternative process of gathering that information.

Zytowski's (1999) Principle 5 (stimulate continuing career development) is addressed on the final page of the KCS report form as "Continuing Your Career Exploration." An online link to the *Occupation Outlook Handbook* (U.S. Department of Labor, 2000) is included on the www.kuder.com Web page. Also, clients are encouraged to learn more about setting goals, discovering similar jobs, networking, and constructing a résumé and/or a portfolio. The Web site contains additional exploration activities and career information for both the client and clinician. The online Kuder Tutorial provides additional interpretation recommendations, along with a counseling session dialogue.

Summary

Each client brings to the counseling session a unique combination of life experiences, work history, personal goals and ambitions, and vocational interests. This chapter included suggestions for explaining interest inventory results in ways that honor each client's particular style and career concerns. Prince and Heiser's (2000) seven-step interpretation model and Zytowski's (1999) five principles are useful for interpreting any vocational interest measure yet were applied in this chapter to the Strong Interest Inventory (Harmon et al., 1994) and the Kuder Career Search (Zytowski, 2002). You are encouraged to use the materials in this chapter as a starting point for developing your own approach, style, and worksheets. You can also use the actual inventory results to assist you in the selection of interventions. For example, clients who score highest on the Holland (1973) Social theme on the SII or have their highest KCS Activity Preference ranking for Communications may prefer conversation, discussion, and/or stories to scores, whereas those from other Holland types or Career Clusters may best appreciate scales with numbers and scores.

The next chapter will merge Anna's results on the Strong Interest Inventory and the Kuder Career Search with cognitive and personality assessments. Vocational interests may be best understood in the total context of a client's life and experiences. We encourage you to consider as many life factors as possible when assisting clients with their career development.

Learning Experience 7.1

Review Anna's Strong Interest Inventory results found in Figure 6.1. The Personal Styles scores on the final page of the report can be compared with scores on the General Occupation Themes and Basic

Interests scales. Complete the graph below using Anna's SII results and the information you know about her from the case study (found in Chapter 8) to begin merging and converging the SII results into a cohesive picture.

Personal Styles	Coinciding General Themes	Basic Interests
(1) Work Style		
Client's score of ___ indicates that he or she _____ _____	_____ _____	
(2) Learning Environment		
Client's score of ___ indicates that he or she _____ _____	_____ _____	
(3) Leadership Style		
Client's score of ___ indicates that he or she _____ _____	_____ _____	
(4) Risk Taking/Adventure		
Client's score of ___ indicates that he or she _____ _____	_____ _____	

NOTE: You may not find General Occupational Themes or Basic Interests that fit every line on this worksheet. First fill in your client's scores and then compare the completed graph to the vocational information you may have about your client from other sources.

Discussion Questions

1. Select either the Strong Interest Inventory or the Kuder Career Search and outline the scales in the order you would choose to discuss them. What is your rationale for presenting the scales in that order?

2. What are some "homework assignments" that you could ask clients to do to add further meaning to their interest inventory results?

3. How might you present interest inventory results to a class or group as opposed to presenting the results to an individual client? Would any procedural changes be necessary?

References

Barak, A., & Friedkes, R. (1982). The mediating effects of career indecision subtypes on career-counseling effectiveness. *Journal of Vocational Behavior, 20,* 120-128.

Bixler, R. H., & Bixler, V. H. (1946). Test interpretation in vocational counseling. *Educational and Psychological Measurement, 6,* 145-155.

Borgen, F., & Grutter, G. (1995). *Where do I go next? Using your Strong results to manage your career.* Palo Alto, CA: Consulting Psychologists Press.

Darley, J. G. (1941). *Clinical aspects and interpretation of the Strong Vocational Interest Blank.* New York: The Psychological Corporation.

Dressel, P. L., & Matteson, R. W. (1950). The effect of client participation in test interpretation. *Educational and Psychological Measurement, 10,* 693-706.

Garfield, N. J., & Prediger, D. J. (1994). Assessment competencies and responsibilities: A checklist for counselors. In J. T. Kapes, M. M. Mastie, & E. A. Whitfield (Eds.), *A counselor's guide to career assessment instruments* (pp. 41-48). Alexandria, VA: National Career Development Association.

Gati, I. (1987). Description and validation of a procedure for the interpretation of an interest inventory score profile. *Journal of Counseling Psychology, 34,* 141-148.

Gati, I., & Blumberg, D. (1991). Computer versus counselor interpretation of interest inventories: The case of the Self-Directed Search. *Journal of Counseling Psychology, 38,* 350-366.

Gustad, J. W., & Tuma, A. H. (1957). The effects of different methods of test introduction and interpretation on client learning in counseling. *Journal of Counseling Psychology, 4,* 313-317.

Harmon, L., Hansen, J., Borgen, F., & Hammer, A. (1994). *Strong Interest Inventory applications and technical guide.* Stanford, CA: Stanford University Press.

Healy, C. C. (1990). Reforming career appraisals to meet the needs of clients in the 1990s. *The Counseling Psychologist, 18,* 214-226.

Hirsh, S. K., & McEvoy, E. (1986). *Using the Strong in organizations.* Palo Alto, CA: Consulting Psychologists Press.

Hoffman, M. A., Spokane, A. R., & Magoon, T. M. (1981). Effects of feedback mode on counseling outcomes using the Strong-Campbell Interest Inventory: Does the counselor really matter? *Journal of Counseling Psychology, 28,* 119-125.

Holland, J. L. (1973). *Making vocational choices.* Englewood Cliffs, NJ: Prentice Hall.

Kuder, F. (1980). Person matching. *Educational and Psychological Measurement, 40,* 1-8.

Matarazzo, J. D. (1986). Computerized clinical psychological test *interpretations:* Unvalidated plus all mean and no sigma. *American Psychologist, 41,* 14-24.

Murphy, K. R. (1987). The accuracy of clinical versus computerized test interpretations. *American Psychologist, 42,* 192-193.

Oliver, L. W. (1977). Evaluating career counseling outcome for three modes of test interpretation. *Measurement and Evaluation in Guidance, 10,* 153-161.

Prince, J. P. (1995). *The Strong Interest Inventory resource: Strategies for group and individual interpretations in college settings.* Palo Alto, CA: Consulting Psychologists Press.

Prince, J. P., & Heiser, L. J. (2000). *Essentials of career interest assessment.* New York: John Wiley.

Randahl, G. J., Hansen, J. C., & Haverkamp, B. E. (1993). Instrumental behaviors following test administration and interpretation: Exploring validity of the Strong Interest Inventory. *Journal of Counseling and Development, 71,* 435-439.

Reardon, R. (1987). Development of the computer version of the Self-Directed Search. *Measurement and Evaluation in Counseling and Development, 20,* 62-67.

Sinnett, E. R., & Albott, W. L. (1987). Computerized interpretation: Additional issues concerning ethics, standards, and regulation of practice. *American Psychologist, 42,* 190-191.

Strong, E. K., Jr. (1943). *Vocational interest of men and women.* Stanford, CA: Stanford University Press.

Toman, S., & Savickas, M. L. (1997). Career choice readiness moderates the effects of interest inventories. *Journal of Career Assessment, 5,* 275-291.

U.S. Department of Labor. (2000). *Occupational outlook handbook.* Washington, DC: Government Printing Office.

Wright, E. W. (1963). A comparison of individual and multiple counseling methods for test interpretation interviews. *Journal of Counseling Psychology, 10,* 126-135.

Zytowski, D. (1999). How to talk to people about their interest inventory results. In M. L. Savickas & A. R. Spokane (Eds.), *Vocational interests: Meaning, measurement and counseling use* (pp. 277-293). Palo Alto, CA: Davies-Black.

Zytowski, D. (2002). *Kuder Career Search: User manual.* Adel, IA: National Career Assessment Services.

8

Adult Case Study

This chapter will give readers an opportunity to move through the interpretive process, step by step, and then through the process of integrating all the data into a formulation of how to help a client. We will begin with a description of a client and then proceed through each of the three categories of test data, highlighting the aspects of the data that are most pertinent to counseling, and then discuss how to consider all the data comprehensively.

The following case was written specifically for this text. Anna is not a "real" client in the sense that she actually exists, but her dilemma represents a composite of issues typical for many community college counseling center clients. To produce Anna's assessment scores, each author considered all aspects of the case in relation to the scales on the measures. The career interest assessment scores were determined by actually completing the items on the Strong Interest Inventory and the Kuder Career Search With Person Match as if the test taker were Anna. The "data" referred to encompass not only test scores but, more broadly, all the information we have about the person, including information she has self-disclosed, as well as the behavioral observations, mental status, and other information we know about her.

Case History

Anna arrived at the counseling center of her community college in the spring term of her first year on campus. She expressed concerns about her academic progress, as well as how to support herself and her two children (a 9-year-old daughter and an 11-year-old son) following a divorce. Her husband provided little child support and did not maintain consistent contact with his children. He never supported her efforts to return to school.

From the intake interview, you learned that Anna is a 35-year-old Caucasian female, a second-generation Austrian American. English is her second language although she speaks English with only a slight accent; most of her peers are not aware of her ethnic heritage. Her parents came to the United States the year they were married. Anna's father completed his education in Austria, and her mother dropped out in her ninth year of schooling. Currently, Anna lives in the same Midwestern urban area as her parents. She spends a lot of time with her now elderly parents, participating with them in church and community activities.

Anna originally enrolled in college to increase her employment opportunities. After graduating from high school with a 2.8 grade point average, she worked in a factory for a year and a half. It was during her employment there that she met her husband. After marriage at the age of 20, Anna quit working to have children. In their 8 years of marriage, Anna bore three children. She did not return to work until her youngest was in the first grade and the family needed additional income following the loss of her husband's job as a factory supervising manager. Her first position after returning to work was as a housekeeper in a nursing home. Anna found that job to be very physically challenging, so after about 3 months she sought employment where she would not need to lift heavy objects and move equipment. She was subsequently hired as a cashier at the local grocery store. She divorced her husband after 8 years of marriage, at the age of 28. The divorce followed several incidents of domestic violence and episodic alcoholic binges on his part. Anna has been working as a cashier for the past 7 years and is very motivated to complete an associate's degree, which she believes will give her more employment options and a better income. She highly values education, to the extreme of pressuring herself to achieve perfection.

During the intake interview, Anna endorsed items indicating a propensity for dysthymia. She complained of being moderately overweight and having low energy, terminal insomnia, increased appetite, mild concentration problems, and difficulty keeping up with her responsibilities. She stated that it seemed to take a great deal of effort simply to meet minimum hygiene needs for herself and her children. Nevertheless, her personal grooming appeared to be fastidious. She also reported having academic difficulties in math and spelling since junior and senior high school. She believed her most immediate concern, though, was selecting a major program of study. The counselor determined that in addition to career assessment, it would also be useful to assess her personality and cognitive functioning.

Report of Findings on Each of Three Domains

Readers are referred to Figure 3.1 in Chapter 3. On that matrix, note that oral feedback to clients is one of four modes of communicating evaluation results. The information in the following section represents not only Anna's particular test results but also the form those results would take if the evaluator were to sit down with her to explain and discuss the results. Of note is the extensiveness of the information to be shared with Anna. It would be advisable to anticipate either scheduling a longer appointment than usual for the feedback or planning on sharing the feedback over two sessions to allow ample time for Anna to process her reaction to the results, as well as ask questions and respond to the evaluation findings.

Cognitive Data

Behavioral Observations

This discussion of Anna's performance on the Wechsler Adult Intelligence Scale—Third Revision (WAIS-III) begins with a general description of Anna's behaviors that were exhibited throughout the WAIS-III assessment. The behavioral observations are relevant because they offer important qualitative information with which we can evaluate the probable validity, or invalidity, of the scores she demonstrated in this test administration.

Anna presented as a woman who appeared to be somewhat older than her stated age of 35. Her grooming and hygiene were appropriate. She appeared to be somewhat overweight. She gave the impression of having low energy, walking and moving slowly. This slowness of movement was observed as she walked from the waiting area to the testing room and continued to be apparent throughout the evaluation. Her response latencies (length of time between when a question was asked and when she responded) lasted from about 3 to 5 seconds. This gave the impression that she was either thinking slowly or carefully formulating a response before offering it. It further gave the sense of a lack of spontaneity and added to the overall sense of slowness.

Anna sat quietly, without initiating conversation, although she seemed to be making a sincere effort to answer questions and converse in a pleasant manner. Her range of affect was somewhat constricted; at no time did she smile or laugh.

She was a diligent worker, persisting at tasks until prompted to stop. Her approach to nonverbal tasks was slow and methodical. She appeared to systemically attempt different problem solutions when the solution she was trying to use did not work. She was very persistent in her solution attempts on the nonverbal items, continuing to work to the limits of the time allowances. She did not inquire as to the accuracy of her responses. On the verbal tasks, she was disinclined to guess even when prompted. Again, the time elapsed between when a question was asked and when she offered a response was long, sometimes with a response latency of 10 to 15 seconds. During that latency period, she would gaze either at her hands, clasped in her lap, or into a corner of the room.

Because of the response latencies and her disinclination to guess at verbal test items not readily familiar to her, this evaluation may have yielded a somewhat depressed estimate of Anna's current intellectual capabilities.

Anna demonstrated the following scaled and standard scores on this WAIS-III administration:

Factor	Standard Score	Percentile	95% Confidence Band
Full Scale	79	8	75-83
Verbal IQ	80	9	76-86
Performance IQ	83	13	77-91
Verbal Comprehension	86	18	81-92
Perceptual Organization	86	18	80-94
Working Memory	71	3	66-80
Processing Speed	79	8	73-90

Verbal Subtests		Performance Subtests	
Vocabulary	8	Picture Completion	11
Similarities	6	Digit Symbol	6
Arithmetic	6	Block Design	7
Digit Span	5	Matrix Reasoning	5
Information	8	Picture Arrangement	8
Comprehension	7	Symbol Search	6
Letter-Number Sequencing	5		

There are several significant WAIS-III findings in terms of clinical implications for counseling Anna. First, Anna's academic difficulties are not surprising considering that her overall test performance was in the borderline to low-average range. However, there are factors that may have contributed to her low-average performance. The two most likely variables are her affect and her primary language. Anna's affect was admittedly depressed, and signs of depression are reflected in her lower Working Memory score. Attention and concentration problems could be the result of her depression and anxiety, which probably interfered with Anna's ability to solve problems and tasks cognitively at an ability level of which she is capable. Further compounding the difficulty, because English is her second language, the lower Working Memory score might be a reflection of the additional concentration she must exert while internally translating from English to her native language. In addition, depending on the nature of the physical assaults she suffered by her husband, it is possible that she sustained some minor brain injury that may be contributing to attentional problems. Realistically, her factor scores are probably a result of both affect and language, and we can only conclude that her abilities are very likely underrepresented in her current WAIS-III scores.

Nevertheless, we can still make some tentative conclusions about her cognitive functioning. Her abilities as assessed by these verbal and nonverbal tasks appear to be approximately equally well developed with the exception of Picture Completion. Because her scaled score on Picture Completion is 4.23 points above her own mean, it constitutes a relative strength for her. In interpreting this, though, we can best serve Anna by thinking not about Picture Completion, per se, but instead about what Picture Completion attempts to measure.

The Picture Completion subtest measures ability to quickly visually scan and to distinguish essential from nonessential details. Again looking back to her developmental history with an abusive husband, Anna may have, by necessity, developed the skill of quickly visually scanning and evaluating her environment. Regardless of how or why those abilities developed, though, visual scanning, alertness to detail, and ability to differentiate essential from nonessential details are significant strengths. This is information that should be taken into consideration when exploring possible career options.

MMPI-2 Data

In Anna's case, career concerns are one component of her presenting problem. The Minnesota Multiphasic Personality Inventory–2 (MMPI-2) data can lend valuable information to the counseling process, in terms of its implications for Anna's career development, as well as general implications for her personality structure, her constellation of symptoms, and the treatment approaches that may be indicated or contraindicated.

The MMPI-2 and other personality inventories can provide crucial information about a client who is seeking career counseling. They can help career counselors assess the client's readiness to engage in the hard work that a career search entails. If the client is distracted by emotional problems or interpersonal stresses, focusing on the tasks of a career search may be difficult. Such inventories also reveal information about the influence of family circumstances on the client's career choice and the amount of support a client can expect from family during the process. In addition, the MMPI-2 can suggest the degree to which the client is able to form a strong therapeutic alliance with the counselor and the client's tendency to trust or distrust the counselor's professional judgments. Finally, data regarding the client's tolerance for stress and ambiguity and his or her general approach to decision making and risk taking can be gathered from the test.

Anna's scores on the MMPI-2 provide an abundance of information essential to effective career counseling. Her scores were as follows:

Validity Scales	Raw Score	T Score
Cannot Say	2	0
L scale	5	57
F	8	65
Fb	5	62
TRIN	6(T)	62
VRIN	6	54
K	16	52
S	11	43

Basic Scales	Raw Score	T Score With K Correction
1	8	56
2	29	67
3	26	58
4	22	63
5	37	48
6	14	64
7	21	66
8	14	57
9	13	42
10	44	67

Content Scales	Raw Score	T Score
ANX	13	64
FRS	10	57
OBS	8	55
DEP	15	66
HEA	10	62
BIZ	2	52
ANG	7	55
CYN	10	51
ASP	4	43
TPA	5	42
LSE	11	63
SOD	15	65
FAM	12	65
WRK	16	63
TRT	7	55

Supplemental Scales	Raw Score	T Score
Mac-R	21	56
APS	25	55
AAS	2	52
MDS	4	58
PK	14	58

Anna cooperated with the testing, answering all the questions and showing no evidence of defensiveness in her responses. She acknowledged problems in coping, understood the items, and answered consistently. As a result, the profile can be considered valid for interpretation.

The pattern of MMPI scores suggests that Anna's major concerns revolve around feelings of depression and anxiety. She appears sad, worried about herself and her future, and has little energy to tackle the demands of her life. She may have difficulty making decisions, concentrating on the tasks before her, and feel excessive fatigue and have other health complaints related to her depressed and anxious mood. She probably feels overwhelmed but may see little way out of her current circumstances. She endorsed items expressing social discomfort, introversion, and low self-esteem. Her social life probably revolves around family and a few friends—making social connections with new people seems especially difficult for Anna, based on this profile. She has been unhappy and frustrated in work situations and expresses significant distress about family relations. She endorsed items that indicate that she feels traumatized by her life, although the test cannot verify any history of trauma. Nevertheless, the presence of features of posttraumatic stress disorder is possible, given her history, and should probably be further evaluated. There is no evidence of substance abuse, problems with aggression or anger control, or any suggestion of any psychotic process of thought disorder. Anna does not come to counseling with any negative presuppositions about mental health professionals. This pattern of scores suggests a person who can be responsive to counseling and appreciative of the support it offers.

Based on this profile, Anna appears to need a career counseling process that simultaneously attends to her depressed and anxious mood and offers her a sense of hope for her future. She needs concrete supports for the present and a structured and supportive approach to making changes for the future. Anna's progress is likely to be slow and steady. Given her current difficulty with coping with stress, homework assignments given to her should be assigned with an awareness that they need to be small and manageable and have a high probability of success until her mood improves. Any career choices she makes ought to take into account her generally introverted personality. The social discomfort she feels is real and certainly can be moderated with intervention, but even when the depression lifts, Anna is unlikely to be comfortable in occupations that demand a high level of self-confidence or risk taking and an extroverted personality.

Career Data

Strong Interest Inventory®

Based on the number of completed responses and the positive Infrequent Responses score, it appears that Anna's results on the Strong Interest Inventory (SII) can be considered valid. She obtained a Holland type of SCA, indicated by her three highest General Occupational Themes of Social-Conventional-Artistic. This code reflects her interest in working with people but also reveals the potential for internal conflict between the aspect of her that prefers order, structure, and rules (Conventional) and the aspect that prefers spontaneity and creativity (Artistic). Anna's Basic Interest Scales predominantly coincide with either her Conventional side (office services, religious activities) or Artistic side (culinary arts, music/dramatics). Anna may find it difficult to find a work role that allows her to express both Conventional and Artistic interests in a Social environment.

Anna's scores on the Personal Styles Scales coincide with her General Occupational Theme, Basic Interests Scales, and Occupational Scales scores. Her Work Style score indicates that she prefers working with people, supporting her highest General Occupational Theme of teaching, speech pathology, and child care. Anna's Learning

Style score reveals that she would prefer to learn by doing rather than learn through lecture and reading. She may find it uncomfortable in academic classrooms that do not include experiential learning situations. Her Leadership Style score shows that she would prefer to do a task herself rather than to lead or manage others, which could coincide with several of her Basic Interests Scale scores (such as office services, culinary arts, or computer activities). Anna's Risk Taking/Adventure score states that she prefers quiet, less risky activities, which could coincide with her Conventional General Occupational Theme.

Overall, her SII results reflect her stated interests and personal styles well while also supporting her previous job choices of nursing home housekeeper and grocery store cashier. Both contain elements of Social and Conventional interests yet could be lacking in opportunities to express Artistic interests. It would be useful to engage Anna in conversation about her Artistic interests to see if those are expressed in her leisure or hobby activities. One weakness of her Occupational Scale scores is that many represent careers that require more education than she is prepared to complete.

Kuder Career Search Data

Anna's Kuder Career Search Activity Preference Profile indicates results similar to her SII results in that her highest preference scores were in human services, nature, office detail, music, communications, and art. These again reflect her two sides, the one that prefers order, structure, and rules (office detail) and the side that prefers spontaneity and creativity (music and art). Again, a socially oriented preference (human services) is her highest percentile score. The definition of *human services* included on her printout states "activities that help other people. Those who score high on this scale may be teachers, counselors, or work for a church. Others are sales persons, child care workers. Many people do volunteer work besides their regular jobs—another way to use this preference" (Zytowski, 1999, p. 4). Teacher, religious activities, and child care worker also appeared as "similar" scores on the Strong Interest Inventory. Anna's Career Clusters also identify vocational areas that match well with her general Activity Preference scores and her SII results, with the highest three being human resources/services, arts and communication, and health services. Pages 8 through 12 of her KCS report provide lists of occupations for each cluster and are grouped by (a) specialized training, (b) community college education, and (c) university education. This multitude of career titles listed at each of the three different educational or training levels opens up the possibilities for increased vocational explorations.

Anna's Person Matches match her to actual individuals successfully engaged in several of the occupations listed on the KCS and were also identified on the SII Occupational Scales (such as teacher, executive secretary, librarian, bank teller, office manager, and religious leader). Yet other occupational titles identified as Person Matches do not appear to coincide with any of the interest assessment scores (credit representative, state legislator, manager, auto tire company, U.S. Army soldier/recruiter, or biological technician). The match for her may not be with the occupational title itself but may be a match with some other aspect of the person.

The only way to identify the similarity between Anna and the matched person is to print each autobiographical sketch and find similarities in their stories, as opposed to looking for similarities in scores. For example, the credit representative's position sounds similar to a bank teller in that it involves establishing new accounts and preparing financial statements. Anna may not identify with this portion of the autobiography, yet she may relate to the phrase, "It is important to have good communication skills and good judgement" (Zytowski, 1999, p. 14). In contrast, Anna may picture herself doing many of the job tasks described by her second Person Match, an executive secretary. Handling correspondence, setting appointments, and coordinating travel may coincide with Anna's interests, but she might also relate to the phrase, "To perform well at this job, it is important to stay cool and calm."

Each individually matched person's autobiography contains some elements that can assist Anna in describing more about herself than she might otherwise through discussing inventoried scores. She can be encouraged to include her own vocational biographies in the sessions, each assisting her in clarifying her career path, self-understanding, and interests. Rather than focusing Anna's career exploration on a handful of occupations, the KCS can broaden the scope of the exploration by including more occupational titles at three different educational levels and by including autobiographies of actual individuals who express interests matched with Anna's in a wide range of careers.

Summary of Career Data

The two interest inventories provide consistent support for Anna's exploring careers or college majors that are Social (or involve working for the welfare of others) and that have a combination of stability and structure while still engaging creativity. Because many of the identified interests include skills in mathematics or numbers, it would be advisable to consider an intellectual assessment. As well, there may be elements of her ethnic background or her history with her former husband that might influence her vocational decisions, so personality assessment could also assist Anna in her vocational choices.

Data Integration From Anna's Test Battery

This section will illustrate how the data set might be interpreted collectively in light of the composite of data across three aspects of Anna's functioning. In some respects, this process of data integration represents the crux of this text—consideration of a multitude of data simultaneously as a means of drawing interpretive conclusions and then generating treatment recommendations.

First of all, the MMPI-2 profile supports our hypothesis that emotional factors may have affected Anna's WAIS-III scores. Her MMPI-2 profile strongly suggests significant depression and anxiety that may have had a detrimental effect on her WAIS-III performance across virtually all the cognitive domains that were sampled. The even distribution of abilities across the verbal and nonverbal realms is quite consistent with her occupational preferences. Anna has diverse interests. The main thing that stands out here is that we cannot draw any conclusions about her WAIS-III beyond the recognition that her affective state is having a detrimental impact on her functioning. We can then conclude that her WAIS-III scores are an underestimate of her true cognitive ability. It is not possible to accurately quantify the magnitude of the underestimate.

In terms of treatment planning, we can gain some general directions. First, here she is in her first semester of school, depressed and anxious. She may be sitting in class worrying about a multitude of other issues, such as supporting her family, doubting her ability to perform in class, and so on. Although she likely possesses the capability to perform satisfactorily in a community college setting, current circumstances are such that she may not perform either up to her potential or at a passing level. Furthermore, failure at this juncture could serve to validate her negative view of herself and her ability. Thus, here is the order and rationales with which treatment strategies would be prioritized. First, address the anxiety/depression immediately. In addition, depending on the degree of impairment in her daily functioning, consider possible referral for evaluation for psychotropic medication. Research (Seligman, 1990) supports taking a cognitive-behavioral approach with clients experiencing depression and/or anxiety. One cognitive (or rational emotive) direction would be to help Anna clearly identify her fears and concerns about finances and other focuses of her worry. Help her generate contingency plans to cope with several "worst-case scenario" situations. Also, identification of her internal dialogue could illuminate areas of cognitive distortion that are contributing to her current affective state.

Next, investigate how she is doing in her classes now. Consider the need for any interventions or advocacy with any of her current instructors. If it did appear that intervention with the instructors was warranted, clearly this advocacy would need to be thoroughly discussed with Anna beforehand. A Release of Information signed by Anna before making the intervention would be essential. Also, discussing her performance in her courses could be framed in the context of her Holland type (Social-Conventional-Artistic), to help Anna understand one way in which some academic courses could be more interesting to her, or easier to do well in, than other classes. Normalizing for her how most students are not interested in every class may help her find a justification or rationale for academic discomfort.

There are a number of longer term counseling goals that seem warranted given the data. One would be addressing social anxiety and subsequent expansion of her support system. Although Anna will never be a "social butterfly," development or expansion of her support system could alleviate some of her feelings of isolation and contribute to her perception of self-efficacy in coping with life's challenges. It is curious that she endorses social interests in paper-and-pencil instruments, yet she has an extremely limited social support system. This discrepancy needs to be explored.

Additional career investigation, possibly through job shadowing, could also help her develop a clearer sense of direction. Doing so might help make a career goal a more tangible entity and help energize her to move forward. Bear in mind that developing the ability to use rational emotive techniques for anxiety management would be an important first step before suggesting that Anna participate in a job shadow. Otherwise, the experience could become the basis for many additional worries and self-doubts. Other interventions that address Anna's vocational concerns could include assisting Anna with a description of her vocational story. Development of a time line and future planning, an explanation of recycling through developmental stages during career changes, a discussion of parental (or family) influences on career choice, and the identification of a life theme as expressed through career could add to the richness of her self-understanding and clarity of her preferences and goals. Finally, further assessments (e.g., values, skills, beliefs), exploration assignments (e.g., job shadowing or reading vocational references), and the discovery of potential gender and/or cultural influences on past, present, and future career concerns could be of benefit.

There seem to be few sources of enjoyment and pleasure in her life. Exploration of possible leisure activities, as well as engagement in some of them, could help augment her sense of well-being. Helping her learn how to consistently create some situations that she enjoys could facilitate her feeling more mastery and enjoyment of her life.

Anna's Report

In this final segment of this chapter, we will provide a report as an example of how to compose a report that integrates test findings from four instruments and how to compose the recommendations from those findings. Referring once again to Figure 3.1, this phase of disclosing evaluation findings occurs in written form. As stated in each of the three chapters about reporting findings (Chapters 3, 5, and 7), succinct, accurate communication of test findings is a critical facet of assessment. If the test findings are not communicated in a manner that the client and referral source can understand, the testing process has been futile.

We discussed in Chapter 3 that in a report describing multiple instruments, a clinician has the option of discussing results test by test or by domain of functioning. Our sample report on Anna is a blending of both styles because her evaluation consisted of one instrument being used in the intellectual and personality domains and two in the career development domain. One other point to note is that the two career instruments use totally different approaches to conceptualize career exploration, and so each offers unique information. Thus, results of those two instruments are initially reported separately.

Psychological Evaluation

Name: Anna Gustafson

Date of Evaluation: July 3, 2001

Date of Birth: June 15, 1966

Evaluator: Maryann Smith, M.Ed., L.P.C.C.

Reason for Referral

Ms. Gustafson is being evaluated due to self-reported difficulties adjusting to the demand of community college. The goal of this assessment is to generate insight as to the nature of her difficulties and to illuminate treatment goals and strategies.

Background Information

Anna Gustafson is a 35-year-old Caucasian female, a second-generation Austrian American. English is her second language. Her parents came to the United States the year they were married. Anna's father completed his education in Austria, and her mother dropped out in her ninth year of schooling. Anna was an only child, and she describes her family of origin as strict but loving. Currently, Anna lives in the same Midwestern urban area as her parents. She spends a lot of time with her now elderly parents, participating with them in church and community activities.

Anna originally enrolled in college to increase her employment opportunities. After graduating from high school with a 2.8 grade point average, she worked in a factory for a year and a half, and during her employment there she met her husband. After marriage at the age of 20, Anna quit working to have children. She had three children and did not return to work until her youngest was in the first grade and the family needed additional income following the loss of her husband's job as a factory supervising manager. Her first position after returning to work was as a housekeeper in a nursing home. Anna left that job after 3 months because it was too physically challenging, and so she gained employment as a cashier at a local grocery store. She divorced her husband after 8 years of marriage following several incidents of domestic violence and episodic alcoholic binges on his part. Anna has been working in the same cashier job for 7 years and is very motivated to complete an associate's degree, which she believes will give her more employment options and a better income. She highly values education, to the extreme of pressuring herself to achieve perfection.

During the intake interview, Anna endorsed symptoms of dysthymia. She complained of being moderately overweight and having low energy, terminal insomnia, increased appetite, mild concentration problems, and difficulty keeping up with her responsibilities. She stated that it seemed to take great deal of effort simply to maintain minimum hygiene needs for herself and her children. Nevertheless, her personal grooming appeared to be fastidious.

Anna reported experiencing academic difficulties in math and spelling since junior and senior high school. She believed her most immediate concern, though, was selecting a major program of study. The counselor determined that in addition to career assessment, it would also be useful to assess her personality and cognitive functioning.

Instruments Used

Clinical Interview

Wechsler Adult Intelligence Scale—Third Revision (WAIS-III)

Minnesota Multiphasic Personality Inventory—2 (MMPI-2)

Strong Interest Inventory (SII)

Kuder Career Search (KCS)

Behavioral Observations

Anna presented as a woman who appeared to be somewhat older than her stated age of 35. Her grooming and hygiene were appropriate. She appeared to be somewhat overweight. She gave the impression of having low energy, walking and moving slowly. This slowness of movement was observed as she walked from the waiting area to the testing room and continued to be apparent throughout the evaluation. Her response latencies (from the time a question was being asked to the time she responded) lasted from about 3 to 5 seconds. This gave the impression that she was either thinking slowly or carefully formulating a response before offering it. It further gave the sense of a lack of spontaneity and added to the overall sense of slowness.

Anna sat quietly, without initiating conversation, although she seemed to be making a sincere effort to answer questions and converse in a pleasant manner. Her range of affect was somewhat constricted; at no time did she smile or laugh.

She was a diligent worker, persisting at tasks until prompted to stop. Her approach to nonverbal tasks was slow and methodical. She appeared to systemically attempt different problem solutions when the solution she was trying to use did not work. She was very persistent in her solution attempts on the nonverbal items, continuing to work to the limits of the time allowances. She did not inquire as to the accuracy of her responses. On the verbal tasks, she was disinclined to guess even when prompted. Again, the time elapsed between when a question was asked and when she offered a response was long, sometimes with a response latency of 10 to 15 seconds. During that latency period, she would gaze either at her hands, clasped in her lap, or into a corner of the room.

Because of the response latencies and her disinclination to guess at verbal test items not readily familiar to her, this evaluation may have yielded a somewhat depressed estimate of Anna's current intellectual capabilities.

On the personality inventory, however, Anna answered all the questions and showed no evidence of defensiveness in her responses. She acknowledged problems in coping, understood the items, and answered consistently. As a result, her MMPI profile can be considered valid for interpretation.

Test Results

Anna demonstrated the following scaled and standard scores on these test administrations:

	WAIS-III		
Factor	Standard Score	Percentile	95% Confidence Band
Full Scale	79	8	75-83
Verbal IQ	80	9	76-86
Performance IQ	83	13	77-91
Verbal Comprehension	86	18	81-92
Perceptual Organization	86	18	80-94
Working Memory	71	3	66-80
Processing Speed	79	8	73-90

Verbal Subtests		Performance Subtests	
Vocabulary	8	Picture Completion	11
Similarities	6	Digit Symbol	6
Arithmetic	6	Block Design	7
Digit Span	5	Matrix Reasoning	5
Information	8	Picture Arrangement	8
Comprehension	7	Symbol Search	6
Letter-Number Sequencing	5		

	MMPI-2	
Validity Scales	Raw Score	T Score
Cannot Say	2	Not applicable
L scale	5	57
F	8	65
Fb	5	62
TRIN	6(T)	62
VRIN	6	54
K	16	52
S	11	43

Basic Scales	Raw Score	T Score With K Correction
1	8	56
2	29	*67*
3	26	58
4	22	63
5	37	48
6	14	64
7	21	*66*
8	14	57
9	13	42
10	44	67

Content Scales	Raw Score	T Score
ANX	13	*64*
FRS	10	57
OBS	8	55
DEP	15	*66*
HEA	10	62
BIZ	2	52
ANG	7	55
CYN	10	51
ASP	4	43
TPA	5	42
LSE	11	63
SOD	15	*65*
FAM	12	*65*
WRK	16	63
TRT	7	55

Supplemental Scales	Raw Score	T Score
Mac-R	21	56
APS	25	55
AAS	2	52
MDS	4	58
PK	14	58

NOTE: Italic and bold italic numbers represent T scores that are at or above the cutoff for clinical significance.

Anna's WAIS-III Full Scale IQ of 79 places her in the borderline range of intellectual functioning in comparison to the standardization sample, which is roughly representative of the general U.S. population. Her Verbal IQ and Performance IQ were obtained with little discrepancy between them, indicating that her verbal and nonverbal abilities have developed at approximately the same rate. However, the discrepancies among the other factor scores of Verbal Comprehension, Perceptual Organization, Working Memory, and Processing Speed strongly suggest that some affective or motivational factors hampered an optimal performance on the WAIS-III. The test scores support the behavioral observation that she was slow to respond. It is hypothesized that her slow response pattern and constricted affect resulted in a conservative estimate of her true cognitive ability. In addition, English is her second language. The extended response latencies and slow problem solutions may have been a reflection of the additional concentration she needed to exert while internally translating from English to her native language.

Nevertheless, Anna did demonstrate a significant strength in her ability to quickly visually scan and distinguish essential from non-essential details. This is information that should be taken into consideration when exploring possible career options.

The pattern of MMPI scores suggests that Anna's major concerns revolve around feelings of depression and anxiety. She appears sad, is worried about herself and her future, and has little energy to tackle the demands of her life. She may have difficulty making decisions and concentrating on the tasks before her, and may feel excessive fatigue and have other health complaints related to her depressed and anxious mood. She probably feels overwhelmed but may see little way out of her current circumstances. She endorsed items expressing social discomfort, introversion, and low self-esteem. Her social life probably revolves around family and a few friends—making social connections with new people seems especially difficult for Anna, based on this profile. She has been unhappy and frustrated in work situations and expresses significant distress about family relations. She endorsed items that indicate that she feels traumatized by her life, although the test cannot verify any history of trauma. There is no evidence of substance abuse, problems with aggression or anger control, or any suggestion of any psychotic process of thought disorder. Anna does not come to counseling with any negative presuppositions about mental health professionals. This pattern of scores suggests a person who can be responsive to counseling and appreciative of the support it offers.

Strong Interest Inventory

Based on the number of completed responses and the positive "Infrequent Responses" score, it appears that Anna's results on the Strong Interest Inventory® can be considered valid. She obtained a Holland type of SCA, indicated by her three highest General Occupational Themes of Social-Conventional-Artistic. This code reflects her interest in working with people but also reveals the potential for internal conflict between the side of her that prefers order, structure, and rules (Conventional) and the side that prefers spontaneity and creativity (Artistic). Anna's Basic Interest Scales predominantly coincide with either her Conventional side (office services, religious activities) or Artistic side (culinary arts, music/dramatics). Anna may find it difficult to find a work role that allows her to express both Conventional and Artistic interests in a Social environment.

Anna's scores on the Personal Styles Scales coincide with her General Occupational Theme, Basic Interests Scales, and Occupational Scales scores. Her Work Style score indicates that she prefers working with people, supporting her highest General Occupational Theme of teaching, speech pathology, and child care. Anna's Learning Style score reveals that she would prefer to learn by doing rather than learn through lecture and reading. She may find it uncomfortable in academic classrooms that do not include experiential learning situations. Her Leadership Style score shows that she would prefer to do a task herself rather than to lead or manage others, which could coincide with several of her Basic Interests Scale scores (such as office services, culinary arts, or computer activities). Anna's Risk-Taking/Adventure score states that she prefers quiet, less risky activities, which could coincide with her conventional General Occupational Theme.

Overall, her SII results reflect her stated interests and personal styles well while also supporting her previous job choices of nursing home housekeeper and grocery store cashier. Both contain elements of Social and Conventional interests yet could be lacking in opportunities to express her Artistic interests. It would be useful to engage Anna in conversation about her Artistic interests to see if those are expressed in her leisure or hobby activities. One weakness of her Occupational Scale scores is that many represent careers that require more education than she is prepared to complete.

Kuder Career Search Data

Anna's Kuder Career Search Activity Preference Profile indicates similar results to the SII in that her highest preference scores were in human services, nature, office detail, music, communications, and art. These again reflect her two sides, the one that prefers order, structure, and rules (office detail) and the side that prefers spontaneity and creativity (music and art). Again, a socially oriented preference (human services) is her highest percentile score. The definition of *human services* included on her printout states, "Activities that help other people. Those who score high on this scale may be teachers, counselors, or work for a church. Others are sales persons, child care workers. Many people do volunteer work besides their regular jobs—another way to use this preference" (Zytowski, 1999, p. 4). Teacher, religious activities, and child care worker also appeared as "similar" scores on the Strong Interest Inventory. Anna's Career Clusters also identify vocational areas that match well with her general Activity Preference scores and her SII results, with the highest three being human resources/services, arts and communication, and health services. Pages 8 through 12 of her KCS report provide lists of occupations for each cluster and are grouped by (a) specialized training, (b) community college education, and (c) university education. This multitude of career titles listed at each of the three different educational or training levels opens up the possibilities for increased vocational explorations.

Anna's Person Matches match her to actual individuals successfully engaged in several of the occupations listed on the KCS and were also identified on the SII Occupational Scales (such as teacher, executive secretary, librarian, bank teller, office manager, and religious leader). Yet other occupational titles identified as Person Matches do not appear to coincide with any of the interest assessment scores (credit representative, state legislator, manager, auto tire company, U.S. Army soldier/recruiter, or biological technician). The match for her may not be with the occupational title itself but may be a match with some other aspect of the person.

The only way to identify the similarity between Anna and the matched person is to print each autobiographical sketch and find similarities in their stories, as opposed to looking for similarities in scores. For example, the credit representative's position sounds similar to a bank teller in that it involves establishing new accounts and preparing financial statements. Anna may not identify with this portion of the autobiography, yet she may relate to the phrase, "It is important to have good communication skills and good judgement" (Zytowski, 1999, p. 14). In contrast, Anna may picture herself doing many of the job tasks described by her second Person Match, an executive secretary. Handling correspondence, setting appointments, and coordinating travel may coincide with Anna's interests, but she might also relate to the phrase, "To perform well at this job, it is important to stay cool and calm."

Each individually matched person's autobiography contains some elements that can assist Anna in describing more about herself than she might otherwise through discussing inventoried scores. She can be encouraged to include her own vocational biographies in the sessions, each assisting her in clarifying her career path, self-understanding, and interests. Rather than focusing Anna's career exploration on a handful of occupations, the KCS can broaden the scope of the exploration by including more occupational titles at three different educational levels and by including autobiographies of actual individuals who express interests matched with Anna's in a wide range of careers.

Based on this profile, Anna appears to need a career counseling process that simultaneously attends to her depressed and anxious mood and that offers her a sense of hope for her future. She needs concrete supports for the present and a structured and supportive approach to making changes for the future. Anna's progress is likely to be slow and steady. Given her current difficulty with coping with stress, the homework assignments given to her need to be manageable and have a high probability of success until her mood improves. Any career choices she makes ought to take into account her generally introverted personality. The social discomfort she feels is real and certainly can be moderated with intervention, but even when the depression lifts, Anna is unlikely to be comfortable in occupations that demand a high level of self-confidence or risk taking and an extroverted personality.

The two interest inventories provide consistent support for exploring careers or college majors that are social (or involve working for the welfare of others) and that have a combination of stability and structure while still engaging creativity. Because many of the identified interests include skills in mathematics or numbers, it would be advisable to consider an intellectual assessment. As well, there may be elements of her ethnic background or her history with her former husband that might influence her vocational decisions, so personality assessment could also assist Anna in her vocational choices.

Interventions that address Anna's vocational concerns may include assisting Anna with a description of her vocational story, development of a time line/future planning, an explanation of recycling through developmental stages during career changes, a discussion of parental (or family) influences on career choice, the identification of a life theme as expressed through career, further assessments (e.g., values, skills, beliefs), exploration assignments (e.g., job shadowing or reading vocational references), and discovering potential gender and/or cultural influences on past, present, and future career concerns.

Anna's MMPI-2 profile supports the hypothesis that emotional factors may have affected her WAIS-III scores. Her MMPI-2 profile strongly suggests significant depression and anxiety that may have had a detrimental effect on her WAIS-III performance across virtually all the cognitive domains that were sampled. We can then hypothesize with confidence that her WAIS-III scores are very likely to be an underestimate of her true cognitive ability. Unfortunately, it is not possible to accurately quantify the magnitude of the underestimate.

Nevertheless, the even distribution of abilities across the verbal and nonverbal realms is quite consistent with her occupational preferences. Anna has diverse interests.

Summary and Recommendations

Anna is a 35-year-old Caucasian woman being evaluated for academic and emotional difficulties in her first year attending community college. The findings of this evaluation suggest a number of conclusions. Although she likely possesses the capability to perform satisfactorily in a community college setting, current circumstances are such that she may not perform either up to her potential or at a passing level. Furthermore, failure at this juncture could serve to validate her negative view of herself and her ability. Thus, the following recommendations are offered in prioritizing treatment strategies:

1. Address her anxiety and depression immediately. Research (Seligman, 1990) supports taking a cognitive-behavioral approach with clients experiencing depression and/or anxiety. Clearly identify her fears and concerns about finances and other focuses of her worry. Help her generate contingency plans to cope with several "worst-case scenario" situations. Depending on the degree of impairment in her daily functioning, consider possible referral for evaluation for psychotropic medication.

2. Assess the need for any interventions or advocacy with any of her current instructors to maximize the chances of her academic success. For example, she may require additional time to complete tests or assignments. In addition, discussing with Anna how her performances in courses could be related to her Holland type (Social-Conventional-Artistic) may help Anna understand one way in which some academic courses could be more interesting to her than other classes. Normalizing for her how most students are not interested in every class may help her find a justification or rationale for academic discomfort.

3. Several longer term goals would include the following:

(a) Addressing social anxiety and subsequent expansion of her support system

(b) More career investigation—possibly some job shadowing

(c) Consistently creating some situations that she enjoys and feels that she is good at to increase her feeling of mastery and enjoyment of her life

By developing a strong, collaborative relationship with Anna, the likelihood of meeting these treatment goals will be improved. She seems to be quite in need of a positive support system, and her therapist will be a key person in helping Anna develop the valuable support she clearly needs. Through attainment of the above identified treatment goals, Anna's prognosis for symptom resolution is quite positive.

Maryann Smith, M.Ed.
Ohio Professional Clinical Counselor Number 1234

Summary

This concludes our case study. We offered readers a scenario of a client situation. It began with a life story and then progressed through test scores, recommendations for her treatment, and examples of methods for competent dissemination of those results and information in both oral and written form. Anna's situation and clinical presentation represent typical client concerns in that many times, a client's issues and difficulties are not limited to one specific aspect of functioning. Instead, the issues span a number of life areas. Competent identification of diagnostic issues and directions for treatment is done by integrating test data that span diverse, yet related, aspects of functioning.

When a clinician is able to competently weave together test scores with background information and presenting concerns to generate treatment recommendations, his or her effectiveness as a helper is increased. When these assessment skills can be applied to improve a client's functioning or life situation, the clinician's efforts to learn this complex process are justified.

Discussion Questions

1. What other issues, besides those raised by Anna's evaluator, look as though they might be relevant in counseling Anna?

2. Is there additional testing you would request for Anna? Why or why not?

3. With the limited information you have about her, what would be your best guess about how Anna will react as she receives her test feedback? What theoretical approach would be justified based on her symptoms, needs, and personality traits?

References

Seligman, L. (1990). *Selecting effective treatments: A comprehensive systematic guide to treating adult mental disorders.* San Francisco: Jossey-Bass.

Zytowski, D. (1999). *Kuder Career Search: Preview manual.* Adel, IA: National Career Development Services.

9

Ethical and Legal Responsibilities in Testing in Clinical Settings

The most fundamental ethical mandate for clinicians in testing is competence—the knowledge, skill, and judgment to select appropriate measures, administer them competently, and interpret them accurately. As Weiner (1989) has remarked, "It is possible in psychodiagnostic work to be competent without being ethical, but it is not possible to be ethical without being competent" (p. 829). Competence in psychological testing is achieved when the professional has successfully completed the following activities:

- A graduate course in psychological testing with emphasis on the psychometric properties of tests and procedures for evaluating the reliability and validity of tests. For complex instruments such as the Wechsler Adult Intelligence Scale (WAIS) and the Minnesota Multiphasic Personality Inventory–2 (MMPI-2), an entire course devoted to the test is advisable.
- Specific study of the particular test(s) to be used that includes but is not limited to careful review of the test manual, reading of related books and articles on the test characteristics and uses, study of sample test results.

- Knowledge of the strengths and limitations of the test and its proper application with diverse populations.
- Supervised experience in the administration, scoring, and interpretation of client test results. This may be accomplished most readily through a formal internship in testing but can also be achieved through peer supervision from another mental health professional already competent in the test(s) of interest.
- Regular continuing education on test features and research. Revised editions of tests get published at regular intervals, and new research is produced that affects the interpretation of test results.

The time it takes to develop these competencies varies according to the background of the professional and the particular instrument. Walsh and Betz (1995) suggested that the greater the likelihood that a test can be misused (or misunderstood), the more stringent the criteria for competency.

There are also some legal restrictions to the use of psychological tests. The licensing requirements of some states and provinces limit the use of some psychological tests to specific disciplines. For example, in states in which only psychologists and psychiatrists are licensed to diagnose mental and emotional disorders, other mental health professionals may need to work under the supervision of psychologists and psychiatrists when using psychological tests. There has been some controversy about the competency of counselors and social workers to use psychological tests (see Clawson, 1997; Marino, 1995); consequently, mental health professionals are encouraged to consult the licensing laws in their jurisdiction for guidance.

Responsibilities to Test Producers

In addition to their competency duties, clinicians must respect both the rights of those who have developed and published tests and the rights of clients who take them. The primary right of test publishers is to maintain control over the security of the tests that they have copyrighted. When qualified clinicians use a copyrighted test, they are implicitly agreeing to protect the security of that test by keeping test materials in their possession and refraining from copying those materials or otherwise disseminating the test items.

The investment that test developers have made in producing a valid and reliable measure gives them the right to profit from their work and control the use of their product. Clinicians fail to honor this ethical obligation when they allow clients to take test materials home because as soon as the client leaves the office, the clinician has lost control over the security of the test. Clinicians have no assurance that the client will return for the next appointment or that the client will not share or copy items with others. Despite the prohibition against uncontrolled administration of tests in the ethics codes of both the American Counseling Association (ACA, 1995) and American Psychological Association (APA, 1992), sending a test home with a client is a relatively common occurrence among both psychologists (Pope, Tabachnick, & Keith-Spiegel, 1987) and counselors (Gibson & Pope, 1993). Allowing a client to take a test out of the office is also unwise from a clinical perspective because then a clinician has no knowledge of the actual conditions under which the test was completed. Perhaps a roommate or family member consulted with the client about the items or even answered the questions for the client. The publisher's copyright also prevents clinicians from extracting items from tests to create their own measures or otherwise plagiarizing them. Test publishers may take legal action unless clinicians receive prior permission for such use.

Responsibilities to Clients

Clinicians also have several ethical obligations to the clients for whom they are considering psychological testing. Anastasi (1992) identified two of the most important. The first is that the test be *relevant* to the needs of a particular client. Completing a psychological test is a stressful, time-consuming, and often costly experience. Test items typically deal with personal information that clients may feel uncomfortable revealing and sometimes provoke concerns about performance—"Will the personality inventory indicate that I am unstable? Or will the intelligence test show that I am dumb?" are questions clients wonder about. Therefore, clinicians should choose tests that are connected to a client's therapeutic goals, compatible with his or her current capacity to endure the testing process, and capable of producing meaningful results.

The second important criterion Anastasi (1992) mentioned is "the hazard of the single score" (p. 611). The ethics codes of the ACA (1995) and APA (1992) echo this concern in their admonition that clinicians always use *multiple criteria for decision making*. No diagnostic or treatment recommendation to a client should be based exclusively on test results. Independent corroborating evidence is essential. So, no matter how elevated a client's score on the depression scales of the MMPI, no diagnosis of depression is justified without other independent evidence of depression. Why? No test, however sound psychometrically, has perfect reliability and validity. Its conclusions in any single situation may be flawed, and too much is at stake for a client to risk such an error. Other sources of evidence include clinical interview data, behavioral observations, reports from reliable significant others, and scores on other tests.

Client Rights in Testing

Clients have several rights identified both in the ethics codes and in regulations governing mental health practice. First, clients have a right to make an informed choice about their participation in testing. They should be informed about the purposes, procedures, uses, and implications of the proposed testing, including any likely benefits or risks involved. If test results are to play a role in important decisions affecting the client (such as eligibility for services or educational placement), clients should fully understand that aspect of testing. Clients have a right to have their questions about the test answered, although disclosing test items and other data that may compromise the security and validity of the results is prohibited. If copies of test reports are to be retained in client files, clients should be advised of that fact. Finally, of course, clients have a right to refuse to participate in any or all parts of testing and to withdraw consent without penalty at any point in the process. Obviously, if tests are to be administered to minors or to others incapable of giving consent, the designated people responsible for the clients must give consent prior to testing.

The second major client right is to feedback about the results of the testing. The ethics codes are quite explicit on this point.

APA *Ethical Principles,* Section 2.09: Explaining Test Results. Unless the nature of the relationship is clearly explained to the person being assessed in advance and precludes provision of an explanation of the results (such as in some organizational consulting, preemployment or security screening, and forensic applications), psychologists ensure that an explanation of the results is provided using language that is reasonably understandable to the person being assessed or to another legally authorized person on behalf of the client. Regardless of whether the scoring and interpretation are done by the psychologist, by assistants, or by automated or other outside services, psychologists take reasonable steps to ensure that appropriate explanations are given (APA, 1992).

ACA *Code of Ethics,* Section E.1.b. They respect the client's right to know the results, the interpretations made, and the bases for conclusions and recommendations (ACA, 1995).

Why are the ethics standards so insistent on feedback? First, the limits of the reliability and validity of psychological tests make them fallible. Therefore, clients ought to have an opportunity to respond to mistaken or misleading conclusions from the test. The opportunity to set the record straight is especially important when educational and clinical decisions will be made at least partially on the basis of test results. Second, feedback with the client offers the mental health professional a chance to clarify confusing or contradictory findings from the test and thereby develop a more accurate and useful test report. For example, a personality inventory may indicate high scores in both extroversion and social discomfort or, conversely, introversion and comfort in social settings. At first, such findings seem contradictory, but a feedback session with a client can reveal hidden aspects of each score that make the pattern clear. In the former case, for instance, a person may seek out the company of others and feel uneasy when alone but may have inadequate social skills to manage interpersonal relationships effectively.

Third, clients are owed feedback as a form of payment for their investment of time and emotional energy in completing the test. Testing raises client anxiety, often pushes clients to confront uncomfortable aspects of their personality and functioning, and can be tedious and intellectually demanding. Mental health professionals who have thrived in academic settings may lose sight of the negative connotation that completing answer sheets holds for clients whose academic experiences were less rewarding. Some clients with low levels of literacy in the language of the test may struggle just to understand the meanings of the words they are reading. When clients are experiencing depression or anxiety or are recovering from a psychological trauma, the sheer effort involved in attending to the items on a test is enormous. Clients make such efforts in good faith, hoping that the test results will help us help them. Providing full feedback in a format they can understand is a way to express our appreciation for their effort and to show them the benefits of their investment.

Finally, the process of describing test results with clients and getting their views on the accuracy of the test findings may be therapeutic in itself. Finn and Tonsager (1992) found that clients who received verbal feedback on their MMPI results experienced significant reductions in symptoms and distress after the feedback session. They also reported no negative consequences, even though the MMPI reveals more deficits in functioning than strengths. In fact, the clients in the study expressed high levels of satisfaction with the feedback and with the whole experience of discussing their results with a psychologist. Their finding is consistent with the views of other scholars who argue that direct and honest feedback about testing promotes therapist-client rapport, client cooperation with treatment, and more positive views of their therapists and mental health professionals in general (Dorr, 1981; Finn & Butcher, 1991; Fischer, 1986).

Research has found that mental health professionals do not share their clients' enthusiasm for feedback about test results. Pope (1992) identified three major reasons that clinicians are reluctant to provide feedback at times. First, they are uncomfortable disclosing results that may appear negative or disappointing to clients. Second, they feel overwhelmed by the task of translating the technical jargon of the test report into language clients can understand. Third, they are unsure of the language to use when test results contain ambiguous or contradictory findings. Although all of these reasons for reluctance are understandable, none justifies avoiding client feedback. When clinicians are experiencing such concerns, they probably indicate a lack of expertise about the test and are best remedied by consultation with other professionals who are able to provide concrete suggestions for dealing with these concerns.

How much feedback is mandated by legal and ethical standards? The professional standards are not especially clear on this point, but the most prudent advice is to provide as full a description of the results as time, interest, and test security allow. Feedback for the tests described in this book usually lasts at least one session but may be much briefer for other tests such as those that focus on a single symptom or skill. Clinicians should postpone discussion of findings that they judge harmful to the client's well-being until the client's state of mind is improved enough to cope with them. Careful preparation for feedback sessions increases the likelihood that they will be productive for both parties. Clinicians should take care to be precise and jargon free in their descriptions of results and to be alert for aspects of the results clients may misunderstand. Feedback sessions should center on the client's experience during the test taking and the relationship of findings to the client's therapeutic goals. When informed consent for testing has included sufficient information to properly orient the client to the test and has identified client goals and concerns about testing, that information can serve as the backdrop for feedback. The aim is to work collaboratively with the client to determine the meaning and impact of the test results for future therapeutic work. The length of feedback is affected, of course, by external pressures. Managed care is not likely to reimburse for extensive feedback time, nor do school personnel have the luxury of scheduling multiple feedback sessions with students in light of their heavy caseloads. Nevertheless, the primary considerations in determining the length of a feedback process should be the following: (a) the client's satisfaction that he or she understands the results, (b) the clinician's assessment that the feedback time has been sufficient to clarify ambiguous aspects of the results, (c) their mutual agreement about the impact of the test results on future therapeutic activities, and (d) the implications of the release of these findings to others if that is necessary.

Of course, there are some circumstances in which there is no ethical or legal obligation to provide feedback about test results. If a client has waived his or her right to feedback prior to testing, then no findings need be disclosed. Similarly, if a court mandates psychological testing, direct communication with the person who took the test is not required, although that person's attorney probably has a right to copies of the test reports. Clinicians must be cautious, however, to ensure that clients who waive their rights to feedback have adequate information to make an informed decision, and that the limits of the clinician's relationship with the person undergoing the testing mandated by the court are clear to all involved.

Clients also have a right to the control of the information gained from testing. No results or reports from testing may be distributed to others without the informed consent and formal release of information from the client. That release should be written and included as part of the client record. Because test data are especially vulnerable to misinterpretation by those untrained in their use and interpretation, clinicians also have a responsibility to see that test data are released only to those competent to interpret them and that clients understand the implications of release. Frequently, courts and attorneys seek test data on clients involved with the courts, and at times subpoenas for these materials ask for raw test data, answer sheets, and the like. When this happens, mental health professionals are placed in a legal dilemma. On one hand, they must honor the copyright rights of producers; on the other hand, they must not ignore subpoenas and court orders. Ideally, clinicians should seek a compromise through the judge involved in the case to have the data released to another competent clinician who can interpret it on behalf of the requesting attorney or have the reports and findings released rather than all the raw data. Needless to say, professionals are encouraged to seek legal assistance when they confront such demands for raw data from the courts. The APA Committee on Legal Issues (1996) published a helpful document that can guide professionals facing these circumstances, and readers are encouraged to add that document to their libraries.

Responsible Use of Test Interpretation Services

Mental health professionals often use computer-based scoring and interpretation services for the psychological and career tests they administer to clients (Butcher, Perry, & Atlis, 2000). Computerized scoring is quick, accurate, and capable of sophisticated analysis of results. McMinn, Ellens, and Soref (1999) found that 85% of psychologists use computer-based services to score psychological tests. Along with the scores, some services provide a typed interpretation of the test results. Computer interpretations of results are used most commonly for complex personality inventories such as the MMPI. How can mental health professionals use these reports responsibly? The best strategy for such reports is to approach them as a "second opinion" about the results, a professional-to-professional consultation. They cannot substitute for the work of the clinician because the scoring criteria they use are not clearly documented (Matarazzo, 1986), and they cannot take into account the unique individual circumstances of the client (Bersoff & Hofer, 1991). These omissions are important to remember because the computerized reports are packaged to appear professional, complete, and carefully crafted and offer a superficial appearance of professionalism. In the end, though, their "bland, impersonal and nonspecific interpretations" (Bersoff & Hofer, 1991, p. 243) can lead professionals to make inaccurate interpretations. Another danger of these computer reports is that they tempt clinicians without sufficient training in testing to use the tests anyway. The current *Standards for Educational and Psychological Tests* (American Educational Research Association [AERA], 2000) prohibit this practice, citing it as unethical and potentially harmful to clients.

In recent years, Internet-based psychological and career assessment services have begun to appear (Sampson & Lumsden, 2000). The range of materials on these Web sites is great, but a cursory exploration of the Web shows dozens of sites that offer personality tests, relationship inventories, employment tests, intelligence tests, and career aptitude measures. Some are well-publicized instruments, and others are self-developed tests not published elsewhere. The availability of these materials on the Web raises important ethical issues ranging from the protection of the rights of test producers to the scientific value of the instruments themselves. Are these tests valid for this use? Can people not competent to interpret them be harmed if they use them? What is the liability of the professionals who offer such services if clients are poorly served by them? None of these questions have acceptable answers yet, and prudent clinicians should be cautious about offering psychological assessments on the Internet to people they do not know and cannot protect from harm with instruments of uncertain scientific value or copyright protections. This medium has promise, but the determination of its ultimate value awaits scientific evidence and rigorous research.

Multicultural Issues in Testing

The codes of ethics exhort clinicians to be alert to the effects of gender, age, race, ethnicity, national origin, religion, sexual orientation, disability, language, or socioeconomic status on both the administration and interpretation of psychological tests. These cautions are important because no test is culture free. The results themselves can give a distorted picture of the functioning of multicultural clients, or clinicians can interpret the findings in a biased way. The best protection against the first error is to ensure that the tests under consideration have normative data for the client's population and are as free as possible from content bias. If no appropriate normative data are available, the clinician should seek a substitute test. If no substitute is useable, then the results should be interpreted cautiously. Content bias comes from the inclusion of items that a particular population has no experience with and cannot answer. For example, urban residents may have difficulty understanding items that rely on a suburban or rural experience, or Native Americans from the desert Southwest may have no experience with evergreen trees. Any items that assumed such knowledge as a part of general intelligence could be described as having content bias. Research suggests that lower scores of ethnically diverse groups on some measures of cognitive ability are at least partially caused by content bias (Lonner & Ibrahim, 1996). One especially helpful guide for the competent and responsible assessment of diverse populations is the *Handbook for Multicultural Assessment* (Suzuki, Meller, & Ponterotto, 1996).

Summary

When using psychological or educational tests, mental health professionals need extensive skill and training to apply the findings in suitable ways with a given individual. They must possess the knowledge and skill to discriminate between valid and invalid findings and to take into account the cultural and social background of the test taker. They must not encourage those unqualified for the activity to engage in it, nor should they use outdated test results in their work. In most instances, clients have a right to feedback about the test. The exact nature of that feedback is not prescribed by the ethics codes, but it must convey as accurate and full a picture of the results as circumstances allow. The history of the profession is replete with examples of mental health professionals misinterpreting test results with diverse and oppressed populations, so counselors and therapists must be especially vigilant not to repeat those violations and to stay current with the literature on multicultural aspects of assessment. Professionals would also be well advised to know how the laws in their jurisdictions affect the assessment process, as state laws vary and change rapidly.

Not only are counselors and therapists bound to protect the rights of clients, but they also have a responsibility to honor the rights of test producers, acting in ways that recognize their legal rights to ownership of and fair profit from test materials. Therefore, they must guard against violations of test security, must not plagiarize test materials, and must seek the option to use such materials only when qualified to do so. In turn, test producers are obligated to provide scientific evidence of the reliability and validity of their tests and other related materials in test manuals. They should assist counselors and therapists in the responsible use of assessment tools as much as possible.

Discussion Questions

1. Research shows that some professionals do not give clients negative feedback from testing; they report only positive results. They tend to justify this decision on the basis of maintaining the therapeutic alliance. What do you think about the ethics and clinical value of this practice?

2. Currently, test producers are asked by professional associations to market their tests only to qualified users. Is that a fair request in a free-enterprise system? What would happen if that restriction did not exist?

3. We have heard clinicians argue that the only workable way to include psychological tests in therapy is to send them home with clients so that they can complete them on their own time. Do you think the ethics codes should be changed to allow for this practice?

4. The MMPI-2 and MMPI-A are widely used in other countries, and research tends to show reliable results from such testing even though the instruments were developed in the United States. Aside from language considerations, what other factors should clinicians keep in mind if they are using these instruments with clients in other countries?

References

American Counseling Association. (ACA). (1995). *Code of ethics and standards of practice.* Alexandria, VA: Author. Available at www.counseling. org/resources/codeofethics.htm

American Educational Research Association. (AERA). (2000). *Standards for educational and psychological tests.* Washington, DC: Author.

American Psychological Association. (APA). (1992). *Ethical principles of psychologists and code of conduct.* Washington, DC: Author. Available at www.apa.org/ethics/code.html

American Psychological Association. (APA). Committee on Legal Issues. (1996). Strategies for private practitioners coping with subpoenas or compelled testimony for client records or test data. *Professional Psychology: Research and Practice, 27,* 245-251.

Anastasi, A. (1992). What counselors should know about the use and interpretation of psychological tests. *Journal of Counseling and Development, 70,* 610-615.

Bersoff, D. N., & Hofer, P. J. (1991). *Legal issues in computerized psychological testing.* Hillsdale, NJ: Lawrence Erlbaum.

Butcher, J. N., Perry, J. N., & Atlis, M. M. (2000). Validity and utility of computer-based test interpretations. *Psychological Assessment, 12,* 6-18.

Clawson, T. W. (1997). Control of psychological testing: The threat and a response. *Journal of Counseling and Development, 76,* 90-93.

Dorr, D. (1981). Conjoint psychological testing in marriage therapy: New wine in old skins. *Professional Psychology: Research and Practice, 12,* 549-555.

Finn, S. E., & Butcher, J. N. (1991). Clinical objective personality assessment. In M. Hersen, A. E. Kazdin, & A. S. Bellack (Eds.), *The clinical psychology handbook* (2nd ed., pp. 362-373). New York: Pergamon.

Finn, S. E., & Tonsager, M. E. (1992). Therapeutic effects of providing MMPI-2 test feedback to college students awaiting therapy. *Psychological Assessment, 4,* 278-287.

Fischer, C. T. (1986). *Individualizing psychological assessment.* Pacific Grove, CA: Brooks/Cole.

Gibson, W. T., & Pope, K. S. (1993). The ethics of counseling: A national survey of certified counselors. *Journal of Counseling and Development, 71,* 330-336.

Lonner, W. J., & Ibrahim, F. A. (1996). Appraisal and assessment in cross-cultural counseling. In P. B. Pedersen, J. G. Draguns, W. J. Lonner, & J. E. Trimble (Eds.), *Counseling across cultures* (4th ed., pp. 293-322). Thousand Oaks, CA: Sage.

Marino, T. W. (1995, December). Battle for testing rights continues. *Counseling Today,* p. 6.

Matarazzo, J. D. (1986). Computerized clinical psychological test interpretations: Unvalidated plus all mean and no sigma. *American Psychologist, 41,* 14-24.

McMinn, M. R., Ellens, B. M., & Soref, E. (1999). Ethical perspectives and practice behaviors involving computer-based test interpretation. *Assessment, 9,* 71-77.

Pope, K. S. (1992). Responsibilities in providing psychological test feedback to clients. *Psychological Assessment, 4,* 268-271.

Pope, K. S., Tabachnick, B. G., & Keith-Spiegel, P. S. (1987). Ethics of practice: The beliefs and behaviors of psychologists as therapists. *American Psychologist, 42,* 993-1006.

Sampson, J. P., & Lumsden, J. A. (2000). Ethical issues in the design and use of Internet-based career assessment. *Journal of Career Assessment, 8,* 21-35.

Suzuki, L. A., Meller, P. J., & Ponterotto, J. G. (1996). *Handbook of multicultural assessment.* San Francisco: Jossey-Bass.

Walsh, W. B., & Betz, N. E. (1995). *Tests and assessment* (3rd ed.). Englewood Cliffs, NJ: Prentice Hall.

Weiner, I. B. (1989). On competence and ethicality in psychodiagnostic assessment. *Journal of Personality Assessment, 53,* 827-831.

Appendix

MMPI-2 Practice Case of Jerome

$\mathbf{N}$otes on the case:

Step 1: Validity Scales

Jerome cooperated with the testing when he answered all the questions and was consistent and attentive to content throughout the test.

Step 2: Review of the Basic Scales

He also showed little defensiveness in his responses and did not seem to present himself as overly virtuous. Jerome was willing to admit a variety of symptoms, although some symptom exaggeration is possible.

Jerome shows only one elevation on the clinically relevant scales, on Scale 8. Coupled with the elevations on the Harris-Lingoes subscales, the following descriptors are suggested:

- Unconventional lifestyle
- Nonconforming
- Somewhat alienated from others
- Feelings of inferiority
- Aloof and uninterested
- Uses fantasy as a defense mechanism
- Immature and self-preoccupied
- May be impulsive, aggressive, or anxious
- Feels misunderstood and mistreated and plotted against
- Family as lacking in love and filled with hostility

- Feelings of loneliness and emptiness
- Unlikely to have experienced a love relationship
- Feelings of depression and despair
- Feels out of emotional control
- Feels impulsive, restless, hyperactive, and irritable
- May experience laughing or crying spells
- May experience times when he does not remember previously performed activities

Jerome's moderate elevation on Scale 10 is also important because it shows a tendency toward social introversion, shyness, lack of involvement with other people, and possible discomfort around the opposite gender.

Step 3: Identification of Inconsistent Findings

Because only one elevation on a clinical scale appeared, chances for inconsistent descriptors are reduced. The most important possible inconsistency may be between the descriptor that suggests restlessness and hyperactivity and Jerome's nonelevated score on Scale 9, the Basic Scale that most directly assesses such feelings. Because the descriptor suggesting these feelings was derived from a Harris-Lingoes subscale that has fewer items and lower reliability than a Basic Scale, this descriptor is less likely to apply to Jerome at this point. However, the feedback session should address this issue.

Step 4: Review of the Content Scales

The Content Scales show no elevations but show six moderate elevations on the following scales: DEP, ANG, CYN, LSE, SOD, and FAM. The descriptors associated with these moderate elevations (not already identified by the Basic Scales) are likely to be the following:

- Significant depressive thoughts
- Feeling blue, unhappy, and uncertain about the future
- Likely to brood, cry frequently
- Possible thoughts of suicide
- Feels condemned or guilty of unpardonable sins
- Feels unsupported
- Has anger control problems
- Feels grouchy and impatient
- Likely to be hotheaded, easily annoyed, and stubborn

- Feels like swearing and smashing things
- Concerned over losing self-control
- May have been physically abusive toward people and objects
- Expects hidden, negative motives from others
- Many misanthropic beliefs
- Negative, distrusting attitudes toward those close to him
- Has low opinion of himself and lacks self-confidence
- Believes others are unlikely to like him
- Feels unimportant and unattractive
- Finds compliments difficult to accept
- Feels overwhelmed by his own faults
- Abusive childhood possible

Taken together, these descriptors fit with the descriptors from the Basic Scales and provide a fuller picture of the problems Jerome is likely to have. The descriptors that do not fit together easily are those that suggest he is both depressed and introverted and those that indicate problems with anger and impulsive action. These need to be explored further in the interview. It is possible that Jerome alternates between feelings of depression and anger, but we obviously need more information from Jerome. The fact that the descriptors all refer to moderate elevations suggests that we need to be cautious about their interpretation and to avoid thinking of these descriptors as representations of serious and intense levels of problems.

Step 5: Review of Supplemental Scales

Because Jerome is not married or in a committed relationship at present, the MDS scale was not scored. The pattern of scores shows elevations on both AAS and PK and a moderate elevation on Mac-R. The following descriptors are likely to apply to these scales:

- Has a lifestyle that could lead to an addictive disorder
- Acknowledges many serious alcohol or drug abuse problems
- Feels intense emotional distress
- Experiences anxiety and sleep disturbance
- Has disturbed intrusive thoughts
- Experiences loss of control over thinking

These findings enrich our understanding of Jerome's possible problems and suggest several important topics to discuss in the feedback session. The findings are generally consistent with prior portions of the test, although the drug and alcohol issues did not appear prior to this point. The possibility that he has intrusive thoughts and feels that his thoughts are out of his control is consistent with the elevation on Scale 8. However, nothing in the test shows that the content of these thoughts may be psychotic. Given his recent history, those thoughts may relate to his former girlfriend, but their specific content should be explored in the feedback session.

Step 6: Review of Critical Items

The critical items are consistent with prior findings and suggest a person who has abused substances and feels depressed, anxious about his own thoughts, and distrustful of others and angry toward them. These items support the view that Jerome may feel suicidal and, along with the findings on DEP, suggest that a suicide assessment in the next session is needed.

Step 7: Reconciling Inconsistencies and Developing Questions for Jerome

The major inconsistency in the findings is the inclusion of descriptors that show not only depression, shyness, introversion, and passivity but also at the same time impulsiveness, hot-headedness, and hyperactivity. The other topics that should be discussed include Jerome's risk for suicide or for physical aggression toward his former girlfriend, his substance use, and his feelings of victimization. The questions derived from these issues may be the following:

- On one hand, the findings suggest that you tend toward shyness, introversion, and submissiveness in relationships, but on the other hand, they suggest a tendency to be quick to get angry and to have some impulses to act on that anger. Have you experienced both these feelings recently? Under what circumstances? Is your anger directed at only one person or group of people?
- The test shows that you admitted problems with substance abuse? Is that a true characterization? If so, can you talk more about the substances you use and the times that you use them? How worried are you about your substance use?

- The test suggests that you feel depressed, hopeless, and over-whelmed sometimes by your thoughts and feelings. It also suggests that you may be having thoughts of suicide. Can we explore that topic further?

Step 8: Preliminary Findings

Validity and Client Test-Taking Attitude. Jerome produced a valid test result by answering the questions honestly and consistently. He showed little defensiveness and was open to admitting a variety of symptoms. In fact, it is possible that he exaggerated symptoms slightly.

Notes on Jerome's Symptoms. Jerome is likely to be experiencing feelings of depression, hopelessness, loneliness, alienation from other people, and loss of emotional control. He may have intrusive thoughts he does not want, feel angry, dislike himself, and feel that others dislike him. He endorsed items that showed a possible risk of suicide or of acting aggressively toward others. He also appears to be abusing substances and to be ready to admit this pattern of behavior. The test presents no evidence of psychotic processes.

Notes on Interpersonal Behavior. Jerome is likely to be shy, socially withdrawn, and uncomfortable with the opposite sex and appears aloof and uninterested in others. Conflict, emotional distance, and a perception of mistreatment, as suggested by the results, probably mark his family relationships. The findings suggest that Jerome is not likely to have had a love relationship, a result contradicted by behavioral evidence, but it is still possible that love relationships are either rare or difficult for him. This point needs to be clarified in the interview.

Behavioral Stability. None of the elevations on this test are extreme, and many descriptors come from moderate elevations. Consequently, no clear conclusions can be drawn about the stability of results, except to suggest that the pattern of shyness, social discomfort, and a preference for solitary activities is likely to be stable.

Diagnostic Considerations. This profile does not clearly support any one diagnosis. Jerome may be clinically depressed, may show symptoms of schizotypal or schizoid personality, may be chemically dependent, and may have anger control problems or a history of trauma leading to posttraumatic stress.

Treatment Considerations. Jerome's shyness and discomfort with people and his general tendency toward cynicism make therapy more difficult. On the other hand, he was open in responding to the test, and his felt level of distress may act as a motivator to engage in therapy. He also enters therapy with no negative perceptions of therapy or mental health professionals.

Name Index

Subject Index

About the Authors

Kathryn C. MacCluskie is a graduate of West Virginia University and is Associate Professor at Cleveland State University. Her area of specialization is teaching clinical skills, with an emphasis on standardized assessment. She has authored several articles and book chapters and recently, with a colleague, published *Becoming an Agency Counselor in the 21st Century*.

Elizabeth Reynolds Welfel is Professor and Coordinator of Counselor Education at Cleveland State University. She earned her doctorate in counseling psychology at the University of Minnesota in 1979 and is a licensed psychologist in Ohio. Prior to her position at Cleveland State, she was on the faculty of the counseling psychology program at Boston College. She is author of two other books, *Ethics in Counseling and Psychotherapy* and *The Counseling Process,* and is coeditor of *The Mental Health Desk Reference.* She has published numerous articles in the professional literature related to responsible professional practice. Her most recent research explores the ethical issues related to the provision of clinical services via the Internet.

Sarah M. Toman is a graduate of Kent State University and is Associate Professor at Cleveland State University. She serves as Research Chair for the National Career Development Association, has published articles and book chapters, and has offered more than 30 presentations at state, national, and international conferences in the field of career development and assessment. She also serves as Secretary for the Association for the Advancement of Gestalt Therapy.